"If, as Dorothy Sayers quipped, the 'only Christian work is good work, well done,' then Crystal Downing has scripted a magnificent Christian work on a fascinating and wonderfully unruly Christian saint whose thoughts on art, beauty, goodness, and cinema reshape the ways in which we might watch films. Downing is no 'hoity-toity film buff' but a creative mind that remakes the experience of filmgoing a religious renaissance of a mystery play."

**Terry Lindvall,** C. S. Lewis Endowed Chair of Communication and Christian Thought at Virginia Wesleyan University and author of *God on the Big Screen* and *Animated Parables*

"Crystal Downing's latest book, *The Wages of Cinema,* is an in-depth study of the ways in which Dorothy Sayers thought, felt, and wrote in cinematic terms in her writings, her novels, and her plays. It is erudite, scholarly, and accurate, and a joy to read. Downing draws on many sources for her ideas and bases her study on materials from important scholars of both Sayers and cinema. I recommend it highly for all who would like to know more about DLS, an exceptional writer, and her gift for dramatization."

**Jasmine Simeone,** secretary of the Dorothy L. Sayers Society

"In *The Wages of Cinema,* Crystal L. Downing takes us to the movies with Dorothy L. Sayers, treating us to a blockbuster of a book that explores the history, theory, and forms of cinema in light of Sayers's biography, theology, and Christian aesthetic. With its thoughtful organization, illuminating examples, and delightful wordplay, Downing's book serves as further proof that Sayers was correct when she wrote that 'a work of creation is an act of love.'"

**Jim Beitler,** professor of English and director of the Marion E. Wade Center at Wheaton College and author of *Seasoned Speech* and *Charitable Writing*

"Through remarkable, original research, Crystal Downing reintroduces us to the vigorous mind, artistry, and faith of Dorothy Sayers. She convincingly details Sayers' many fascinations and intersections with theater, photography, and cinema, arguing that the creator of the famous Lord Peter Wimsey mysteries exuded genius far beyond the printed page. Through this renewed biographical lens, Downing casts the light of Sayers' well-known Christian aesthetic theories upon the cinema, sharpening our view of the spiritual power of film and reintroducing us to the wisdom of this truly incisive thinker and artist."

**Joseph G. Kickasola,** professor of film and digital media and director of the Baylor Communication in New York program at Baylor University

"A rich and necessary exploration of the intersection of Christian thought and cinematic aesthetic through the lens of Dorothy L. Sayers. Thought-provoking and insightful, this work offers a fresh perspective on cinema's artistic and spiritual dimensions. A must-read for those who seek a deeper understanding of film history, theory, and the theological insights that enrich both."

**Krista Imbesi,** associate professor of film and media arts at Messiah University

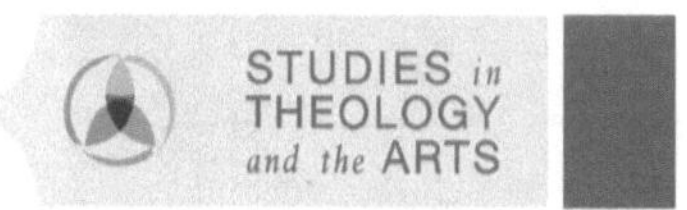


# THE WAGES OF CINEMA

## A CHRISTIAN AESTHETIC OF FILM IN CONVERSATION WITH DOROTHY L. SAYERS

Crystal L. Downing

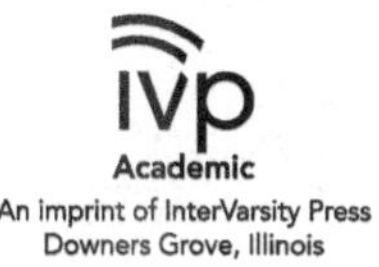


An imprint of InterVarsity Press
Downers Grove, Illinois

InterVarsity Press
P.O. Box 1400 | Downers Grove, IL 60515-1426
ivpress.com | email@ivpress.com



InterVarsity Press® is the publishing division of InterVarsity Christian Fellowship/USA®. For more information, visit intervarsity.org.



Cover design: Faceout Studio
Interior design: Daniel van Loon
Image: © dial-a-view / DigitalVision Vectors via Getty Images

ISBN 978-1-5140-0880-5 (print) | ISBN 978-1-5140-0881-2 (digital)

**Library of Congress Cataloging-in-Publication Data**
Names: Downing, Crystal, author.
Title: The wages of cinema : a Christian aesthetic of film in conversation with Dorothy L. Sayers / Crystal L. Downing.
Description: Downers Grove : InterVarsity Press, 2025. | Series: Studies in theology and the arts series | Includes bibliographical references and index.
Identifiers: LCCN 2024047200 (print) | LCCN 2024047201 (ebook) | ISBN 9781514008805 (paperback) | ISBN 9781514008812 (ebook)
Subjects: LCSH: Motion pictures–Religious aspects–Christianity. | Motion pictures–Moral and ethical aspects. | Sayers, Dorothy L. (Dorothy Leigh), 1893-1957–Influence. | Motion pictures–Study and teaching. | LCGFT: Film criticism.
Classification: LCC PN1995.9.C49 D69 2025 (print) | LCC PN1995.9.C49 (ebook) | DDC 791.43/6823–dc23/eng/20241028
LC record available at https://lccn.loc.gov/2024047200
LC ebook record available at https://lccn.loc.gov/2024047201

For Debra, who has projected the light of Christ

through the multiple reels of my life

# Contents


Acknowledgments ix

Abbreviations xi

Introduction: Truth, Beauty, and Goodness 1

1 The Religious Origins of Cinema 21

2 The Stigmata of Theater Versus the Stigma of Film 43

3 The Theater of War:
Effects on Film and Faith 69

4 From Silent Film to Sound Work 96

5 The Mind of the Filmmaker:
Endorsing a Christian Aesthetic 119

6 Film Theory:
Making Meaning of Cinematic Form 143

7 Seeing Women:
From *King Kong* to *Barbie* 170

8 Love on Screen:
Finding the Real Thing 191

Coda: Sayers and Cinema: Intersecting Histories 217

Index 239

# Acknowledgments

*The Wages of Cinema* was made possible by the Marion E. Wade Center, in Wheaton, Illinois, which contains the most comprehensive collection of published and unpublished materials by and about Dorothy L. Sayers in the world. Privileged to serve as Wade codirector, along with my codirector husband, C. S. Lewis scholar David C. Downing, I was aided in my work by assistant director Marjorie Lamp Mead, archivist Laura Stanifer, cataloguer Jill Walker, and former cataloguer Elaine Hooker, who insisted I see the *Barbie* movie. Equally important were office manager Melissa Doogan, who repeatedly lifted my spirits, and office assistant Olivia D'Souza, who proofed an early draft of the book and worked on the index. Former office assistant Shawn Mrakovich and her husband, Pete, not only created joy through their friendship but also nurtured my thoughts about film, drawing attention to some unpublished Sayers materials at the Wade while also discussing significant movies with my husband and me. Members of the Wade Advisory Board provided encouragement as well, becoming friends in the process, most especially Walter and Darlene Hanson, Stan and Jeannette Bakke, and Jim and Britta Beitler. Conversations with Wheaton College archivists Sarah Stanley and Katherine Graber helped sustain me, fertilizing both mind and spirit. Thanks also go to my brilliant students at Messiah College (now University), which honored me with the title Distinguished Professor of English and Film Studies. The InterVarsity Press editor for this work, Rebecca Carhart, deserves recognition as well, wisely guiding me through major revisions that have made this a better book. Finally, thanks go to my screening partner for over four decades, David C. Downing.

# Abbreviations

*Letters* 1 Reynolds, Barbara, ed. *The Letters of Dorothy L. Sayers*. Vol. 1, *1899 to 1936: The Making of a Detective Novelist*. New York: St. Martin's, 1995.

*Letters* 2 Reynolds, Barbara, ed. *The Letters of Dorothy L. Sayers*. Vol. 2, *1937–1943: From Novelist to Playwright*. Cambridge, UK: Carole Green, 1997.

*Letters* 3 Reynolds, Barbara, ed. *The Letters of Dorothy L. Sayers*. Vol. 3, *1944–1950: A Noble Daring*. Cambridge, UK: Carole Green, 1998.

*Letters* 4 Reynolds, Barbara, ed. *The Letters of Dorothy L. Sayers*. Vol. 4, *1951–1957: In the Midst of Life*. Cambridge, UK: Carole Green, 2000.

# Introduction
# Truth, Beauty, and Goodness

The cultural power of narrative cinema has long captured the attention of priests, pastors, and professors who write books assessing film through the lens of Christian faith. Extracting spiritual insight from secular films as well as Jesus movies, many celebrate the revelatory truths or moments of transcendence generated in and by cinema. Their inspirational books have done a service for Christendom.

*The Wages of Cinema* offers a different kind of service. Unlike most books by Christians, it emphasizes the history of film as well as the development of secular theories about the artistry of its form. This is important. Christians who would consider naive any evangelist who proclaims, "I don't care about Christian theology; I just save souls from hell," often display similar naivete when it comes to film, extracting salvation messages from movies while displaying no knowledge of film theory. They seem unaware that, in the early decades of cinema, cineastes (filmmakers as well as lovers of cinema) argued about the essence of the medium just as bishops in the early centuries of Christianity argued about the essence of Jesus as the medium of salvation. Earnest followers of film have long recognized the need to focus on the medium itself rather than merely on their own uplifting experiences as viewers. In full endorsement of Christian orthodoxy, then, *The Wages of Cinema* seeks to reflect, even if on a screen darkly, what theologians study: historical development of doctrine about the medium.

Debates about *how* Christ functioned as the medium of salvation were not resolved until the Fourth Ecumenical Council at Chalcedon in 451 CE. Even then, disagreements continued between the Eastern and Western church, anticipating disagreements centuries later between Protestants and Roman Catholics. The same might be said of scholarly debates about the medium of cinema, debates exacerbated by the development of digital media, such that a "film" is no longer photographed on celluloid *film*. Nevertheless, attentiveness to cinematic techniques displayed on the screen, though never saving us from sin, might save us from obsession with the wages of cinema, which includes judging a movie by how much money it makes or awards it garners, or else by counting the number of sinful scenes and hellish words it contains.

## A Guide Through Sin and Cinema

To explain the sins that landed people in hell, Dante Alighieri did something unusual as he began writing the *Inferno* in the early fourteenth century: he inserted a human guide. His *Divine Comedy*, as the completed poem was later called, is still read six hundred years after its composition, largely due to the dynamic between Dante as first-person narrator and his guide through the inferno and purgatorio.

Inspired by the fact that Dante's explicitly Christian work about the wages of sin continues to be studied even at secular universities, *The Wages of Cinema* similarly employs a guide to direct our journey through the complex circles of cinema, including infernal debates among film scholars. Whereas Dante chose as guide Virgil (70–19 BCE), the author of the *Aeneid*, this book invokes an author who translated the *Inferno* and *Purgatorio* into English, Dorothy L. Sayers (1893–1957), whose faith was reignited partially due to an "infernal film," as she called it.[1] The primary difference is that Sayers had much greater acquaintance with the movie industry than Dante's guide had with Christianity, since Virgil died before the birth of Jesus. Nevertheless, as Sayers notes, "The Church of Rome has always held that Virgil . . . was a Prophet of Christ."[2] Similarly, this book demonstrates that Sayers is a prophet of cinema, largely due to her Christian aesthetic, which harmonizes with secular film scholarship. Unlike books that tend to extract theological messages while ignoring techniques of the cinematic medium, *The Wages of Cinema* views film through the lens of Sayers's theology of art, thus echoing what Christianity preaches, that is, the importance of a medium that entered into and changed history.

---

[1]Dorothy L. Sayers, unpublished letter to Muriel St Clare Byrne, April 2, 1935. Sayers's unpublished correspondence will be cited throughout this book by means of its location at the Marion E. Wade Center, in Wheaton, Illinois. In this case, Muriel's letter is Wade 186/16: the first number indicates the file, and the second indicates the page number(s) in the file.

[2]*Letters* 1:144. Though Virgil died in 19 BCE, he was considered a prophet, as C. S. Lewis explains, because he began a poem with, "The great procession of the ages begins anew. Now the Virgin returns, the reign of Saturn returns, and the new child is sent down from high heaven." Lewis, *Reflections on the Psalms* (New York: Harcourt, 1986), 101.

Sayers's qualifications as guide are impressive. Not only did she matriculate to Oxford University "having topped the whole country" in a "nationwide test," but her fellow Oxford graduate, C. S. Lewis, later considered her a profound influence on his spiritual life.[3] In addition to enjoying Sayers's translations of Dante's *Inferno* and *Purgatorio,* Lewis considered "indispensable" a book Sayers wrote about the relationship between creativity and Christianity, *The Mind of the Maker*—a book that others have found indispensable as well.[4] Cultural historian and philosopher Jacques Barzun, a contemporary of Lewis, warmly praised what he called Sayers's "aesthetic theology," and eighty years later Christian artist Makoto Fujimura quoted from *The Mind of the Maker* in his Yale University Press book *Art and Faith: A Theology of Making* (2020). And, as will become clear, Fujimura is not the only twenty-first-century Christian to endorse the continued relevance of Sayers to conversations about faith and the arts.[5]

*The Wages of Cinema,* of course, narrows the conversation to visual art in the medium of film, beginning with a little-known fact: Sayers literally sought wages from cinema. Before detective fiction provided her a viable income, the cash-strapped twenty-something wrote film scenarios in collaboration with a silent film director. Later, during the height of her fame as the author of best-selling detective novels, a film studio commissioned Sayers to write an original detective story, turning it into a 1935 movie called *The Silent Passenger.* And Sayers's last published novel, *Busman's Honeymoon,* itself sprinkled with allusions to cinema, was transformed into a 1940 film starring Hollywood celebrities. Some scholars might offer these examples to argue against Sayers's interest in cinema, citing the fact that Sayers so abhorred *The Silent Passenger* (the "infernal" movie) that she never again had "anything to do with films," as James Brabazon puts it. Another biographer, David Coomes, said something similar over a decade later: "Sayers never touched the film world again."[6]

---

[3]Francesca Wade, *Square Haunting: Five Writers in London Between the Wars* (New York: Crown, 2021), 92.

[4]C. S. Lewis, *Miracles: A Preliminary Study* (New York: Macmillan, 1947), 101.

[5]Jacques Barzun, "Aesthetic Theology," *Nation* 154 (February 21, 1942): 238. Barzun coined the phrase "aesthetic theology" for this review of Sayers's 1941 book *The Mind of the Maker*. See Makoto Fujimura, *Art and Faith: A Theology of Making* (New Haven, CT: Yale University Press, 2020). See also Paul Kuritz, professor emeritus from Bates College, who quotes Sayers in *Theater and Film: A Christian Perspective* (Enumclaw, WA: Redemption, 2007). Kuritz's book, however, takes a different tack than does *The Wages of Cinema.*

[6]James Brabazon, *Dorothy L. Sayers: A Biography* (New York: Scribner's, 1981), 155; David Coomes, *Dorothy L. Sayers: A Careless Rage for Life* (Batavia, IL: Lion, 1992), 118.

Unpublished correspondence proves otherwise. *The Wages of Cinema* demonstrates not only Sayers's continuing interest in movies, but also that her Christian aesthetic reinforces secular theories about film form, much as the non-Christian Virgil illuminated Christian theology for readers of Dante. Perhaps not coincidentally, film theory, as it is called, was initially developed by contemporaries of Sayers who were screening the exact same movies she was.

## Behind the Screen

Because almost every single letter celebrating cinema was screened out of the four-volume collection of Sayers's published letters, *The Wages of Cinema* relies on archival research, projecting light on little-known material. For example, in letters to her parents, Sayers enthusiastically praises movies she has just screened, occasionally adding drawings of interesting shots. A decade after she tried to break into the film industry, she published an essay in *Sight and Sound*, a world-renowned journal produced by the British Film Institute. In the 1940s she discussed film adaptation with Michael Powell, the much-lauded British director who mentored Oscar-winning Martin Scorsese. In the 1950s Sayers socialized with stage and film star Dame Sybil Thorndike, who shared the screen with the likes of Marilyn Monroe and Sir Laurence Olivier. As late as 1955, Sayers wrote friends that she was planning to screen *Pinocchio*, the award-winning 1940 Disney cartoon, which had recently been rereleased in England.[7]

Even the heading of this section, "Behind the Screen," suggests the relevance of cinema to Sayers's life. Not only did she enjoy Charlie Chaplin movies, perhaps even screening *Behind the Screen*, which Chaplin released in 1916 when Sayers was often attending cinema, but *Behind the Screen* also names a serial detective story to which Sayers contributed. Written for BBC radio by multiple members of the Detection Club, an exclusive London organization established in 1930, the collaborative story is one of Sayers's many contributions to the club, including a term as president. Conversations at events surely focused on films adapted from club members' novels, including multiple movies by Alfred Hitchcock.[8] Helen Simpson, Sayers's best friend in the

[7]These film events will be discussed later. For *Pinocchio*, see Dorothy L. Sayers to "Bar and Muriel," April 1, 1955 (Wade 185/94).

[8]For film adaptations of books written by Sayers's friends in the Detection Club, see Martin Edwards, *The Golden Age of Murder: The Mystery of the Writers Who Invented the Modern Detective Story* (London: HarperCollins, 2015), 31, 49, 105, 113, 115, 117, 144, 154, 212, 389, 423-24.

Detection Club, wrote dialogue for Hitchcock after he had successfully adapted one of her novels for the screen. And the first president of the Detection Club, G. K. Chesterton, often referred to cinema in his writings, having costarred with George Bernard Shaw in *How Men Love*, a 1914 cowboy movie directed by J. M. Barrie, the author of *Peter Pan*. Sayers, who screened *Peter Pan* after it was made into a 1924 silent film, identified Chesterton as probably the most profound influence on her "mental makeup."[9] It is no wonder that references to cinema are scattered throughout Sayers's unpublished letters.

Also scattered throughout her letters are references to sin, that which screens us from reconciliation with our Creator. Sayers's commitment to Christian orthodoxy arises from her firm belief that "all have sinned and fall short of the glory of God" (Rom 3:23). Though impatient with evangelical pietism, the Anglo-Catholic Sayers firmly believed that accepting God's gift of salvation through Jesus Christ released humans from "the wages of sin," a biblical phrase she inserted into her detective fiction, even before her faith was reignited in middle age.[10] Humbled by the wages of her own sin and frustrated with the wages from cinema, Sayers came to a startling conclusion: "What we make is more important than what we are—particularly if 'making' is our profession."[11] This statement applies to the writing of movie treatments as well as novels, poetry as well as essays, translations as well as literary criticism, plays as well as letters, all forms of making that engaged Sayers. Feeling burdened by consequences of a sin she kept hidden her entire life, even from her closest friends, Sayers rejoiced in her ability to offer gifts that, *if made well*, reflect the glory of a Maker who offers the gift of forgiveness to all who will accept it.

Creative making, Sayers believed, reflected the three virtues celebrated by famed Greek philosopher Plato: the good, the true, and the beautiful. However, according to her view of art, the *good* is "good craftsmanship, 'beauty' is artistic beauty, and 'truth' is structural truth."[12] And she would find it quite

[9]For an example of references to film, see G. K. Chesterton, *The Everlasting Man* (New York: Dover, 2007), 21-22. For Sayers's screening of *Peter Pan*, see *Letters* 1:228. For her reference to Chesterton's influence, see *Letters* 1:394.

[10]See, for example, Dorothy L. Sayers, *Strong Poison*, in *Dorothy L. Sayers: On the Case with Lord Peter Wimsey* (New York: Wings Books, 1991), 60; and Dorothy L. Sayers, "Blood Sacrifice," in *Dorothy L. Sayers: In the Teeth of the Evidence and Other Mysteries* (New York: HarperCollins, 1993), 160.

[11]*Letters* 2:221-22.

[12]Dorothy L. Sayers, *The Mind of the Maker* (New York: HarperCollins, 1979), 97.

disconcerting that craft, beauty, and structure are rarely explored in books about cinema and faith.

## Seeing Versus Doubting

Christians who doubt the theological importance of visual beauty might feel led to cite the famous comment by Jesus to Thomas, "Blessed are those who have not seen and yet have believed" (Jn 20:29). Thomas, of course, doubted Christ was alive because he missed seeing Christ's postresurrection appearances (Jn 20:24), leading to his famous moniker, "doubting Thomas." Sayers, however, points out that "the one absolutely unequivocal statement, in the whole Gospel, of the Divinity of Jesus" comes from doubting Thomas after he sees with his own eyes the medium of salvation: "My Lord and my God" (Jn 20:28). Quoting from the original Greek to prove her point, Sayers asserts that Thomas uses the word *God* "without qualification, and in the most unambiguous form of words."[13] Hence, when she wrote a script for the incident that was aired on BBC radio, she prepared listeners for Thomas's "unambiguous" proclamation by having him say, "Seeing's believing," a line that people writing about the relationship between faith and film have repeatedly employed.[14]

One such book, *Seeing Is Believing,* has as its subtitle *The Revelation of God Through Film,* reminding us of the revelation of the incarnate God to Thomas. Indeed, author Richard Vance Goodwin invokes the doubting Thomas story to argue, "Film images can be religiously powerful and even conducive to revelation. . . . We might take our cue from another of Jesus' blessings: 'Blessed are your eyes because they see' (Mt 13:16)."[15] Sayers would emphatically agree, drawing attention not only to images on the screen, but also to *how* we *see* them, whether via close-up, point-of-view shot, over-the-shoulder shot, deep focus, rack focus, shot-reverse-shot, and so on, terms that will be illustrated in the course of this book. As Matthew puts it in his Gospel, "The eye is the lamp of the body. If your eyes are healthy, your whole body will be

---

[13]Dorothy L. Sayers, *The Man Born to Be King: A Play-Cycle on the Life of Our Lord and Savior Jesus Christ* (Grand Rapids, MI: Eerdmans, 1943), 315.

[14]Sayers, *Man Born to Be King,* 336. See Richard Vance Goodwin, *Seeing Is Believing: The Revelation of God Through Film* (Downers Grove, IL: InterVarsity Press, 2022); Robert Benne, *Seeing Is Believing: Visions of Life Through Film* (Lanham, MD: University Press of America, 1998); Margaret R. Miles, *Seeing and Believing: Religion and Values in the Movies* (Boston: Beacon, 1996).

[15]Goodwin, *Seeing Is Believing,* 17.

full of light. But if your eyes are unhealthy, your whole body will be full of darkness" (Mt 6:22-23). The Greek word translated "healthy" in this passage "implies *generous*."[16] *The Wages of Cinema*, then, is about inculcating healthy, generous eyes, eyes that focus on visual detail rather than merely searching for Christian messages.

## Detecting Visual Details

Attention to visual detail informs Sayers's fiction-making career from the start, perhaps because she began conceptualizing her first mystery novel while still working on silent film scenarios. In *Whose Body?* (1923), the work that launched her reputation as a detective novelist, a man entirely naked except for pince-nez on his nose is discovered dead in a bathtub. Sayers's amateur sleuth, Lord Peter Wimsey, proceeds to solve the mystery by noticing multiple signs professional detectives have missed. It takes viewers with special lenses, like Lord Peter with his monocle, to separate the significant from the incidental.[17]

The same could be said of cinema. Most people go to movies seeing only the narrative incidents portrayed on screen, failing to detect significant details that embody the mystery of cinematic art. Books about Christianity and film all too often follow suit, authors saying little about a movie that could not be gleaned simply by reading its screenplay.[18] When Christian investigators do focus on screen imagery, they often fixate on one particular sign, such as a cruciform pose, identifying a Christ-figure with no supporting evidence from the rest of the film. As Robert K. Johnston aptly notes in *Reel Spirituality*, "There is a danger, as anyone teaching in the field of Christianity and the arts knows, in having overenthusiastic viewers find Christ-figures in and behind every crossbar or mysterious origin."[19] Sayers recognized a similar problem

---

[16]John H. Walton and Craig S. Keener, eds., *NIV Cultural Backgrounds Study Bible* (Grand Rapids, MI: Zondervan, 2016), 1622, emphasis added.

[17]I also make this point in "The Power of Imagination: The Seeing of Sayers and Cinema," *Journal of Christian Legal Thought* 12, no. 2 (2022): 52. This five-page essay in fact could serve as an abstract of what I argue in *The Wages of Cinema*.

[18]I also explore this problem in *Salvation from Cinema: The Medium Is the Message* (New York: Routledge, 2016). However, in the earlier book I assess scholarship in the field of "religion and film," discussing multiple religions. Giving greater attention to the history of cinematic form, *The Wages of Cinema* narrows to the particularity of Christianity.

[19]Robert K. Johnston, *Reel Spirituality: Theology and Film in Dialogue* (Grand Rapids, MI: Baker Academic, 2000). 53. For similar cautions against the "discovery" of Christ-figures in film, see Christopher Deacy,

almost eighty years earlier, having Lord Peter inform Detective Inspector Charles Parker that all too many investigators "find what they are looking for."[20]

Most Christian film sleuths parallel Charles Parker. A man of integrity and insight who reads Bible commentaries and works of theology, Parker serves as collaborator and friend for Lord Peter in Sayers's early novels. However, he always seems to be one step behind the nonreligious Wimsey, who detects the truth through greater sensitivity to visual detail. Expecting her readers to notice clues as well, Sayers criticizes mystery authors who do not expose readers to clues before the mystery is solved.[21] In other words, she expects readers, whether of books or of films, to be cognizant of visual subtleties. When a correspondent questioned whether Christians should go to the movies, Sayers replied, "It is *easier* to say that all films are wicked than to select them with care, and learn to tell good art from bad." And she summarized the importance of such care with a theological point: "Did God make beauty and give artists their genius for nothing? Did He *intend* them for traps and temptations? Surely it is rather blasphemous to think that."[22] Instead, she wanted Christians to value the architectural beauty of a movie as much as its story line.

## The Architecture of Cinema

A year after Sayers published *Whose Body?*, Hungarian poet and film critic Béla Balázs denounced those who elevated story over the craft of cinema: "A person who judges a film by its storyline seems to me to resemble someone who says of a love poem: 'What's so special about this poem? She is beautiful and he loves her!'" Over forty years later, Alfred Hitchcock bemoaned that the "mass audience has had no education in technique of cinema" and "think only of story."[23] Famous film theorist Christian Metz identified the same problem around the same time: "The rule of the 'story' is so powerful that the image, which is said to be the major constituent of film, vanishes behind the plot it

---

"Theology and Film," in *Theology and Film: Challenging the Sacred/Secular Divide*, ed. Christopher Deacy and Gaye Williams Ortiz (Malden, MA: Blackwell, 2008), 5-6, 27-28.

[20]Dorothy L. Sayers, *Whose Body?* (New York: Avon, 1961), 118. For a précis of cinema references in Peter Wimsey detective fiction, see Philip L. Scowcroft, "Dorothy L. Sayers and the Cinema," *Sidelights on Sayers* 4 (April 1984): 20-22.

[21]Dorothy L. Sayers, introduction to *The Omnibus of Crime*, ed. Dorothy L. Sayers (New York: Payson and Clarke, 1929), 9-47. Sayers makes clear that Lord Peter is not a Christian in *Mind of the Maker*, 131.

[22]Dorothy L. Sayers to Miss S. Bates, July 22, 1948 (Wade 28/5), emphasis original.

[23]Quoted in Gene Adair, *Alfred Hitchcock: Filming Our Fears* (Oxford: Oxford University Press, 2002), 100.

has woven."[24] Things have changed little since these pronouncements, with story still ruling the way people discuss film.

This is not to say that Sayers dismissed the power of story. When C. S. Lewis asked her to write an essay in honor of novelist and Dante scholar Charles Williams, she titled her contribution ". . . And Telling You a Story," focusing her discussion on Dante's ability, in the *Divine Comedy,* to communicate theological insight through narrative. However, she makes clear in the essay that the *form* of Dante's story, its "architectural beauty," as she calls it, is its "*chief* glory."[25] Sensitive to the glory of well-crafted form, Sayers had long expressed impatience with Christians who produce stories merely "to *illustrate* certain doctrine or church activities," especially annoyed when the stories were "blasphemously incompetent" movies produced by a "religious film society."[26]

Sayers believed that "for any work of art to be acceptable to God it must first be right with itself. That is to say, the artist must serve God in the technique of his craft," and she reinforced her point with the example of cinema: "Actors for religious films and plays should be chosen for their good acting and not chosen for their Christian sentiment or moral worth regardless of whether they are good actors or not." She later says something very similar about the need for excellent production values: "There is nothing (except the expense) to prevent the filming of a Life of Christ—but here again, the properly qualified people are rare, and the making of a film is a complicated job, in which a good script can be sabotaged by unintelligent production."[27] Sayers believed Christians should endorse art not simply for art's sake but for God's sake as well.

## Art for Art's Sake: Sayers and Sontag

The Latin words *ars gratia artis,* "art for the sake of art," were appropriated in 1917 by Goldwyn Pictures, which used the famous aphorism to frame a roaring

---

[24]Christian Metz, *Film Language: A Semiotics of the Cinema,* trans. Michael Taylor (Chicago: University of Chicago Press, 1974), 45. Metz's statement was originally published in French in 1964.

[25]Dorothy L. Sayers, ". . . And Telling You a Story," in *Further Papers on Dante* (London: Methuen, 1957), 36, emphasis added.

[26]*Letters* 2:261, emphasis added. In 2020 Steven Vredenburgh expressed similar dismay over a film made by Christians. See "Evangelizing Atheism: Missing the Mark in Recent Christian Film," *Christian Scholar's Review* 50, no. 1 (Fall 2020): 61-84.

[27]*Letters* 2:261, 200-201.

lion for its new trademark. Of course, anyone familiar with the history of American film will find the motto exceedingly ironic, since art for art's sake was the last thing studio heads worried about. Nevertheless, it is significant that Goldwyn borrowed a phrase from nineteenth-century aesthetes, retaining the motto after the 1924 Metro-Goldwyn-Mayer merger. Both Goldwyn and MGM wanted to expand their audiences by appealing to more sophisticated viewers, ones who valued art for its own sake.

Familiar with the "art for art's sake" movement promoted by Oscar Wilde, with whom her father socialized at Oxford University, Sayers gave Peter Wimsey a similar aesthetic. At the very start of *Whose Body?*, the aristocratic Lord Peter is traveling to an auction in order to bid on a "Folio Dante," clearly motivated by its physical form—a rare 1481 edition of *The Divine Comedy*—rather than by its content, which could be read in a far cheaper edition.[28] Later in the novel, after a medical student admires the Dante folio, Peter proceeds to discuss detective stories with him by focusing on form—"*how* the story was put together"—much as she would later focus on the "architectural beauty" of Dante.[29] One wonders whether it is more than coincidence that, in *Whose Body?*, Sayers places the murdered corpse in an architect's bathtub. After all, she was concentrating on the architecture of film stories—how they were put together—when she began to conceptualize her first novel.

Appreciation for how stories are put together can lend beauty to even the ugliest images, as when Dante powerfully describes the tortures of hell. In 1944, as Allied forces were uncovering Nazi atrocities, Sayers wrote,

> Art that is the true image of experience is true art, even though the experience is ugly or immoral (as the image of God is still the image of God, even in a wicked man); but you can't make untrue, or venal, or incompetent art into good art, by putting it in a church or extracting morals from it, any more than you can get the Holy Spirit out of a tin of petrol.[30]

With these words Sayers anticipated by decades a perspective made popular by scholar Susan Sontag in the 1960s, the same decade in which Hitchcock and Metz were descrying obsession with film stories. Arguing that one should "cherish works of art which, considered in terms of 'content,' are morally objectionable,"

---

[28]Sayers, *Whose Body?*, 10.

[29]Sayers, *Whose Body?*, 145.

[30]*Letters* 3:27.

Sontag offers grace even to the visually stunning Nazi propaganda films made by Leni Riefenstahl, *The Triumph of the Will* (1935) and *The Olympiad* (1938). After Béla Balázs helped Riefenstahl direct a 1932 film that he cowrote with her, Riefenstahl removed his name from the credits due to his Jewish origins; nevertheless, the Jewish Sontag continued to praise the *craft* of Riefenstahl.

Often quoted by film scholars, Sontag thoroughly believed, "What is needed, first, is more attention to form in art," ending her famous essay "Against Interpretation" with a metaphor about the problem of extracting morals: "Our task is not to find the maximum amount of content in a work of art, much less to squeeze more content out of the work than is already there." Furthermore, like Sayers, Sontag repeatedly alludes to Dante while discussing the importance of attending to "the sensuous surface of art," what theologian Hans Urs von Balthasar famously calls "seeing the form."[31] Like von Balthasar, Sayers considered the importance of form to be inseparable from Christian faith. When she writes in 1941 that a true artist "retains so much of the image of God that he is in love with his creation for its own sake," Sayers anticipates by more than sixty years Christian cinephiles who argue that "human creativity" should "be seen as analogous to God's creativity because it reflects the all-pervasive consequences of creation in *imago Dei*."[32]

Contemplating the *imago Dei* with more and more intensity as she aged, Sayers took very seriously the Bible verse that inspired it: "God created humans in his image, in the *image of God* he created them; male and female he created them" (Gen 1:27 NRSV). Summarizing Sayers's sense of this verse, theologian Laura Simmons slyly puns on the word *make*: "Genesis suggests that the desire and the ability to *make* things are what *make* humans most like God and that we are closest and truest to the image of God within us when we are engaged in the act of creation."[33] This is the theological principle that Fujimura borrowed from Sayers, quoting her near the start of his book *Art and Faith*

---

31 Susan Sontag, *Against Interpretation and Other Essays* (New York: Farrar, Straus & Giroux, 1967), 25, 12, 14, 13. For Sontag's Dante references, see 13, 25, 27. See also Hans Urs von Balthasar, *Seeing the Form*, vol. 1 of *The Glory of the Lord: A Theological Aesthetics*, trans. Erasmo Leiva-Merikakis (New York: Crossroad, 1983).

32 Sayers, *Mind of the Maker*, 221; Robert Pope, "Speaking of God and Donald Duck: Realism, Non-realism and Animation," in *Cinéma Divinité: Religion, Theology and the Bible in Film*, ed. Eric S. Christianson et al. (London: SCM Press, 2005), 169.

33 Laura K. Simmons, *Creed Without Chaos: Exploring Theology in the Writings of Dorothy L. Sayers* (Grand Rapids, MI: Baker Academic, 2005), 139. Simmons's chapter "Creativity and Art" (133-43) provides a helpful introduction to Sayers's theology of art.

as saying, "The characteristic common to God and man is apparently . . . the desire and the ability to make things." Several pages later he echoes Sayers by stating, "We are *Imago Dei,* created to be creative, and we are by nature creative makers."[34]

Christians interested in cinema could take the *imago Dei* one step further, noting that the God in whose image we are created also takes delight in *seeing* the goodness of creation. The Hebrew word for "seeing" is repeated seven times in fewer than thirty verses in Genesis 1: "And God *saw* that it was good. . . . And God *saw* that it was good." The *imago Dei,* in other words, encompasses not only creative making but also the ability to see the goodness of created form.

### Cinematic Docetism Versus Christian Dogma

Ironically, all too many books about faith and film echo a heresy that developed in the early centuries of Christianity, what Sayers calls "that Docetic and totally heretical Christology which denies the full Humanity of Our Lord."[35] Based on a Greek word that means "to seem," docetism is associated with Bishop Marcion (ca. 85–ca. 160 CE), an earnest follower of Christ who believed that Jesus only *seemed* to be human. Antagonistic to the idea that God would take on flesh, Marcion denounced the incarnation, believing the idea to be "a disgrace to God" since the human body is "stuffed with excrement."[36] As Diarmaid MacCulloch summarizes, Christ's "Passion and Resurrection in history were," for docetists, "not fleshly events, even if they *seemed* so; they were heavenly play-acting."[37] MacCulloch's metaphor about playacting harmonizes with Sayers's explicit alignment of docetism with any kind of storytelling in which the creator/author seems "antagonistic to the medium he is working in," much as Marcion was antagonistic to God working in the medium of flesh.[38]

Christian discussions of film, then, sound docetic when they ignore the medium itself. For example, one author proclaims his focus to be "Christian

---

[34]Makoto Fujimura, *Art and Faith: A Theology of Making* (New Haven, CT: Yale University Press, 2020), 6, 14, ellipsis original.

[35]Dorothy L. Sayers, introduction to *Man Born to Be King*, 2. For other references to docetism in relation to the radio plays, see *Letters* 2:73, 282.

[36]See Jaroslav Pelikan, *The Christian Tradition: A History of the Development of Doctrine*, vol. 1, *The Emergence of the Catholic Tradition (100–600)* (Chicago: University of Chicago Press, 1971), 75.

[37]Diarmaid MacCulloch, *Christianity: The First Three Thousand Years* (New York: Viking, 2010), 124, emphasis added.

[38]*Letters* 2:267.

truths that are *illustrated* in popular films," another celebrates movies for "*carrying* and *conveying* religious hopes and values," and a third "calls us to go to the movies to hear and see sermons."[39] Such statements reduce film to a content-delivery system, much as second-century docetists reduced Jesus to a content-delivery system. Disturbed by the way Christian critics "mined" movies "for the sake of theological nuggets," one Catholic film reviewer states, like Sayers decades before him, that "the essence of art can't be reached by skipping over its materiality, its sensuous surface."[40]

*The Wages of Cinema* therefore argues that, just as Jesus should not be considered a mere conveyor of God's spirit on earth, movies should not be treated as mere conveyors of spiritual insight. This harmonizes with what secular film scholars have been saying for decades: "A film *enacts* ideological meaning through its form."[41] Sayers's description of effective detective fiction could in fact summarize artistic cinema: "The essential facts of the HOW arrange themselves to form a synthesis (by which time, of course, they usually include the WHY as well)."[42] Indeed, film scholar James Monaco echoes Sayers when he argues, "The drama of film, its attraction, lies not so much in what is shot (that is the drama of the subject), but in *how* it is shot and *how* it is presented."[43] In other words, the *how* of cinematic form establishes the *why* of movie meaning.

The same might be said of the drama of salvation. As Sayers put it in 1938, "The dogma is the drama."[44] Seeking to combat heresies such as docetism, bishops in ecumenical councils determined that dogma about *how* must explain *why* Jesus can save humanity from the wages of sin. After the First Council of Constantinople (381 CE) confirmed the hypostatic union of God

---

[39]James Hogan, *Reel Parables: Life Lessons from Popular Films* (Mahwah, NJ: Paulist, 2007), 1; Christopher Deacy, *Screen Christologies: Redemption and the Medium of Film* (Cardiff, UK: University of Wales Press, 2001), 14; Tony Campolo, foreword to Gareth Higgins, *How Movies Helped Save My Soul: Finding Spiritual Fingerprints in Culturally Significant Films* (Lake Mary, FL: Relevant Media Group, 2003), x, emphases added.

[40]Richard Alleva, "'I Would Toss Myself Aside': Confessions of a Catholic Film Critic," *Image: A Journal of the Arts and Religion* 20 (Summer 1998): 105. I also use the phrase "content-delivery system" in *Salvation from Cinema*, 24.

[41]David Bordwell, Kristen Thompson, and Jeff Smith, *Film Art: An Introduction*, 11th ed. (New York: McGraw Hill, 2017), 60, emphasis original.

[42]*Letters* 1:389.

[43]James Monaco, *How to Read a Film: The Art, Technology, Language, History, and Theory of Film and Media*, rev. ed. (New York: Oxford University Press, 1981), 137.

[44]"The Dogma Is the Drama" names an essay Sayers first published in *St. Martin's Review Literary Supplement* (April 1938): 20.

in Christ proclaimed at Nicaea in 325, the Council at Chalcedon (451 CE) clarified the *how* of the union: not two separate natures in one body, as suggested by Christ-loving followers of Nestorius, but Jesus as *both* fully God *and* fully human simultaneously. In other words, both/and thinking grounds Christian orthodoxy, explaining why Sayers wrote an entire play to celebrate both/and thinking initiated at the first Council of Nicaea in 325, titled *The Emperor Constantine* (1951).

## The God Born to Be Man

Sayers applied both/and thinking to dramatic scripts, whether written for stage, screen, or radio. In her introduction to the published version of *The Man Born to Be King*, the title of her twelve radio plays about the life of Jesus, Sayers states, "My object was *to tell that story* to the best of my ability, within the medium at my disposal—in short to make as good a work of art as I could. For a work of art that is not good and true *in art* is not good or true in any other respect, and is useless for any purpose whatsoever—even for edification."[45] In her eleventh play, *The King of Sorrows*, Sayers therefore alludes to the hypostatic union through dialogue she gives to Mary, the mother of Jesus: "You cannot *see* the immortal truth till it is born in the flesh of the fact."[46] Sayers thus advocates a hypostatic union between inspirational story and artistry of the medium, implying that a Christian response to cinema should reflect similar both/and thinking, that a well-crafted movie should be valued for both its form (the visual facts of the film) and the immortal truth of its content.[47] Indeed, she later argues that "Christian revelation" should not be separated from "truth about Art": "We have merely allowed them to exist side by side in our minds; and where the conflict between them became too noisy to be overlooked, we have tried to silence the clamour by main force, either by brutally subjugating Art to religion, or by shutting them up in separate prison cells and forbidding them to hold any communication with one another."[48]

---

45Sayers, introduction to *Man Born to Be King*, 4, emphasis original.

46Sayers, *Man Born to Be King*, 289, emphasis added.

47Craig Detweiler similarly argues for "a both/and approach to theology and film," an approach that unites "the best in aesthetic evaluation" with "a firm emphasis on the message, the story, the meaning of movies." However, he does not discuss the history and theory of film form. See Detweiler, *Into the Dark: Seeing the Sacred in the Top Films of the Twenty-First Century* (Grand Rapids, MI: Baker Academic, 2008), 43.

48Dorothy L. Sayers, "Towards a Christian Aesthetic," in *Christian Letters to a Post-Christian World: A Selection of Essays* (Grand Rapids, MI: Eerdmans, 1969), 70. Sayers originally wrote the essay for a 1944 lecture.

## The Union of Form and Content

In her first novel, Sayers establishes that Lord Peter values his rare folio Dante for the glory of its form. But she also has him figure out how to solve the identity of the victim in the bathtub only after reflecting on the Christian contents of his rare book: "While communing with Dante, he made up his mind." After visiting his main suspect, he arranges to exhume the murdered body. As two gravediggers join him in the cemetery, narrative elements from Dante's *Inferno* are played out before his eyes: "Two Dantesque shapes with pitchforks loomed up." Unnerved, Wimsey calms down when he feels Parker's trench coat beneath his fingers. Parker's presence, like the contents of Parker's Christian theology, provides comfort in the face of death, causing Wimsey to reflect, "You clung on now for fear you should get separated." Like Lord Peter and Detective Inspector Parker, then, form and content should not be separated. Sayers does not separate Wimsey and Parker even after they identify the victim. Following the Dante-like exhumation, "Lord Peter was playing Bach and Parker was reading Origen," the former relishing message-free beauty, the latter assessing the content of an early church theologian.[49]

As though coming full circle from her first published novel, Sayers ended her career synthesizing the form and content of Dante. While translating Dante's *Inferno* into English, she addressed a Virgil Society in 1948, arguing for the need to unite form and matter.[50] Whereas many English editions of Dante's first two books focus primarily on accurately translating the great Italian's *content*, Sayers wanted to also capture Dante's *form*, imitating his rhyme scheme. Furthermore, she arranged to have her publisher, Penguin Books, include diagrams and illustrations to aid in the understanding of Dante's architectural schema.[51] As Barbara Reynolds notes in *The Passionate Intellect*, Sayers believed that Dante "*saw* what he wrote: it was not just a matter of words. And she was equally convinced that few translators took the trouble to *see* the picture which the words evoke."[52]

---

[49]Sayers, *Whose Body?*, 161, 170, 175.

[50]Dorothy L. Sayers, "Dante's Virgil," in *Further Papers on Dante*, 53.

[51]Sayers even created some of her own linocut illustrations to capture elements from the narrative. Reynolds includes not only Sayers's illustrations and diagrams but also comments from scholars who critiqued her use of terza rima in *The Passionate Intellect: Dorothy L. Sayers' Encounter with Dante* (Kent, OH: Kent State University Press, 1989), 64-65.

[52]Reynolds, *Passionate Intellect*, 138, emphasis original.

From Peter to *Paradiso*, then, Sayers recognized the importance of seeing what others have missed, suggesting a relationship that she would explore with more and more passion. As she explains in a letter outlining her career, Sayers was committed not only to telling truth but also to "the right use of my own medium," thus guaranteeing an accurate "image of that truth." This explains what attracted Sayers to Dante in the first place: "his power of using words to make *a visual picture*."[53]

We should therefore take note that an Italian adaptation of *The Inferno* (*L'Inferno*, 1911), one of the first feature films to attract international attention, was released in Britain in October 1912, the same month Sayers matriculated at Somerville College in Oxford, where she frequented the town's six cinemas.[54] This explains why Sayers evaluated Dante's *Inferno* in cinematic terms. In a 1946 lecture she praised Dante's text by saying, "We see the whole action as though it were shown on a screen."[55] A decade later, she wrote Italian scholar Barbara Reynolds that Dante's "pace and fluidity and his variation of tempo get lost unless one can see the poem reeling out like a film." It may be no coincidence, then, that Sayers affirms the visual power of Dante with imagery that sounds as if she were talking about the darkened space of a cinema theater:

> The pictures that come floating up out of the dark sea of the unconscious link themselves together into an associative pattern, until gradually, some kind of significance seems to emerge. But to strip off the imagery and present the naked intellectual content is next door to impossible, for the images *are* the content, and the significance scarcely exists apart from them.[56]

*The Wages of Cinema* argues as well that "the images *are* the content." Images are linked "into an associative pattern" on the screen, often with "unconscious" effects, as film theorists have famously argued. Those theorists would also

---

[53]*Letters* 4:140; Sayers, "Dante's Imagery: I. Symbolic," in *Introductory Papers on Dante* (New York: Barnes & Noble, 1969), 1, emphasis added.

[54]David C. Cook, *A History of Narrative Film*, 2nd ed. (New York: Norton, 1990), 39. The number of cinemas in Oxford comes from a 1914 report cited in Colin Harding and Simon Popple, *In the Kingdom of Shadows: A Companion to Early Cinema* (Madison, WI: Fairleigh Dickinson University Press, 1996), 209. Unpublished letters testify to Sayers's delight with movies she screened during her years at Oxford.

[55]Dorothy L. Sayers, "The Eighth Bolgia," in *Further Papers on Dante*, 106. I also quote this line in "Through the Screen: Dorothy L. Sayers's Journey to New Worlds," *VII: Journal of the Marion E. Wade Center* 36 (2019): 7. In this essay I give additional evidence that Sayers probably screened *Dante's Inferno*.

[56]*Letters* 4:331; Sayers, "Dante's Imagery," 1, emphasis original.

endorse Sayers's assertion that "to substitute the explanation" for a work of art merely serves to "disintegrate the image."[57]

## A Guide to the Projection of Wages

Sayers also serves as a worthy guide to cinema through her affirmation of historical knowledge. Convinced that God entered human history as Jesus Christ, Sayers knew that attention to history was imperative for intelligent faith. Hence, for her 1949 translation of Dante's *Inferno*, she provides a twenty-two-page overview of Italian politics to contextualize the various historical figures that Virgil and Dante encounter in hell.[58]

Inspired by Sayers, *The Wages of Cinema* begins with history as well: the history of theater, illustrating how the stage not only provided paradigms still employed in movies today but also influenced Christianity. Chapter two then discusses important figures in the history of narrative cinema to illustrate dramatic differences between stage and screen, closing with discussion of an award-winning film that addresses the vexed relationship between theater and film. A radically different kind of theater informs chapter three: the theater of war. Sayers lived through both world wars, and her experiences can help Christians assess the artistry of war films.

It was during World War II that Sayers refined her Christian aesthetic, and chapter four looks at how the history of synchronized sound in cinema contributed to her theory. Chapter five then demonstrates how Sayers's theology of creativity not only illuminates the artistry of famous filmmakers but also provides language with which Christians can adjudicate differences between mass entertainment and cinematic art. Secular theories about such artistry are the subject of chapter six, showing how the discourse known as film theory reinforces Sayers's Christian aesthetic. Chapter seven then narrows the focus to one theoretical approach to cinema: feminist film theory. Sayers, who refused to call herself a feminist, can help Christians understand and address the marginalization of brilliant women artists who powerfully influenced the film industry.

---

57Dorothy L. Sayers, "The Poetry of the Image in Dante and Charles Williams," in *Further Papers on Dante*, 183-84. For film theory parallels, see Jean-Louis Baudry, "The Apparatus: Metapsychological Approaches to the Impression of Reality in Cinema," in *Film Theory and Criticism: Introductory Readings*, 6th ed., ed. Leo Braudy and Marshall Cohen (New York: Oxford University Press, 2004), 206-23.

58Dorothy L. Sayers, introduction to *The Comedy of Dante Alighieri the Florentine: Cantica I, Hell*, trans. Dorothy L. Sayers (Harmondsworth, UK: Penguin, 1949), 17-39.

Chapter eight ties together multiple strands of the book by discussing love, which is the origin of salvation from the wages of sin: "For God so loved the world that he gave his one and only Son, that whoever believes in him shall not perish but have eternal life" (Jn 3:16). Love on screen, however, usually gets reduced to sex acts. The last chapter therefore focuses on the visual artistry of films that subvert Hollywood clichés about erotic love, invoking insights from *The Four Loves* by Sayers's friend C. S. Lewis while celebrating the Love behind Sayers's Christian aesthetic.

*The Wages of Cinema* closes with a coda, a chapter that can be read either before or after the rest of the book. It is written for those who want to learn more about the qualifications of Dorothy L. Sayers as a Christian guide to film form, showing how her life intersects not only with the origins of cinema but also with some of the greatest filmmakers of all time. It will help explain why Sayers despaired that only when "a new film has cost many thousands"—and now millions—of dollars do many think "that it must be a good film." It further shows why she worried over young people crowding movie theaters, "gaping at film-stars in plutocratic surroundings and imbecile situations and wishing with all their heart that they too could live like the heroes and heroines of these witless million-dollar screen stories." Her goal, like the goal of this book, was to encourage viewers in "a less commercial . . . more religious conception of what work ought to be."[59]

This does not mean that *The Wages of Cinema* discusses only artsy films that few people have seen, as though written by a "hoity-toity film buff," to use the words of William Romanowski.[60] Encouraging Christians to become creative viewers of many different genres of film, it discusses *King Kong* movies and other box-office hits, such as *Barbie* (2023), as well as little-known movies. Inspired by Sayers, it includes lengthy, in-depth analyses of cinematic techniques in some movies while only briefly alluding to other films. In the process, it follows the example of the *Divine Comedy*: just as Dante sometimes explores parts of Inferno and Purgatorio with little input from Virgil, so also this book invokes historians and cinephiles with little input from Sayers. Nevertheless,

---

[59]Dorothy L. Sayers, "Living to Work," in *Unpopular Opinions* (London: Gollancz, 1946), 124-25.

[60]William Romanowski, *Cinematic Faith: A Christian Perspective on Movies and Meaning* (Grand Rapids, MI: Baker Academic, 2019), 2. Though taking a radically different approach than I do, Romanowski attends to the importance of film aesthetics.

her Christian aesthetic grounds this entire study, as when she said of Dante, "The best that the interpreter can do is to contemplate the image with an open and a humble mind in the hope that it may communicate . . . something of the reality which it images." Applied to cinema, this means contemplation of the work itself, what Susan Sontag calls "the explicit, complex, and discussable technology of camera movements, cutting, and composition of the frame that goes into the *making* of the film."[61]

By demonstrating how the Christian lens of Dorothy L. Sayers fits onto the projectors of non-Christian theorists such as Sontag and many others, *The Wages of Cinema* models both/and thinking, providing a fresh approach to the relationship between film and our both/and Lord, an incarnate God who told his disciples, "The worker deserves his wages" (Lk 10:7). All workers, of course, are important to the artistry of a well-made film, but a book such as this cannot name each one, so it uses the director's name to represent the entire film crew. Sayers went so far as to suggest that everyone involved with a theater (or cinema) production functioned like an effective church. And because she adored live theater even more than narrative cinema, we now turn to the ancient theatrical origins of narrative cinema.

[61]Dorothy L. Sayers, "Dante and Charles Williams," in *Further Papers on Dante*, 184; Sontag, *Against Interpretation*, 13, 12.

# 1

# The Religious Origins of Cinema

Christians who write about film often fail to consider its connection to the stage—an oversight especially problematic for those who talk about movies in terms of the stories they tell.[1] After all, theater presented stories for viewing audiences millennia before moving images were a glint on the lenses of nineteenth-century cameras. Greek theater even preceded the gospel message, influencing it in multiple ways. This chapter therefore argues that a full appreciation for the relation between Christianity and film necessitates knowledge about the history of theater. Oxford-educated Dorothy L. Sayers, who not only read classical drama but also wrote scripts for both stage and screen, can help us see theater with new eyes.

## The Seeds of Cinema

Without a doubt, the seeds of narrative cinema were incubated on theatrical stages.[2] In the silent era, filmmakers often adapted stage plays, such as those starring Sarah Bernhardt (1844–1923), who reprised her famed theatrical roles for the screen. When "talkies" took off in 1927, studios recruited Broadway stage writers to compose dialogue. French filmmaker Marcel

---

[1]For exceptions see Paul Kuritz, *Theater and Film: A Christian Perspective* (Enumclaw, WA: Redemption, 2014); Gerard Loughlin, *Alien Sex: The Body and Desire in Cinema and Theology* (Malden, MA: Blackwell, 2004); and Terry Lindvall, *Sanctuary Cinema: Origins of the Christian Film Industry* (New York: New York University Press, 2007). Kuritz discusses theater and film as important expressions of the *imago Dei* but does not explore historical parallels or medium distinctions between the two. Loughlin provides a two-page summary of medieval theater (*Alien Sex*, 51-52) to argue for the religious function of film. Lindvall discusses theater in the context of Christian resistance to it (*Sanctuary Cinema*, 28-34), making the point that Christians in the early twentieth century considered film far more "salubrious" than the vulgarity of the popular stage. Christian "effort to distance film from theater" (35) may explain why people who write about Christianity and film overlook the theatrical origins of cinema.

[2]For a comprehensive study of this incubation, see A. Nicholas Vardac, *Stage to Screen: Theatrical Origins of Early Film: David Garrick to D. W. Griffith* (Cambridge, MA: Harvard University Press, 1949).

Pagnol went so far as to argue, in 1933, that "talking films" demonstrate "the art of recording, preserving, and diffusing theater." Even into the 1960s, as James Monaco notes, "Much of the best British cinema . . . was closely connected with the vital theater of that period." In addition to common words borrowed from theater—*protagonist, prop, scenery*—one of the most important terms in film scholarship comes from the French stage: *mise-en-scène.* Meaning "the fact of putting into the scene," mise-en-scène originally referred to everything theater audiences saw on the stage in any one scene.[3] In film it means everything cinema audiences see on the screen in any one shot.

We should not be too surprised, then, that significant figures in the history of cinema had direct ties to theater:

- Louis Daguerre (1787–1851), one of the fathers of photography, was a theatrical set designer.
- D. W. Griffith (1875–1948), sometimes called "the man who invented Hollywood," started out as a stage actor and playwright.
- Another founding father of Hollywood cinema, Cecil B. DeMille (1881–1959), began his career acting, directing, and writing for the stage, from which he borrowed lighting devices for his films.
- Soviet filmmaker Sergei Eisenstein (1898–1948), originally a theatrical set designer, argued that cinema was an extension of theater.
- In addition to directing what many regard as the finest films ever made—*The Grand Illusion* (1937) and *The Rules of the Game* (1939)—Jean Renoir (1894–1979) wrote and directed plays, and his film *The Golden Coach* (1953) "pays homage to Italian classical theater."[4]
- George Cukor (1899–1983), director of Hollywood classics such as *Philadelphia Story* (1940) and *My Fair Lady* (1964), started out as a stage manager and theater director.
- As artistic director and vice president of MGM studios, Irving Thalberg (1899–1936) filmed staged performances of every Broadway play the

---

[3]Marcel Pagnol, translated and quoted in Robert Stam, *Film Theory: An Introduction* (Malden, MA: Blackwell, 2000), 58; James Monaco, *How to Read a Film: The Art, Technology, Language, History, and Theory of Film and Media,* rev. ed. ((New York: Oxford University Press, 1981), 269; David Bordwell and Kristin Thompson, *Film Art: An Introduction,* 2nd ed. (New York: Knopf, 1986), 119. As the authors make clear, "Mise-en-scene is at bottom a theatrical notion: the filmmaker stages an event to be filmed" (151).

[4]Kristin Thompson and David Bordwell, *Film History: An Introduction,* 3rd ed. (New York: McGraw Hill, 2010), 348.

studio purchased in order "to provide a blueprint of the pacing and diagramming of scenes, the timing of individual lines for laughter and dramatic impact."[5]

- Howard Koch (1901–1995), a playwright who received an Oscar for his contributions to *Casablanca* (1942), published an essay about the similarities between writing for the stage and writing for the screen.[6]
- Sir Laurence Olivier (1907–1989), founding director of Britain's National Theater, appeared in over fifty movies, several of which he directed.
- Elia Kazan (1909–2003), Turkish-born director of film classics such as *A Streetcar Named Desire* (1951) and *On the Waterfront* (1954), was also considered "the preeminent stage director of his generation."[7]
- Orson Welles (1915–1985) cofounded the Mercury Theater, where he directed Broadway stage productions before directing and starring in one of the greatest films in history: *Citizen Kane* (1941).
- Originally a playwright and theater director, Sweden's greatest filmmaker, Ingmar Bergman (1918–2007), once commented, "I am much more a man of the theatre than a man of the film."[8]
- Rainer Werner Fassbinder (1945–1982), who helped energize new German cinema, was active in the theatrical scene as actor, director, and playwright.

We could add to the list Dorothy L. Sayers and her close friend Muriel St Clare Byrne, a specialist in Elizabethan drama, both of whom wrote for the stage as well as trying their hands at screenwriting. As famous film theorist André Bazin summarizes, "the relations between theater and cinema are much older and closer than is generally thought."[9]

Even denouncers of theater and cinema have much in common. In his magisterial work *Theo-drama,* Hans Urs von Balthasar outlines the antitheater teachings of Christian theologians such as Tertullian (160–220 CE) and Augustine (354–430 CE), polemics that anticipate the antimovie attitudes of

[5]Quoted in Barry Day, *Coward on Film: The Cinema of Noël Coward* (Lanham, MD: Scarecrow, 2005), 14.

[6]Howard E. Koch, "A Playwright Looks at the 'Filmwright,'" *Sight and Sound* 19, no. 5 (1950): 210-14.

[7]Michael Almereyda, "Everybody Part of Everybody Else," in booklet included with the Criterion Collection DVD of *On the Waterfront* (2013), 9.

[8]Quoted in Lise-Lone Marker and Frederick J. Marker, *Ingmar Berman: Four Decades in the Theatre* (Cambridge: Cambridge University Press, 1982), 6.

[9]André Bazin, "Theater and Cinema: Part One and Part Two," in *What Is Cinema?*, trans. Hugh Gray (Berkeley: University of California Press, 1967), 1:81.

Christians in the twentieth century. When bishops at the Fourth Council of Carthage (399 CE) wanted to excommunicate anyone attending theater on a Sunday, they foreshadowed followers of Canon William Sheafe Chase, pastor of Brooklyn's Christ Episcopal Church, who proclaimed in 1908 that attending cinema on Sunday was a "desecration."[10]

This genealogical connection between stage and screen is essential to *The Wages of Cinema* because theater, having nurtured narrative cinema from its very start, was developed in response to the wages of sin. As Sayers succinctly puts it, "All drama is religious in origin," initially watched not simply for "entertainment" but as "an act of communal worship."[11]

## The Religious Origins of Drama

While the Hebrews were sacrificing lambs on their altars to Yahweh, the Greeks were sacrificing goats on their altars to Dionysus, the god of wine and fertility. Both forms of sacrifice were about new life: the sacrifice of the Jewish lamb for reconciliation with God, the sacrifice of the Greek goat to guarantee the resurrection of crops in spring. Furthermore, like the Hebrews, who sang and danced in honor of Yahweh (Ex 15:20-21), the Greeks performed hymns called dithyrambs in honor of Dionysus.[12]

Theater began with the embellishment of these dithyrambs, as choruses of up to fifty males danced around the sacrificial goat while singing stories about the life of Dionysus. The event became known as "the goat song," from which we get our word *tragedy*: *tragos* = male goat; *ōdē* = song, or "ode." A tragedy, then, establishes that a sacrificial goat (or lamb) must shed its blood for human life to continue. This explains the plots of classical tragedies, in which powerful individuals, having defied the gods and/or human laws, must die so that harmony can be restored to society.

---

[10]Hans Urs von Balthasar, *Theo-drama: Theological Dramatic Theory*, trans. Graham Harrison (San Francisco: Ignatius, 1988), 1:93-97. Von Balthasar notes that, as late as 1917, Roman Catholic clerics were forbidden to attend theater (104n52). Canon Chase is quoted in William Romanowski, *Reforming Hollywood: How American Protestants Fought for Freedom at the Movies* (New York: Oxford University Press, 2012), 17.

[11]Dorothy L. Sayers, introduction to *The Man Born to Be King: A Play-Cycle on the Life of Our Lord and Saviour Jesus Christ* (Grand Rapids, MI: Eerdmans, 1943), 2.

[12]Todd E. Johnson and Dale Savidge note, "Religious theatre goes back further than the Greeks. . . . Early tribes of hunters used drama, often in the form of dance, to ask the gods for help with the coming hunt and to thank the gods for success on their return." Johnson and Savidge, *Performing the Sacred: Theology and Theatre in Dialogue* (Grand Rapids, MI: Baker Academic, 2009), 150n13.

A key development in Greek theater occurred in 534 BCE, when a dithyramb singer named Thespis began to "answer" the rest of the chorus in the guise of a character from one of the Dionysian myths. Thespis thus created the first known actor, which explains why stage actors to this day are sometimes called thespians. Several decades later, Aeschylus (ca. 525–ca. 456 BCE) added a second "answerer" to a play, inventing costumes to distinguish the two.[13] Sophocles (ca. 497–ca. 406 BCE) not only added a third answerer but also invented scenery—a word that comes from the Greek *skēnē*: the closed space at the back of the open-air Athenian stage. The most dramatic development, however, was initiated by Euripides (ca. 480–ca. 406 BCE), who separated the chorus from the action, making character portrayals seem more lifelike. The greater the realism, of course, the easier it was for audiences to see thespians as people acting out a story rather than as mere celebrants of religious rites.

## From Greek Theater to the Greek New Testament

The Greek language changed considerably in the four hundred–plus years between Euripides and the Gospel writers, just as the English language changed considerably in the four hundred–plus years between Chaucer (d. 1400) and Jane Austen (d. 1817). Nevertheless, in both instances numerous words from one culture helped shape messages to follow, if even with considerably different spelling and/or alphabet systems.

For example, during the height of classical theater (500–300 BCE), the Greek word for "answerer" was *hypokritēs*. Jesus would have been very aware of the *hypokritai* (plural) performing on stages in his own day. According to Carsten Peter Thiede, "There were theatres all over Galilee, Judaea, Samaria, and in Jerusalem. One of them, the theatre of Sepphoris in Galilee, was actually built while Jesus was living a mere four miles away in Nazareth." Some scholars go so far as to suggest that Jesus, trained as a "builder," may have even aided in its construction.[14]

[13]In an essay on the *Godfather* films, John R. May argues, "The two generations of the Corleone family recall pointedly the tragic world of . . . Aeschylus's *Oresteia*." May, "The Godfather Films: Birth of a Don, Death of a Family," in *Image and Likeness: Religious Visions in American Film Classics*, ed. John R. May (New York: Paulist, 1992), 72.

[14]Carsten Peter Thiede, "A Critic of the Critics: Dorothy L. Sayers and New Testament Research," *Inklings* 12 (1994): 141-42.

Whether or not he ever saw a theatrical performance, Jesus clearly knew that *hypokritai* wore distinctive masks by which audiences could identify characters on stage. The Greek word for mask was *prosōpon,* which literally means "face." To this day, the medical community uses the term *prosopagnosia* for a condition in which people cannot recognize faces, the Greek word for "face" coupled with one that means "not knowing" (as in *agnostic*). This lends special significance to a verse in Matthew in which Jesus exhorts, "When you fast, do not look somber as the hypocrites [*hypokritai*] do, for they disfigure their faces [*prosōpa*] to show others they are fasting" (Mt 6:16). The Gospels, written in Hellenistic (Koine) Greek (300 BCE–300 CE), therefore employ *hypokritēs* to describe people putting on an act for self-serving purposes.

Matthew quotes forms of the word *hypocrite* five times more than the other three Gospel writers combined, sometimes in combination with other theatrical terms. For example, he reports that the Pharisees, attempting to trick Jesus, "sent their disciples to him, . . . saying 'Teacher, we know that you are sincere, and teach the way of God in accordance with truth, and show deference to no one; for you do not regard people with partiality'" (Mt 22:16 NRSV). Literally, that last phrase reads, "you do not regard the *prosōpon* of men." They thus admit to Jesus that he does not judge individuals by their masks—their roles, reputations, or status in society. Ironically, their words come true when Jesus sees under their own masks, saying, "Why are you putting me to the test, you *hypokritai*?" (Mt 22:18 NRSV). In the next chapter, Matthew quotes Jesus using the word *hypokritēs* seven times to condemn the scribes and Pharisees (Mt 23:13-29). Luke, in his Gospel, literalizes the theatrical metaphor when he writes, "Keeping a close watch on him, they sent spies, who *pretended* [*hypokrinomenous*] to be sincere" (Lk 20:20), thus alluding to a conflict between the authenticity of Christ and the theatrical pretenses of his enemies.[15]

Significantly, the Greek word for "conflict" is *agōn,* explaining the terms *protagonist* and *antagonist,* borrowed from Greek theater. Though Gospel writers clearly establish priests and Pharisees as the antagonists of Jesus, forms of the word *agōn* appear primarily in the Epistles, as in "Fight [*agōnizou*] the good *agōn* of the faith" (1 Tim 6:12). The writer to Timothy was probably

[15]My understanding of New Testament Greek relies on George V. Wigram and Ralph D. Winter, *The Word Study Concordance* (Wheaton, IL: Tyndale, 1978). See esp. 778.

thinking of Olympic *agōns*, as was the author of Hebrews, who includes the viewing audience as well: "Therefore, since we are surrounded by such a great a cloud of witnesses, . . . let us run with perseverance the *agōn* marked out before us" (Heb 12:1). *Agōn* appears nowhere in the Gospels other than in alternate forms employed by Luke. For example, while recounting Jesus praying in the garden of Gethsemane, Luke writes, "In his *anguish* [*agōnia*] he prayed more earnestly, and his sweat became like great drops of blood falling down on the ground" (Lk 22:44 NRSV). The word *anguish* captures well the internal conflict (*agōn*) Jesus feels over his mission, as though his human fears were competing with his divine understanding. Though all three Synoptic Gospels recount Christ's agonized prayer, "Father, if it is possible, may this cup be taken from me" (Mt 26:39; see Mk 14:36; Lk 22:42), Luke is the only writer to use the word *agōnia*, which appears frequently in Greek drama.

## The Acts of the Greeks and the Acts of the Apostles

According to a tradition established by Christian historian Eusebius of Caesarea (ca. 260–ca. 339 CE) and confirmed by Jerome (ca. 347–420 CE), the writer of the Third Gospel and the Acts of the Apostles is the same man mentioned in the letter to the Colossians, "Our dear friend Luke, the doctor" (Col 4:14). While Garry Wills makes a compelling case that the author of Acts could not have traveled with Paul or known him very well (if at all), there is good reason to assume that the author of Acts knew Greek culture well, which influenced the way he recounted incidents in Paul's life.[16]

Paul preaching in front of the Areopagus in Athens provides a good example. As part of his message to the Athenians, Paul quotes from Greek literature, saying of God, "For in him we live and move and have our being" (Acts 17:28). This line, originally describing the Greek god Zeus, is taken from a poem by Epimenides, a poet living in Crete during the sixth or seventh century BCE. Paul invokes the literary allusion to suggest that the Athenian search for an "unknown god" (Acts 17:23) has been fulfilled, the unknown God performing on the stage of the world through Jesus.[17] Athens, of course,

---

16Garry Wills, *What Paul Meant* (New York: Viking Penguin, 2006), 11-12, 30-37, 157-66. Wills's expressed goal is to prove that Paul's "letters stand closer to Jesus than do any other words in the New Testament" (10).

17The Epimenides source was discovered by Professor J. Rendel Harris, who published his findings in *The Expositor* (April 1907): 333-35. Others suggest, "Paul is quoting Aratus and is also suggesting the words of

was also home to the Theater of Dionysus, where gods were often seen on stage. However, as Paul's listeners well knew, those gods were merely *hypokritai*, humans acting like gods, whereas Paul stunningly suggests that God literally became flesh in Christ.

Paul in fact used Greek theater to communicate the good news about Christ in his testimony before King Agrippa in Caesarea. While recounting his Damascus road experience, Paul explains how, after a bright light from heaven made him fall to the ground, he heard Christ's voice speaking "in the Hebrew tongue" (Acts 26:14 KJV). When he translates the voice into Greek for Agrippa, however, he employs a phrase used by the playwright Euripides in *The Bacchae*: "Saul, Saul, why persecutest thou me? It is hard for thee *to kick against the pricks*" (Acts 26:14 KJV). The plot of Euripides's play lends this quotation special meaning.

Premiering at the Theatre of Dionysus in 405 BCE, *The Bacchae* begins with Dionysus explaining his dual nature. Because his heavenly father, Zeus, impregnated a woman on earth, Dionysus claims to be both god and human. Doubting such an outrageous story, skeptics imprison Dionysus. But, due to his divine nature, Dionysus breaks free of his tomb-like containment, only to have his disciples, the Bacchae, perform miraculous works in his name.

The parallels with the gospel message are obvious, adding power to a conversation between the disguised Dionysus and a doubter named Pentheus. Dionysus counsels Pentheus,

> Better to yield him [Dionysus] prayer and sacrifice
> Than *kick against the pricks*, since Dionyse
> Is God, and thou but mortal.[18]

Paul seems to have included "kick against the pricks" to better influence his listeners about salvation through Christ. Agrippa, the primary listener in this case, was educated in the court of the Roman emperor and hence well acquainted with Greek theater. He therefore would have caught Paul's allusion to a divine human who could bring new life. Indeed, after Paul's narration,

---

Cleanthes in his 'Hymn to Zeus.'" See Peter Fraser and Vernon Edwin Neal, *ReViewing the Movies: A Christian Response to Contemporary Film* (Wheaton, IL: Crossway, 2000), 106.

[18]Euripides, *The Bacchae*, trans. Gilbert Murray (Project Gutenberg, 2011), 47, www.gutenberg.org/files/35173/35173-h/35173-h.htm.

Agrippa states, if even suspiciously, "Do you think that in such a short time you can persuade me to be a Christian?" (Acts 26:28).

In contrast, two other accounts of the Damascus road experience do not include the theatrical allusion (Acts 9:4; 22:7), both simply ending Christ's statement with "Saul, Saul, why do you persecute me?" If all three accounts included "kick against the pricks," we might assume that the phrase was a common idiom in first-century Roman culture. Quoting it only for Agrippa endorses something Paul states in his letter to the Corinthians: "I have become all things to all people, that I might by all means save some" (1 Cor 9:22 NRSV). To Agrippa, Paul has become a lover of theater—or at least someone familiar with Euripides.

Christians today might do the same with cinema, which also carries the marks of Greek theater. In fact, French film director Robert Bresson (1907–1999) describes his process of filmmaking using language reminiscent of the dismemberment and rebirth of Dionysus that generated Greek theater: "A film is born in my head and I kill it on paper. It is brought back to life by the actors and then killed in the camera. It is then resurrected into a third and final life in the editing room where the dismembered pieces are assembled into their finished form."[19] Though Bresson's films are considered some of the most artistic in the history of cinema, lowbrow movies also display techniques developed by Greek and Roman dramatists. Even the Academy Awards follow classical convention, the very word *academy* originating from the location where Plato taught Aristotle, the philosopher who describes the development of Greek theater in his *Poetics* (ca. 335–323 BCE).

## From Satyr Plays to Comedy

As dithyrambs to Dionysus became more and more embellished, competitions developed, awards given to the best dithyrambs. Interestingly, *competition* is another translation of the Greek word *agōn*. Hence, by the time of Aeschylus, *agōns* among playwrights had been formalized such that each playwright submitted four plays as part of the competition: three tragedies and one satyr play. The latter tended to lampoon ancient gods and heroes from Greek mythology, often using vulgar language and obscene sight gags.

---

[19]Quoted in David Bordwell, Kristin Thompson, and Jeff Smith, *Film Art: An Introduction*, 11th ed. (New York: McGraw Hill, 2017), 17.

Because satyrs were followers of Dionysus, the god of wine, their antics seemed to symbolize the excess associated with drunkenness, actors often tying to their groins humorously gigantic phalluses. Satyr plays thus anticipate the gross-out vulgarity of teen-oriented comedies in our own day, which seek to outdo one another in obscenity.

Only one complete satyr play has survived—*The Cyclops* by Euripides—perhaps telling us something about the artistry of the genre. Like most movies made to elicit laughs from adolescents, satyr plays may have not been considered worth preserving. In contrast, the comedy genre, which appeared a century after satyr plays, can offer sophisticated commentary on contemporary cultural issues.

The word *comedy* originates from Greek terms meaning "revel song," and Aristophanes (ca. 450–ca. 385 BCE) is usually considered the best exemplar of "old comedy." Though borrowing fake phalluses and other vulgar sight gags from satyr plays, Aristophanes's extravaganzas, graced by passages of beautiful poetry as well as comic originality, had purposeful content: to expose the self-serving behavior of his contemporaries, both highborn and lowborn. Writing plays that satirized politics and personalities—including the personality of Dionysus—Aristophanes was accused of slander when the sharp edge of his scripts cut too deeply.

We might compare the topicality of Aristophanes to movies that make fun of contemporary political and religious issues. For example, in summer 2012, as the presidential race between Mitt Romney and Barack Obama began to heat up, Warner Brothers released a movie called *The Campaign*. Starring Will Ferrell and Zach Galifianakis as Southern politicians running against each other for a seat in Congress, the movie spoofs the use of Christian rhetoric and corporate financing in the contemporary election marketplace. Like comedies by Aristophanes, it alludes to actual persons in the news. The movie's portrayal of the wealthy and manipulative Motch brothers (John Lithgow and Dan Aykroyd) is a thinly veiled satire of the Koch brothers, whose foundations have supplied Republican candidates and causes with millions.

Aristophanes did much more than satirize his contemporaries, however. Making the chorus larger than in tragedies, he divided it in two, setting up an *agōn* between the groups and the *hypokritai* with which they identified. In cinema, the closest thing we get to the feel of old comedy *agōns* may be musicals, wherein choruses of bystanders sing and dance in response to the dramatic tension established between the primary actors. Take, for example, *West Side Story*, the 1961 film adaptation of a 1957 Broadway musical. Inspired by the *agōn* between Montague and Capulet families in Shakespeare's *Romeo and Juliet*, the film sets up an antagonism between two teenage gangs in Manhattan: the Jets and the Sharks. Though the movie holds the record for the most Academy Awards granted a musical (ten Oscars, including Best Picture)—a record that Steven Spielberg's critically acclaimed remake in 2021 could not surpass—many viewers today will find the synchronized song-and-dance routines of supposedly vicious gang members unintentionally humorous, more like Aristophanes than the filmmakers intended.

## Aristophanes and Deus Ex Machina

In addition to politics and religion, Aristophanes mocked the conventions of theater itself. Perhaps the most famous convention is deus ex machina, meaning "god from the machine." When tensions among characters became too tangled for logical resolution, Greek playwrights would lower an actor onto the stage from a crane-like machine, as though he were a god descending from heaven. This god would resolve the dilemma or rescue the hero through judgment or command, sometimes whisking the character away on the machine. True to his comic craft, Aristophanes, in one of his plays, mocks Euripides's overuse of deus ex machina by lowering an actor pretending to be Euripides onto the stage.

The Latin term *deus ex machina* was made popular by Horace (65–8 BCE), the most famous Roman poet during the reign of Augustus, the Caesar who "issued a decree that a census should be taken of the entire Roman world" (Lk 2:1). Using the Greek theatrical device as a metaphor for any contrived resolution to a plot, Horace warned writers against use of deus ex machina, as did Aristotle before him: "The unraveling of the plot, no less than the complication, must arise out of the plot itself, it must not be brought about by the *deus ex machina*."[20] Thanks to Horace's *Ars Poetica* (*The Art of Poetry*), "deus ex machina," used even in translations of Aristotle, has become a phrase that refers to any arbitrary problem-solving device, whether on stage or screen.

---

[20]Aristotle, *Poetics*, in *Critical Theory Since Plato*, ed. Hazard Adams (New York: Harcourt Brace Jovanovich, 1971), 57.

## DEUS EX MACHINA IN CINEMA

Deus ex machina is explicitly invoked in Joseph Mankiewicz's 1959 film adaptation of a play by Tennessee Williams, *Suddenly Last Summer,* nominated for three Academy Awards. A controlling mother named Violet (Katharine Hepburn) makes her first appearance while being lowered from the second story of her mansion in an open elevator, an image not included in the original 1958 play. Her first words in the film, unlike the play, make the allusion clear: "Sebastian always said 'Mother, when you descend, it's like the goddess from the machine.'" Indeed, seeking to save the reputation of Sebastian, Violet tries to play God by hiring a neurosurgeon to lobotomize her niece (Elizabeth Taylor) to stop her from recounting her son's horrific Dionysian death.

Not coincidentally, Sebastian's demise closely parallels an episode in *The Bacchae,* the play by Euripides from which Paul quotes in Acts. Like the mother in *The Bacchae,* who discovers her son was dismembered and eaten, Violet is forced to confront her complicity with her son's violent death. *Suddenly Last Summer* ends with another image not included in the original play—Violet ascending alone in her elevator, failing in her role as deus ex machina.

Lloyd Baugh asserts that the Greek convention is employed in movie Westerns any time a hero's "origins, his arrival, his powerful goodness and his departure" are left "unexplained."[21] Far more simplistic are movies in which we see characters, traumatized by unbearable situations, suddenly wake up. They are lifted out of sleep just as characters in Greek and Roman tragedies were lifted off the stage by the deus ex machina. Establishing that a terrifying scenario "was only a dream," filmmakers can titillate audiences without having to write intellectually viable scripts.

Consider *The Invasion,* a 2007 film featuring multiple well-known actors: Nicole Kidman, Jeremy Northam, Daniel Craig, and Roger Reese. The movie begins with the space shuttle Patriot crashing to earth, carrying with it an extraterrestrial life form that infects humans, turning them into emotionless automatons as soon as they enter REM sleep. These infected humans feel the need to spread the disease by regurgitating into the food or faces of others, causing their victims to fall asleep. As Carol (Kidman) and Ben (Daniel Craig) seek to evade infection through violent chase scenes, they appear to be the

---

[21]Lloyd Baugh, *Imaging the Divine: Jesus and Christ-Figures in Film* (Kansas City, MO: Sheed & Ward, 1997), 157.

only healthy people in the country except for a team of scientists ensconced at a military fort. After Ben is infected, Carol and her son are nearly captured by diseased automatons until a helicopter lands on top of a building in Baltimore and whisks them away to safety.

As a machine descending from above, the helicopter functions as deus ex machina almost literally. But the movie's figurative deus ex machina is more outrageous. Even though most humans were infected, those protected in the military fort somehow manufacture enough antibodies to reverse the disease. And, happiness of all happinesses, the inoculated people totally forget their infection, each thinking it was only a bizarre dream. Deus ex machina! Of course, we are never told how these recovered people explain the devastation surrounding them: dead bodies and crashed cars on the streets, buildings looted and burned. Instead, the last scene of the movie shows Carol living in a gorgeous house with her handsome recovered lover, Ben, who remembers nothing of his infection. Even Euripides would be ashamed.

## Mocking the Machina in Cinema

Aware of such contrived ex machina endings, some filmmakers, like Aristophanes before them, mock the use of deus ex machina. At the end of *Dodgeball: A True Underdog Story* (Rawson Marshall Thurber, 2004), we see a chest with "deus ex machina" written on it—clearly alluding to the outrageous plot twists by which loose ends in the movie have been tied up and protagonists rewarded.

Far cleverer is Woody Allen's award-winning 1995 comedy *Mighty Aphrodite*. The title itself tells us that Allen was thinking of the Greeks, since Aphrodite was their goddess of love, beauty, and procreation. Allen begins *Mighty Aphrodite* with the shot of an ancient Greek stage, on which appears a chorus wearing masks. Though mostly set in contemporary New York, the film includes characters from famous Greek tragedies: Oedipus, Tiresias, Jocasta, and Cassandra. We should not be too surprised, then, that the film's tensions are resolved through deus ex machina. The Aphrodite of the story is Linda, played by Mira Sorvino, who won an Oscar for her role. Seeking to break free from her life as a prostitute, the goodhearted Linda wants to reconcile with a suitor who rejected her once he learned of her past. As Linda drives to the city in a desperate attempt to win him back, a helicopter suddenly lands, delivering to Linda a man who gives her a new life through marriage and a child. As though dropped by a crane, the helicopter is clearly Allen's comic reference to a deus ex machina that resolves everything for the protagonist. We might even conclude that Allen was mocking the helicopter scene from *The Invasion* if it weren't for the fact that *Mighty Aphrodite* preceded the Nicole Kidman vehicle by over a decade.

### Remaking the Machina: Science Fiction

While Greek theater developed machines that brought imagined gods to earth, cinematic science fiction imagines machines themselves as gods. The *Matrix* movies (one in 1999, two in 2003, and another in 2021), as well as both *Total Recall* films (1990 and 2012), play on the idea of deus ex machina by having their characters' brains literally attached to machines. After wrenching our emotions with terrifying scenes, the movies repeatedly return us to shots of the protagonists' bodies in the machines. Hence, like audiences in ancient Greece, we see protagonists escape the devastating consequences of their experiences through machines. However, these films make the escapes more ambiguous, encouraging viewers, along with the protagonists, to question the distinction between reality and machine-made fiction, an ambiguity that reflects contemporary viewers' vexed relationship with artificial intelligence and other computer technology that defines, if not controls, their actions. Not coincidentally, credits for *The Matrix Revolutions* (2003) announce that the final Matrix machine encountered by Neo (Keanu Reeves) is called "Deus Ex Machina." Like a scene straight out of Euripides, Neo is carried off by Deus Ex Machina after it helps him destroy his antagonists, the Smiths.

### From New Comedy to Movie Comedy

While the old comedy of Aristophanes satirized political and religious issues of his day, the new comedy that followed focused on the perils of private life. Menander (ca. 341–290 BCE), the most famous representative of Athenian new comedy, is quoted by the apostle Paul, "Do not be misled: '*Bad company corrupts good character*'" (1 Cor 15:33).

Plautus (ca. 254–184 BCE), a Roman playwright who translated Menander's work into Latin, became a master of the plot devices of new comedy, humorously portraying ordinary people and family life. Many contemporary Hollywood films echo new comedy's focus on the family, including its humor. Take, for instance, the outrageous scenarios of the Ben Stiller / Robert DeNiro comedies *Meet the Parents* (Jay Roach, 2000), *Meet the Fockers* (Jay Roach, 2004), and *Little Fockers* (Paul Weitz, 2010). The name "Focker" itself echoes the Plautine love for vulgar wordplay.

New comedy stock characters are clear ancestors of stock characters in Hollywood movies. For example, a common figure in Plautus was the *servus callidus*, Latin for "clever servant," who functioned as talkative companion to and brilliant tactician for the protagonist, called *adulescens* in Roman drama. (The Latin *adolescere* means "to ripen" or "grow old," explaining the origin of our word *adolescent.*) Accompanying the *adulescens*, the *servus callidus* compares to the buddy or sidekick in contemporary movie comedies, a companion aiding and many times challenging or ridiculing the protagonist. *The Lone Ranger* movies (1956, 1958, 2013), based on a television series of the same name, established Tonto as a sidekick comparable to characters from Plautus. Indeed, even though Tonto takes a subordinate position, the name with which he addresses the Lone Ranger, "Kemosabe," makes mild mockery of the protagonist. Reflecting the wordplay loved by Plautus, "Kemosabe" sounds like the Spanish phrase *quien no sabe*: "the one who does not know."

Influenced by Plautus, Terence (195/185–159 BCE) seems to have lived the life of the *servus callidus*. Sold as a slave to a Roman senator, Terence was so brilliant that his master (from whom he took the name Terence) set him free after educating him. By the time he was twenty-five, Terence had written six plays so celebrated that they were referenced by Shakespeare in the sixteenth century and President John Adams in the nineteenth.

Terence appropriated the stock characters employed by Plautus, thus perpetuating identifiable roles still seen in contemporary film:

- *Miles gloriosus* (Latin for "braggart soldier") is the arrogant man who desires the same woman as does the *adulescens*, causing the hero great trauma while deceiving the female. The *miles gloriosus*, then, is two-faced, a characteristic literalized in *The Dark Knight* (Christopher Nolan, 2008) when district attorney Harvey Dent (Aaron Eckhart) appears with a face divided in two, one handsome, the other horrific. Though the film starts with the handsome Dent dating Rachel Dawes (Maggie

Gyllenhaal), Batman's love interest, it ends with Dent in mortal combat with Batman.

- *Senex* (Latin for "old man") can be either an old man competing with the *adulescens* for a young woman's affection or a father resisting the overtures of the *adulescens* for his daughter's attention. Both kinds of *senex* appear in Franco Zeffirelli's 1967 film adaptation of *Taming of the Shrew* by Shakespeare, who explicitly mentions Terence in the play. Other times, *senex* takes the form of a wizened figure who counsels the hero with sage, often enigmatic, advice, like Gandalf in Peter Jackson's film adaptations of Tolkien's *Lord of the Rings* and *The Hobbit* novels. *Senex* also anticipates a stock movie character dubbed "the magical Negro" by director Spike Lee, who has dramatized *agōns* ignited by race relations in multiple award-winning films such as *BlacKkKlansman* (2018). The "magical Negro," according to Lee, is a Black man who aids a White protagonist by channeling supernatural power and/or insight rather than by exercising critical thinking or character depth. Commonly cited examples of the racism underlying "the magical Negro" are Bagger Vance (Will Smith) in *The Legend of Bagger Vance* (Robert Redford, 2000) and John Coffey (Michael Clarke Duncan) in *The Green Mile* (Frank Darabont, 1999).[22]
- *Meretrix* (Latin for "prostitute") functions as a temptation for the *adulescens* but also can be the goodhearted fallen woman, such as Linda in *Mighty Aphrodite*. In an essay exploring "The Image of Woman in Contemporary (Religious) Film," Diane Apostolos-Cappadona argues that the "convention of the 'fallen woman' with the heart of gold" is fulfilled by Michelle Pfeiffer's Countess Olenska in *The Age of Innocence* (Martin Scorsese, 1993). By contrasting Olenska with "the virginal maiden" played by Winona Ryder, Apostolos-Cappadona alludes to another stock figure from ancient theater, *virgo*.[23]
- Latin for "young maiden," *virgo* is the sweet ingenue who engenders competition among the *adulescens*, the *miles gloriosus*, and the *senex*, her character serving as a motivator for male action more than having much depth of its own.

---

[22]See Matthew Hughey, "Cinethentic Racism: White Redemption and Black Stereotypes in 'Magical Negro' Films," *Social Problems* 3 (August 2009): 543-77.

[23]Diane Apostolos-Cappadona, "From Eve to the Virgin and Back Again: The Image of Woman in Contemporary (Religious) Film," in *New Image of Religious Film*, ed. John R. May (Kansas City, MO: Sheed & Ward, 1997), 124, 122. Though she attributes these stock figures to Victorian convention, Apostolos-Cappadona does a good job of assessing how the mise-en-scène reinforces the women's characters.

One cannot help wondering whether the conventional characters of *virgo* and *senex* influenced a powerful Christian tradition of Joseph as a *senex* called by God to wed the *virgo* Mary. By the second century CE, the husband of Mary had been established as a widower, a means by which the church could suggest that the siblings of Jesus mentioned in the Gospels were not biological (Mt 12:46-50; 13:55-56; Mk 3:32; 6:3; Lk 8:19-20). The *virgo* married the *senex* Joseph, who brought with him children from his previous marriage. By the seventh century Joseph was said to have been in his nineties when he married the fourteen-year-old girl, an age that ensured Mary's perpetual virginity after giving birth to Jesus.[24]

## Senecan Tragedy and Christian Tragedies

Jesus was born around the same time as the most famous writer of Latin tragedies, the philosopher Seneca (ca. 4 BCE–65 CE), who wrote Greek-inspired plays filled with violence and gore. Mel Gibson's *The Passion of the Christ* (2004), with its graphic torture and bloodshed, seems straight out of Seneca, who, like Jesus, died according to the commands of Roman authorities.

Hired to tutor a twelve-year-old named Nero, Seneca remained his adviser when Nero ordered the construction of more theater spaces after he became Caesar in 54 CE. Thirsting, perhaps, for greater visual stimulation than Seneca's stylized violence on stage, Nero became the first imperial sponsor of theatrical Christian torture. In fact, according to a tradition established by Eusebius of Caesarea, the apostle Paul was beheaded in Rome during Nero's reign. As Nero became intoxicated with power, he even accused Seneca of infidelity, finally ordering him to die by suicide. So, like his contemporary Jesus, who willingly went to the cross, Seneca willingly killed himself by cutting open his veins and bleeding to death.

The Nero-like thirst for graphic blood-and-guts violence, of course, influences cinema today, with viewers differing little from those who filled the Roman Coliseum to watch humans get eviscerated. While consumers that pay for real-life torture may be more deplorable than filmgoers who know that what they see is illusion, there is something vastly disturbing about cinematic

[24]A document written around 145 CE known as the Protoevangelium of James is the earliest known source to suggest the perpetual virginity of Mary after the birth of Jesus. It also established that Joseph was a widower, with children from a previous marriage. The document asserting that Joseph was ninety is called History of Joseph the Carpenter. See Bart D. Ehrman and Zlatko Plese, *The Apocryphal Gospels: Texts and Translations* (New York: Oxford University Press, 2011).

close-ups on eyeballs being pierced, arms severed, and brains scrambled, close-ups that paying audiences in Rome usually did not see.

Partially due to its dehumanizing violence (literally de-humanizing), theatrical murders died out in the fifth century, their demise influenced by Christian protesters. One monk, while attempting to stop gladiators from murdering one another, was stoned to death by spectators, their bloodlust aroused by the theatrical battle. As Hans Urs von Balthasar notes, "By the time Christianity arrived, there was little left [to theater] but a noisy, popular entertainment; it was principally coarse and lewd and often cruel, so that even the pagans themselves turned away from it."[25] Hence, Roman emperors began to prohibit theatrical displays, such that, as David Bevington bluntly puts it, "drama ceased to exist."[26] Before it ceased to exist, however, Roman theater profoundly influenced the development of Christian theology.

## THEATER AND THEOLOGY

Romans borrowed numerous conventions from Greek culture, including the wearing of masks during theater productions. However, rather than using the Greek word for mask, *prosōpon*, Romans used the Latin word *persona*. A stock character's role was indicated by the *persona* worn, leading to the idea that personhood, even for individuals offstage, was a function of the roles played in society. We still retain the concept of role-playing in our words *impersonate* and *personnel*; to impersonate is to act like someone else, and business personnel have certain roles to play in a company.

Some linguists suggest that *persona* originally meant "to breathe through," since the actor under a mask had to breathe through it to make the character seem alive. This etymology lends special meaning to Tertullian's Latin description of the Trinity, which he formulated around 200 CE: *tres Personae, una Substantia*. God, in other words, though one substance, *breathes* through three separate persons, who have different roles to play.[27]

---

[25]Von Balthasar, *Theo-drama*, 89.

[26]David Bevington, *Medieval Drama* (Boston: Houghton Mifflin, 1975), 3. Bevington's statement is based on the lack of textual evidence for drama between 500 and 900 CE. Other theater historians, however, identify nontextual theatrical activities during the period: traveling minstrels and mimes, as well as religious rites and festivals. See Oscar G. Brockett, *History of the Theatre*, 9th ed. (Boston: Allyn & Bacon, 2003), 74.

[27]Sounding like Plato, Tertullian disparages theater, arguing "All plays . . . arouse strong emotions." Quoted in von Balthasar, *Theo-drama*, 94n1.

Having borrowed *personae* from Roman theater to explain an essential doctrine of their faith, Western Christians were also the ones to resurrect theater several centuries after the fall of the Roman Empire. In the tenth century, European churches began to embellish their Easter services, with priests acting parts while they recited the liturgy. Two or three portrayed the women who visit Christ's tomb, while another pretended to be the angel who asks them, *Quem quaeritis?*—Latin for "Whom do you seek?" Because manuscripts from France, Germany, Italy, and England contain the phrase, often repeating it, these dramatic liturgies have become known as *quem quaeritis* plays.

Hence, like classical Greek drama, which began with celebrations over the death and resurrection of a god, Christian drama of the medieval period began by celebrating the death and resurrection of the God "above all gods" (Ps 95:3). At its very start (both times), theater thus focused on new life, a body put to death so others could live. Gaston Baty goes so far as to suggest, "Although Aeschylus and Sophocles could foresee neither the dogma nor the ethics of the Gospels, they acted in accordance with a Catholic aesthetics."[28] Nevertheless, as Sayers argues, each bloody and tragic event in Aeschylus and Sophocles is "mere domestic incident" compared to the founding event of Christianity, when "a number of quite commonplace human beings, in an obscure province of the Roman Empire, killed and murdered God Almighty—quite casually, almost as a matter of religious and political routine."[29] The casualness of the crucifixion, of course, reinforces the doctrine of Christ's resurrection. Something amazing must have happened in order to ignite a movement that changed the world.

*Quem quaeritis* plays were so thoroughly about Christian doctrine that many were performed without a congregation present. In such cases, the point was not to entertain or to educate the common people, as is often assumed. Instead, priests or monks acted out *quem quaeritis* to incarnate, for its own sake, the profundity of incarnation, God taking on flesh in order to conquer the wages of sin by rising from the dead. "Whom do you seek?" captures the essence of Christianity—seeking the savior who left an empty tomb.

Due to its powerful significance, the phrase *Quem quaeritis?* eventually entered into dramatic liturgies written for Christmas services. In a twelfth-century

---

28Quoted in von Balthasar, *Theo-drama*, 1:119.

29Sayers, introduction to *Man Born to Be King*, 5.

manuscript from Fleury, France, shepherds go to Bethlehem only to be greeted by midwives asking, *Quem quaeritis, pastores, dicite?* (Whom do you seek, shepherds, say?). In the same Fleury text, Herod asks the magi, *Quem quaeritis . . . ?*[30] As its playwright well knew, Christianity is about seeking Jesus, the medium of salvation, both at his birth in a physical body and after his death in the resurrected body.

The importance of Christ's body led to the next development in medieval drama, English Corpus Christi plays, often called mystery plays. Literally meaning "the body of Christ," Corpus Christi was a holiday instituted by the Roman Church in 1311. Scheduled to fill in the gap between the holy days of Easter and Christmas, the Corpus Christi Feast celebrated the doctrine of transubstantiation, the holy moment during Mass when bread and wine turn into the body and blood of Christ. By 1318 many British towns sponsored processions for the feast day, in which priests and clerics would walk through the streets in full regalia holding up a box containing the Eucharist host.

In northern England, these processions eventually developed into Bible stories performed on wagons by different guilds. As in parades today, townspeople would stand along the designated route, waiting to see the pageants roll by.[31] Audiences were thus given an overview of Christian history in minidramas, from the fall of Lucifer, at the start of the procession, through the birth, death, and resurrection of Christ, to the last judgment at the end. Inspired by the importance of the incarnated body of Christ, these medieval Corpus Christi plays drew attention to how common human bodies—not just priests' bodies—might incarnate biblical truths. And the plays themselves drew attention to the body: Noah and his wife hitting each other as he tries to get her on the ark; Isaac desperately trying to talk Abraham out of killing him; Joseph worrying that Mary has cheated on him due to his old age; the scribes and Pharisees trying to trap Jesus with the body of a woman taken in adultery; Roman soldiers ineptly trying to nail the body of Jesus to the cross, adding humorous double meaning to his prayer, "Father, forgive them, for they do

---

30"The Service for Representing Herod," from *The Fleury Playbook*, in Bevington, *Medieval Drama*, 58, 61.

31Not all Corpus Christi festivals used pageant wagons. Some towns employed multiple stage scaffolds arranged in a circle, where audience members would move around to see the action on the various stages (Bevington, *Medieval Drama*, 479-80).

not know what they are doing" (Lk 23:34).[32] Corpus Christi playwrights, in other words, endorsed the assumption that God celebrated embodiment through the incarnation.

## From Corpus Christi to Corpus Sayers

Sayers had in mind Corpus Christi cycles, or "mystery plays," as they were known, when in 1940 she agreed to write a cycle of plays about Jesus for the Children's Hour on BBC radio. In letters to the director of religious broadcasting, she contrasts the freedom medieval playwrights had "to let Christ say anything that seemed natural and appropriate" with the problematic British "prohibition against representing Our Lord directly on the stage or in films." Believing that radio drama got around that prohibition, Sayers wrote plays that included complex psychological, social, and political issues relevant to her own day, justifying the complexity with the benefits of cinema, which had made children "far more sophisticated than we ever were at their age."[33] Hence, when personnel at the BBC asked Sayers to dumb down her plays, Sayers tore up her contract. After heated correspondence, the BBC removed Children's Hour personnel from oversight of the project, thus encouraging a broader audience, like the audiences of all ages that watched medieval Corpus Christi plays.

Deciding to broadcast Sayers's twelve plays over a ten-month period, beginning in late December 1941, the BBC scheduled a press conference in which Sayers read dialogue from her upcoming plays. Journalists turned the theatrical moment into a tragedy worthy of Aeschylus, playing up the fact that Sayers not only failed to use King James English but sometimes had her disciples speaking slang. Christians all over England mounted a censorship campaign, demanding the broadcasts be taken off the air. Ironically, because of the controversy, thousands of people indifferent to Christianity listened to the broadcasts, writing Sayers to say that they finally understood the gospel message, which changed their lives. In the introduction to her published version of her Jesus plays, *The Man Born to Be King* (1943), Sayers states that insistence on King James English is a "singular piece of idolatry" that "imposes difficulties upon the English playwright from which the Greek tragic poets

[32] The Middle English reads, "What they wirke wotte they nought," in *The York Crucifixion of Christ*, in Bevington, *Medieval Drama*, 578.

[33] *Letters* 2:147, 146, 214.

were free."[34] She later wrote a correspondent about the problem with "bibliolatry," saying, "The Pharisees, after all, read their Bibles from cover to cover, and were none the better for it—they might have done better to wrestle with the great human problems of Aeschylus or Euripides."[35]

Due to the power of theater to capture truth, both of human nature and about Christ, *The Man Born to be King* radio cycle was broadcast four years in a row. It was the "nearest modern approach to a genuine Mystery Cycle," wrote Sayers in 1955, noting, "Last year, portions of the Mediaeval Mystery Cycles have been revived, for the first time since the 16th century."[36] Sayers, in other words, was important to the revival of religious drama in England as well as the revival of faith for thousands.

How, then, might resurrection, the originating event of both Christianity and theater, apply to cinema? Film critic Charles Champlin suggests an answer, explaining that what keeps him going to the movies is a "constant hope of *resurrection*. You have to hope that the next one you see is the one that's going to knock you into the aisle and make you come alive and restore your *faith in the medium*."[37] Though faith in Jesus Christ as the medium of salvation radically transcends all other kinds of faith, both religious and artistic, Champlin's words force us to consider how the medium of film differs from that of theater, the subject of the next chapter.

---

34Sayers, introduction to *Man Born to Be King*, 3.

35*Letters* 3:524-25. Sayers alludes to Greek theater repeatedly in her detective fiction. See, e.g., Dorothy L. Sayers (with Robert Eustace), *The Documents in the Case* (New York: Harper & Row, 1987), 136, 208; Sayers, "The Incredible Elopement of Lord Peter Wimsey," in *Hangman's Holiday* (New York: HarperCollins, 1995), 55.

36Dorothy L. Sayers, "Sacred Plays," in *Episcopal Churchnews*, January 9, 1955, 22. My sincerest thanks go to Laura Simmons for drawing my attention to this essay, the first of a three-part series.

37Quoted in Jeffrey Overstreet, review of *Conversations at the American Film Institute with the Great Moviemakers—The Next Generation*, ed. George Stevens Jr. (New York: Knopf, 2012), *Books and Culture* 18, no. 4 (July/August 2012): 8, emphasis added.

2

# The Stigmata of Theater Versus the Stigma of Film

While ignoring the theatrical precedents for cinema, much of the work on Christianity and film discusses movies no differently than if the narratives were enacted on a stage. *The Wages of Cinema* therefore suggests that viewers who endorse the incarnation must not only consider the many parallels between stage and screen but also intelligently assess the radically different ways each medium incarnates its message.

Dorothy L. Sayers, even while admitting, "My heart and my interest are very much with the living theater," clearly recognized that film could often do things better than theater could. In an unpublished letter she says of her tenth detective novel, *The Nine Tailors* (1934), "A very good film-producer with a conscience might make something of it . . . but it would die flat inside a theatre." And she once cautioned the Society for Promoting Christian Knowledge about representing Dante's *Divine Comedy* in a theatrical pageant. Far better, she suggests, would be "the *Inferno* in Glorious Technicolor," but only if "produced by a very great artist" who was willing to spend an extraordinary amount of money.[1] Sayers repeatedly emphasized that it was "necessary always to bear in mind the conditions imposed by the medium," an opinion that echoes Aristotle, whose *Poetics* seeks to "distinguish" different kinds of art by assessing "the medium" of imitation.[2]

The first half of this chapter therefore seeks to distinguish the different conditions imposed by stage and screen, tracing how cinema struggled to get out

---

[1]*Letters* 3:281; Dorothy L. Sayers to Seymour Green, June 18, 1952 (Wade 524a/4); *Letters* 3:237.

[2]Dorothy L. Sayers, introduction to *The Man Born to Be King: A Play-Cycle on the Life of Our Lord and Saviour Jesus Christ* (Grand Rapids, MI: Eerdmans, 1943), 13; Aristotle, *Poetics*, in *Critical Theory Since Plato* (New York: Harcourt Brace Jovanovich, 1971), 48-49. In 1935, Sayers delivered a lecture focused on Aristotle's *Poetics*, titled "Aristotle on Detective Fiction," which was later published in *Unpopular Opinions: Twenty-One Essays* (London: Gollancz, 1946), 178-90.

from under the shadow of its theatrical predecessor. The second half highlights an award-winning film that illuminates the distinctive artistry of both art forms, helping to generate reflection about our own viewing practices. Sayers, who proclaimed Christ's incarnation as the medium of salvation, will provide terminology that can help Christians think more carefully about the medium of cinema.

## THE EMBODIMENT OF ART: THE STIGMATA OF THEATER

Living, breathing bodies have always been the medium of theater, an embodiment that cinema, from its very start, photographed onto celluloid, a medium that moved through projectors much as Corpus Christi plays moved through the streets of their sponsoring towns. The difference, however, is dramatic (pun intended). Unlike staged productions, finished films are almost exactly the same wherever they are projected, whether shown to a group of screaming ten-year-olds or to a rapt audience at the Venice Film Festival.[3] In contrast, the embodiment of theater affects every performance. Not only do various productions of the same play differ, due to set design, costuming, lighting, choreography, and characterization, but even the same production can differ from performance to performance. One night an actor might speak or gesture differently because he accidentally tripped on stage, causing the other actors to compensate for the unexpected changes. Furthermore, as any actor will tell you, the living, breathing bodies in the audience influence what happens on stage, their responses either energizing actors or entirely deflating them.

For Sayers, as theologian Laura Simmons notes, "a play was literally an incarnation."[4] Sayers goes so far as to argue that live theater exemplifies what the Christian church should be like: "I recognize in the theatre all the stigmata of a real and living church."[5] The term Sayers uses here, *stigmata*, the plural

[3]I write "almost always the same" rather than "exactly the same" since scratches on celluloid and the material conditions of a film's screening can change viewer perception. As Paolo Cherci Usai noted in 1987, each time a film is shown "its aesthetic changes, since each copy ends up possessing an identity of its own, distinct from all the others." Usai, "The Unfortunate Spectator," *Sight and Sound* (Summer 1987): 173. His point has less force today with the digitizing of movies, but nevertheless the location of a screening—in a 1940s art deco theater, a mall multiplex, or on a computer or phone screen—will affect perception.

[4]Laura K. Simmons, *Creed Without Chaos: Exploring Theology in the Writings of Dorothy L. Sayers* (Grand Rapids, MI: Baker Academic, 2005), 54.

[5]Dorothy L. Sayers, "The Church's Responsibility," in *The Life of the Church and the Order of Society, Being the Proceedings of the Archbishop of York's Conference: Malvern 1941* (London: Longmans, 1942), 59.

form of *stigma*, comes from an ancient Greek word meaning "mark" or "brand." Traditionally, of course, the word *stigmata* refers to marks appearing on someone's body that correspond to the wounds on Christ's crucified body, wounds that first appeared on the body of St. Francis of Assisi (ca. 1181–1226). Whereas the plural *stigmata* has sustained its religious connotations, *stigma* has become a negative term, usually defined as "a mark of disgrace or infamy."[6] Neither *stigma* nor *stigmata* appears in the Greek New Testament except for one amazing instance: Paul ends his letter to the Galatians saying, "I bear on my body the marks [*stigmata*] of Jesus" (Gal 6:17).

Hence, when Sayers says a theater troupe bears "the stigmata of a real and living church," she suggests an entire community can be branded by their common "feeling and interest."[7] As theologian David Brown notes, Greek drama was "essentially a communal experience, accentuated by the key role given to the chorus," and he makes a parallel with Christian worship: "Christian liturgy is like ancient drama a 'mythic' act."[8]

Furthermore, the mythic act depends on the acknowledged interdependence of community members, who together incarnate one body, as recounted in Scripture: "The body is a unit, though it is made up of many parts. . . . Those parts of the body that seem to be weaker are indispensable" (1 Cor 12:12, 22 NIV 1984). Both a church and a theatrical troupe succeed only when bodies with diverse gifts work together, valuing all gifts equally. Costume designers and lighting technicians contribute as much to productions as do actors on stage and directors behind the scenes. Sayers, in fact, gladly changed dialogue she had composed when a theatrical director or actor explained why a particular statement didn't work on stage; she knew that each contributor to a theatrical production had a gift that contributed to the success of the whole.

## The Stigma of Cinema

Cinema, of course, also necessitates numerous bodies working together to bring a film to completion, unseen members of the crew such as sound mixers and lighting technicians considered as indispensable as actors and directors.

---

[6]Unless otherwise noted, all definitions and etymologies in *The Wages of Cinema* come from the *Oxford English Dictionary Online*: www.oed.com.

[7]Sayers, "Church's Responsibility," 60.

[8]David Brown, *God and Mystery in Words: Experience Through Metaphor and Drama* (Oxford: Oxford University Press, 2008), 157.

British director Michael Powell, who discussed cinema with Sayers, believed "the camaraderie of a film company" arose from "the combined enthusiasm towards a common end," a definition that also applies to a church.[9] Nevertheless, cinema still lacks the incarnational power of live theater, wherein the *real presence* of flesh-and-blood bodies, both on and off the stage, can affect performances. This leads Babak Ebrahimian, who has directed both stage plays and movies, to state, "Theater's essence is located in its *presence*, whereas cinema's essence is located in its *distancing*," with film signaling "an *absence*" since shooting and editing occurred "in the past."[10]

Such absence stigmatized cinema in its early decades, impeding its artistic development. Early filmmakers followed the precedent of theater, shooting their stories scene by scene as though performed on a stage with the camera as audience. Rather than conceptualizing the distinctive power of their medium, they separated their scenes with techniques that functioned like curtains opening and closing under a proscenium arch: a *dissolve*, where one image slowly disappears as an image for the next scene slowly appears over it, or a *fade-out*, where the screen becomes slowly black until the brightening screen of a *fade-in* announces the beginning of the next scene. These devices were invented by magician-turned-filmmaker Georges Méliès, who regarded cinema, as famous French film theorist André Bazin notes, to be "nothing more than a refinement of the marvels of the theater."[11] A powerful influence on French filmmakers in the 1950s, Bazin titled a section of his famous book *What Is Cinema?* "Theater and Cinema." He knew that efforts to reproduce marvels of the stage merely contributed to film's stigma as a second-rate form of entertainment.

Cognizant of this stigma, Stanley Kauffmann suggests that historical origins may explain the tension between the medium of film and that of theater: "The crucial historical difference between theater and film is this: the theater began as a sacred event and eventually included the profane. The film began as a profane event and eventually included the sacred."[12] *Profane*,

[9]Michael Powell, *A Life in Movies: An Autobiography* (New York: Knopf, 1987), 93.

[10]Babak A. Ebrahimian, *The Cinematic Theater* (Lanham, MD: Scarecrow, 2004), 3-4.

[11]André Bazin, "Theater and Cinema—Part One," in *What Is Cinema?*, trans. and ed. Hugh Gray (Berkeley: University of California Press), 1:78.

[12]Stanley Kauffmann, "Notes on Theater-and-Film," in *Theater and Film: A Comparative Anthology*, ed. Robert Knopf (New Haven, CT: Yale University Press, 2005), 161.

notably, means "outside the temple." Because cinema did not start with live bodies performing rituals around a religious altar, it therefore had to develop a different kind of stigmata, its artistry depending not on what actors do but on what is done to the photographic image. Hence, like cuts on the flesh of St. Francis, cuts in the filmic medium are the stigmata of cinema. Furthermore, just as St. Francis continued to move after bearing the stigmata, film images continue to move after they are cut and spliced together. Creating something more powerful than the story it tells, film editing challenges viewers to inspect the stigmata of the medium itself—much as Jesus challenged doubting Thomas to inspect the cuts in his resurrected body (Jn 20:27). Like Thomas, who was initially suspicious of Christ's resurrection, viewers suspicious of film art can be transformed through close inspection of cinematic stigmata.

## From Stigma to Stigmata: Edwin S. Porter

Helping to generate the stigmata of cinema was Edwin S. Porter (1870–1941), production head at Thomas Edison's New York studios. Around 1903, Porter began to borrow not only techniques developed by Méliès in France but also those of the Brighton School of filmmakers in England, the most significant being the splicing together of multiple *shots* rather than multiple theatrical *scenes*.[13] To understand the difference, consider a hypothetical movie about a couple falling in love, marrying, and having children. Before Porter, American camera operators, who were also the film's directors, might shoot a scene of the couple meeting just as it might be acted on a theater stage. At the end of the scene, rather than a curtain closing, a fade-out / fade-in might initiate staging of the wedding scene, followed by a dissolve to a new scene of multiple children playing a game with the two adoring parents. Porter, in contrast, would leave out parts of the wedding, cutting from one image to another as follows:

- a brief take of the bride walking down the aisle
- a brief take of the groom putting the ring on her finger
- a shot of the bride and groom exiting the church as people throw rice

[13]As Kristin Thompson and David Bordwell note, "Porter has often been credited with virtually all the innovations of the pre-1908 period," but credit should go to these European forebears who inspired him. See Thompson and Bordwell, *Film History: An Introduction*, 3rd ed. (New York: McGraw Hill, 2010), 20.

In this hypothetical scenario, Porter reduces to thirty seconds what might take numerous minutes to perform on stage, even while maintaining a sense of continuity for viewers. With the extra time provided by what became known as *continuity editing,* Porter could tell a more complicated story. As film historian David A. Cook summarizes, "Porter had hit upon the absolutely essential fact that cinematic narrative depends not upon the *arrangement of objects or actors within a scene* (as does the theater and, to a large extent, still photography) but upon the *arrangement of shots in relation to one another.*"[14]

Porter also moved the camera while filming, establishing another stigmata of cinema. The significance of such a move, both literally and figuratively, can be illustrated by its contrast with techniques used by Méliès around the same time. When the French magician decided to present a view from the front of a rocket as it sped through outer space in his iconic film *A Trip to the Moon* (1902), Méliès placed a huge papier-mâché moon on a dolly and moved it toward the camera, rather than moving the camera toward the prop. In contrast, for *The Great Train Robbery* (1903), Porter created a panning shot by pivoting the camera horizontally to follow bandits scrambling down a hill.[15] Porter's film also provides one of the earliest examples of *crosscutting,* splicing together shots from different locations to suggest simultaneity of action.[16] Though advancing the craft of cinema immensely, Porter's innovations still carried with them the precedent of theater, as when a staged production may show two actions happening at the same time by placing actors on different parts of the set and alternating dialogue back and forth between the two groups.

Even the places people go to watch movies, still called movie *theaters* to this day, reflect theatrical precedents. In 1905 the first storefront space dedicated exclusively to projecting moving pictures opened in Pittsburgh. Charging only a nickel, the owners employed the term *nickelodeon* for their business, the second part of the name coming from a Greek term for a roofed-over theater stage: *odeon.* Nevertheless, in a matter of only three years, ten

---

[14]David A. Cook, *A History of Narrative Film,* 2nd ed. (New York: Norton, 1990), 28, emphasis original.

[15]In France, Pathé filmmaker Ferdinand Zecca was using panning shots around the same time, and he developed crosscutting by 1905.

[16]Some historians attribute the new grammar of cinema to Porter's film that preceded *The Great Train Robbery,* titled *Life of an American Fireman,* produced in 1902. But because the earlier film takes two radically different forms in its earliest prints, *The Great Train Robbery* provides a less ambiguous example of Porter's creative intentions. For an overview of the two copies of Porter's earlier film, see Cook, *History of Narrative Film,* 21-24.

thousand nickelodeons were lighting up the faces of one million Americans a day. To meet the demand, studios often shot, edited, and distributed a single one-reel movie per week. Reeling in lots of money through their assembly-line processes, most production companies had little motivation to assess and develop stigmata of the medium itself, preferring to keep their movies under twelve minutes.

## Turning Film into a Moving Medium: D. W. Griffith

At the height of the nickelodeon phenomenon, which made his *Great Train Robbery* famous, Edwin S. Porter codirected a six-minute movie called *Rescued from an Eagle's Nest,* starring an unknown stage actor named David Wark Griffith (1875–1948). Several months later, Griffith landed an acting job at American Mutoscope and Biograph Company. When a Biograph director fell ill, Griffith was asked to take over. It was the same year that Porter had initially hired him, 1908. Griffith, however, proceeded to exceed Porter in creativity. Though swiveling the camera to create a panning shot, Porter was merely copying what stage audience members could do—sit in one location and swivel their heads to watch actors run off the stage. Griffith, in contrast, varied viewers' distance from the action. In doing so, he added a psychological component to the stigmata of film, creating different points of view on the same event.

Take, for example, the hypothetical wedding scene discussed above. Rather than film the entire ceremony or even reduce the ceremony to three comparable shots, he might splice together different perspectives on the wedding: a brief *medium shot* (from the waist up) of the veil-covered bride walking toward the camera holding flowers, followed by a *long shot,* the camera a long distance from the action, in order to show the full bodies of the rest of the wedding party at the front of the church. But then Griffith might startle viewers by inserting a *close-up* on the groom's face, capturing subtle apprehension—something staged drama cannot do.

Through the close-up, a presumed heartwarming event takes on new connotations, causing viewers to feel apprehension as well. Just as they begin to wonder about the groom's attitude, Griffith might cut to a medium shot on the groom as he turns his head to look at something other than the bride. When viewers next see a close-up on the beaming smile of a middle-aged man in a church pew, they realize that this is the person on whom the groom has turned his attention—in a *motivated point-of-view shot* (the groom's motivated point of view). The camera might then cut back to a medium shot of the groom weakly smiling, relaxing his shoulders, and turning his head back to look at the bride coming down the aisle. All of this, of course, would take less time to view than to read this description. But in that brief collection of multiple perspectives, created by a lens at different lengths from the subject matter, a filmmaker can offer subtleties of the groom's psychology without the need for either words or histrionic actions.

## Griffith's Psychological Message: Angled Shots and Crosscutting

Griffith also developed the *low-angle shot,* setting the camera on the floor to shoot up an actor's body, creating a sense that the character is powerful and/or ominous. For example, after the close-up that captures the emotional distress of the groom in the wedding scene, a low-angle shot on the older man in the pew would have a different psychological effect on viewers than a medium shot that showed him smiling from his seat. Making the man appear to fill the church to the ceiling, a low-angle shot would generate a sense that the father used his power to force the wedding to occur, his smile seeming sinister rather than joyful.

Griffith intensified the psychological response of viewers through another stigmatic technique still employed today. In 1909 he put together a melodrama called *The Lonely Villa,* in which robbers attempt to invade a house containing a defenseless woman and her children. While Porter had crosscut between escaping bandits and the posse chasing them, Griffith cut back and forth among *three* simultaneous actions:

- robbers attacking the house from without
- a traumatized woman seeking to protect her children from within
- a man racing from town to the rescue

Even though other filmmakers tried their hand at *crosscutting* to communicate simultaneity of action, Griffith did something new that heightened the suspense for viewers. As the film cuts back and forth among the three parallel actions, the length of each shot (each *take*) gets shorter and shorter, thus causing the attack to feel closer and closer. The increasingly short takes create a feeling of rapidity, mimicking the sped-up heartbeat of someone feeling suspense—including those in the audience. Not just the story but the medium itself created a psychological response, even though *The Lonely Villa* lasted only eight minutes.

## Returning to Europe: *Films D'Art*

The development of the "feature film" (three reels or more) was influenced by the Société Film d'Art, an association of businessmen in France who wanted to elevate the status of movies by making them more literary. By doing so, they aimed to develop a market of more sophisticated viewers than the working-class people who flocked to nickelodeons. Begun in 1908, the Société was so successful that numerous other companies copied their style, producing multireel movies that are now known as *films d'art*: movies based on highbrow novels and plays, including tragedies by Sophocles. In 1912, one three-and-a-half-reel *film d'art* became a smash hit even in the one-reel-addicted United States. Called *La Reine Elizabeth*, the movie starred famed stage actress Sarah Bernhardt as Queen Elizabeth, the monarch under whom English theater reached its apex through the work of William Shakespeare.

Ironically, *films d'art* impeded the artistic development of cinema, for they primarily aimed to reproduce the stigmata of theater. As Cook summarizes, "Productions of the Société Film d'Art were merely photographed plays; their directors made no concession whatever to the filmic medium."[17] Hence, in 1913, a Russian intellectual named Leonid Andreyev called for the need "to distinguish cinema from theatre, to determine precisely the basic creative elements of each and thus to set each on its own true path."[18] His point was echoed two years later by famed American poet Vachel Lindsay, who published a book called *The Art of the Moving Picture* (1915). In a chapter titled "Thirty Differences Between the Photoplays and the Stage," Lindsey writes, "Many of the moving pictures discussed in this book are rewritten stage dramas. . . . But in order to be real photoplays the stage dramas must be overhauled. . . . The successful motion picture expresses itself through

[17]Cook, *History of Narrative Film*, 54.

[18]Quoted in David Bordwell, *On the History of Film Style* (Cambridge, MA: Harvard University Press, 1997), 30.

mechanical devices that are being evolved every hour."[19] Lindsay published these words during the Great War, which affected the European film industry in different ways.

### CINEMA BETWEEN THE WARS

Whereas World War I devastated the French film industry, it fertilized the German. General Erich Lundendorff, commander-in-chief of the German army, encouraged the merger of multiple film companies, evidently hoping to dominate Europe through cinema, if not through war. To aid the conglomeration, established in 1917 as Universum Film Aktiengesellschaft, the government oversaw construction, near Berlin, of "the largest and best equipped studio in the Western world."[20] Alfred Hitchcock worked at Universum Film Aktiengesellschaft studios early in his career, where he watched F. W. Murnau direct *The Last Laugh* (1924). As Hitchcock recounts, "The Germans placed great emphasis on telling the story visually—if possible with no titles or at least very few. *The Last Laugh* was almost the perfect film. It told its story even without subtitles—from beginning to end entirely by the use of imagery, and that had a tremendous influence on me."[21]

Powerfully influencing films produced by Universum Film Aktiengesellschaft was Robert Wiene's *The Cabinet of Dr. Caligari* (1920), a film that intrigued Sayers. To construct and paint the sets, Wiene hired artists influenced by a prewar movement in painting, theater, and architecture, wherein external images were meant to express internal psychological states. Known as Expressionism, this artistic movement thus entered cinema through *Caligari*, which employed angularly distorted sets and unrealistic lighting effects to communicate the psychological disorientation of the film's protagonist. Inspired by *Caligari*'s striking production design, German Expressionist films such as *Nosferatu* (Murnau, 1922) and *Metropolis* (Fritz Lang, 1927) employed stylized sets and exaggerated acting techniques to create similarly eerie effects.

Unfortunately, the strangely lit and distorted sets in *The Cabinet of Dr. Caligari* differ little from effects that could be produced on a stage, thus

---

[19]Vachel Lindsay, *The Art of the Moving Picture* (New York: Macmillan, 1915), www.gutenberg.org/ebooks/13029.

[20]Cook, *History of Narrative Film*, 120-21.

[21]Quoted in Donald Spoto, *The Dark Side of Genius: The Life of Alfred Hitchcock* (Boston: Da Capo, 1999), 68.

subordinating film, once again, to the precedence of theater. This caused Soviet filmmaker Sergei Eisenstein to denounce *Caligari* as a "barbaric carnival of the destruction of the healthy human infancy of our art, this common grave for normal cinema origins, this combination of silent hysteria, particolored canvases, daubed flats, painted faces, and the unnatural broken gestures and action of monstrous chimaeras."[22] By referring to "infancy of our art" and "cinema origins," Eisenstein reveals his intense desire to distinguish the stigmata of cinema from that of theater, to the point of stating, "In my 'revolt against the theater' I did away with a very vital element of theater—the story."[23] Though later regretting his stigmatizing of story, Eisenstein became famous for developing the stigmata of cinema.

## The Evolution of Film Stigmata: Soviet Montage

The Soviet Union had long affirmed the power of film, largely due to D. W. Griffith's *Intolerance* (1916), which captured the attention of Vladimir Lenin. Believing that the movie promoted views sympathetic with communist ideology, Lenin arranged to have *Intolerance* shown throughout the USSR after the Bolshevik Revolution, ultimately leading to the world's first film school in 1919. Analyzing Griffith's techniques with their students, founders of the Moscow Film School concluded that the editing together of shots, done so provocatively by Griffith, constituted the essential stigmata of cinema. Borrowing the word *montage* from a French word for "assembling," they argued that montage verified Lenin's view that "cinema is the most important of all the arts," for it has power to shape people's view of reality.[24]

To prove this point, one of the founders of the film school, Lev Kuleshov (1899–1970), made an experimental film in which he cut from a close-up on a famous actor's face to shots of radically different objects. As the authors of *Film Art* summarize, "When the face was intercut with a bowl of soup, viewers reportedly said the man looked hungry. When the same facial shot was

[22]André Bazin, "The Evolution of the Language of Cinema," in Gray, *What Is Cinema?*, 26; Sergei Eisenstein, "Dickens, Griffith, and the Film Today," in *Film Form: Essays in Film Theory*, ed. and trans. Jay Leyda (New York: Harcourt Brace Jovanovich, 1949), 203.

[23]Sergei Eisenstein, "Through Theater to Cinema," in Leyda, *Film Form*, 16. Eisenstein later changed his opinion about the importance of story, but he probably did so to appease Stalinist expectations that "cinema was called upon to embody the philosophy and ideology of the victorious proletariat" (17).

[24]Quoted in Sergei Eisenstein, "A Dialectic Approach to Film Form," in Leyda, *Film Form*, 63.

intercut with a dead woman, he was taken to look mournful." Though Kuleshov used the exact same headshot each time, viewers thought the actor's expression subtly changed as he was situated in new locations, implied by the juxtapositions. Known as "the Kuleshov effect," the results "demonstrated editing's power over the viewer's sense of space." Director Michael Powell later pronounced, "All of us in Europe went mad about the Russian Revolutionary films and our editing was changed forever and for good."[25]

Though a supporter of the Bolshevik Revolution, Eisenstein distinguished himself from the Kuleshov school by insisting that montage should *not* be understood merely as an assembly or linkage of shots that imply either location or human psychology. Instead, the essence of cinema, as Eisenstein argues in a famous collection of essays titled *Film Form*, results from shots in "collision. By the conflict of two pieces in opposition to each other. By conflict. By collision."[26] Like the conflict incited by revolutionaries against the White Army in Russia in 1917, or the collision between Marxism-Leninism and capitalism, Eisenstein believed montage would revolutionize bourgeois cinema practices.

Eisenstein illustrates the power of montage in his pro-Bolshevik film *The Battleship Potemkin* (1925), often considered "the most perfect and concise example of film structure in the history of the cinema."[27] For example, he cuts from a shot of mutinous Potemkin sailors throwing the battleship surgeon overboard to a close-up of white maggots feeding on dark meat, then to a close-up of the staff surgeon's pince-nez caught on rigging where he was tossed into the sea. The jarring juxtaposition of images implies that the surgeon's demise results from his failure to see the horrible conditions on the Potemkin. Indeed, earlier in the film the surgeon had inspected the infested meat through his pince-nez and dismissed the problem.

Eisenstein reinforces the failure of seeing by having a woman on shore, also wearing pince-nez, shot through one eye. In his book on film theory, he uses the sequence to emphasize the importance of montage as the essential language of cinema: "Woman with pince-nez. Followed immediately—without

[25]David Bordwell, Kristin Thompson, and Jeff Smith, *Film Art: An Introduction*, 11th ed. (New York: McGraw Hill, 2017), 226, 225, emphasis added; Powell, *Life in Movies*, 182.

[26]Sergei Eisenstein, "The Cinematographic Principle and the Ideogram," in Leyda, *Film Form*, 37.

[27]Cook, *History of Narrative Film*, 157.

transition—by the same woman with shattered pince-nez and bleeding eye: impression of a shot hitting the eye."[28]

## The Stigma Remains

Despite the international acclaim Eisenstein received for *The Battleship Potemkin*, the stigma of film lasted well after the film's 1925 release. Famed British actor Sir John Gielgud admits that he hesitated to act in a Hitchcock film in the 1930s because, as he states, "in those days, it was considered beneath one's dignity, as a stage actor, to accept employment in films."[29] Only by the 1960s did Gielgud regularly appear in movies, receiving his first Oscar nomination for a role in *Becket* (Peter Glenville, 1964). Like many celebrated thespians, he had surmounted the stigma of film, perhaps seduced by the wages of cinema as much as by the distinctive stigmata of the medium itself.

Significantly, Gielgud's brother Val developed a friendship with Dorothy Sayers. Serving as her BBC radio producer, Val corresponded with Sayers for almost two decades. However, he was far less friendly toward film, perhaps influenced by his brother's stigmatizing of cinema. During a 1948 visit to New York City, Val became disgusted with Hollywood's influence on the Broadway theater scene:

> It seemed to me that over all brooded the shadow of Hollywood. . . . In a number of cases it became apparent that Hollywood was financing the theatre: either in the hope of persuading the public that film-stars were after all actors, or in the belief that the *real* actors and *genuine* playwrights whom the film-moguls were compelled to employ had better be given some sort of employment in conditions bearing some slight resemblance to *reality*.[30]

Gielgud's assessment could serve as commentary on an Oscar-winning film set on Broadway over sixty years later, *Birdman: The Unexpected Virtue of Ignorance* (Alejandro González Iñárritu, 2014). In a review of the film for *The New Yorker*, Richard Brody alludes to the stigma of cinema when he summarizes "the theme of *Birdman*" to be "the higher artistic dignity of acting in

---

28Eisenstein, "Dialectic Approach to Film Form," 55-56.

29Quoted in Charlotte Chandler, *It's Only a Movie: Alfred Hitchcock, a Personal Biography* (London: Simon & Schuster, 2005), 102.

30Val Gielgud, *One Year of Grace: A Fragment of Autobiography* (London: Longmans, Green, 1950), 50, emphasis added.

theatre."[31] Iñárritu, however, challenges such stigmatizing by presenting a film that celebrates the stigmata of cinema. What follows is an extended discussion of cinematic techniques in the film, intended to demonstrate how the medium incarnates its message.

### *Birdman* and the Unexpected Virtue of Cinema

The film focuses on Riggan Thomson (Michael Keaton), who, twenty years previously, became a movie star by playing a winged superhero named Birdman. Unable to escape his identification with comic book antics on screen—a "shadow of Hollywood" that still broods over him—Riggan wants to prove that he is a *real* artist. He therefore decides to produce, direct, and act in a Broadway play he scripted himself, an adaptation of a story by Raymond Carver. As opening night of the play approaches, however, Riggan encounters Tabitha (Lindsay Duncan), a famous theater critic, who tells him she will single-handedly "kill" Riggan's play by writing a vicious review. She venomously proclaims, "I hate you and everyone you represent." In other words, she reviles crowd-pleasing movie stars who, in her opinion, are "blissfully untrained, unversed, and unprepared to even attempt real art"—the "real art" of live theater.

Tabitha's power as critic certainly reflects attitudes about "real art" on Broadway. As Val Gielgud reports in his memoir,

> The opinion of the professional critics achieved an altogether disproportionate importance. If they damned a play it disappeared before the public could have any opportunity of finding out whether the experts might not be mistaken. If they praised it, it became a "smash-hit," the prices of seats soared into the empyrean, and it became almost impossible for the ordinary person to buy a seat even if he could pay for it.[32]

"Real art," then, can be as much a creation of the critic as of the playwright, a point endorsed by Iñárritu decades later. The word *real*, in fact, threads its way through the film, stitching together various motifs while suturing viewers into a film that contrasts theater and film. In the process, it grapples with something even more profound: contrasting definitions of truth and "the real."

---

[31] Richard Brody, "Birdman Never Achieves Flight," *New Yorker*, October 27, 2014, www.newyorker.com/culture/richard-brody/birdman-never-achieves-flight.

[32] Val Gielgud, *One Year of Grace*, 49.

Iñárritu and his cowriters signal that this is their goal by repeatedly inserting the names of real people into the dialogue, especially the names of recognizable actors and their films. For example, the play's associate producer, Jake (Zach Galifianakis), tells Riggan that Woody Harrelson cannot join the cast due to his commitment to the next *Hunger Games* movie, and therefore Riggan should consider hiring Jeremy Renner, star of *The Hurt Locker*. These, among other references to actual cinema stars, undermine clear-cut distinctions between reality and fiction. Even Riggan's past, as a fictional superhero, alludes to the past of the real Michael Keaton, who, twenty years previously, turned down the temptation of fifteen million dollars to star in a third *Batman* movie.[33]

Iñárritu establishes, in addition, that fiction competes with the real on stage as well. An actor recruited at the last minute for Riggan's play, Mike Shiner (Edward Norton), breaks character during an audience preview because water has been substituted for the *real* gin he had been drinking during rehearsals. In protest he not only breaks the glass of fake gin by throwing it against a stage wall but also breaks the realism of the scene. His temper tantrum, however, is very real, so much so that we as viewers of *Birdman*, like Shiner's theater viewers, at first think it is part of the scripted stage play. Which is most real?

After breaking character by breaking the glass, Shiner breaks the fourth wall: a phrase used in theater to describe scripted moments when stage actors turn to audience members and address them, thus breaking the illusion that they are contained behind the four walls of a room. Like mise-en-scène, the phrase "breaking the fourth wall" was borrowed from theater by cineastes. In the case of *Birdman*, however, Shiner does something unusual: he goes off script to contemptuously address audience members, ordering them to "get off" their "cell phone screens and have a *real* experience" of "truth" portrayed on stage. But then he proceeds to contemptuously denounce the staged production, stating, "The only thing that is *real* on this stage is the chicken," as he pulls poultry out of the refrigerator. Clearly, Shiner desires to intensify the

---

[33]According to Dana Stevens, Iñárritu and his collaborators did not write *Birdman* with Keaton in mind, but the coincidence adds to the relevance of their story. See Stevens, "Birdman: Or, the Not-Unexpected Virtues of Michael Keaton and Emmanuel Lubezki," *Slate*, October 16, 2014, www.slate.com/articles/arts/movies/2014/10/birdman_starring_michael_keaton_reviewed.html.

stigmata of theater, in which real bodies, drinking real gin, perform on stage to give viewers a real experience.

Shiner gets adulation on the front page of the arts section for the power of his temper tantrum and is quoted as saying, "Raymond Carver is the reason" he became an actor, a biographical tidbit he stole from Riggan's life. Meanwhile, the newspaper buries Riggan in the middle of the arts section, his picture one-tenth the size of Shiner's front-page photograph. Tellingly, the dismissive article about Riggan appears to the right of a full-page advertisement for Lumber Liquidators, the shot lingering on a close-up of the huge letters to make sure we get the pun. Because actors refer to the stage as "the boards," the shot implies that Riggan's attempt to gain respectability on the lumber of the boards is being liquidated. The pun is reinforced by another that accompanies it, as we hear a voice, presumably the thoughts of Riggan, say, "He's playing you, Riggan!" Indeed, Shiner is playing him in both senses of the phrase: playing a trick on him by acting (playing) Riggan's real self. As the newspaper implies, Shiner's "real art"—his ability to act—overpowers Riggan's truth.

The tension between real art and the real world becomes tragic in the last scene of Riggan's play. Before he goes on stage, his daughter Sam (Emma Stone) contemptuously tells Riggan that, because he doesn't use Facebook or Twitter, "You're the one that doesn't exist. . . . You're not important; get used to it." Several minutes later we see Riggan saying very similar lines scripted into his play. After walking in on the character of his wife in bed with Shiner's character, his stage character laments, "I don't exist. I'm not even here," repeating, "I don't exist," before shooting himself in the head. Which failure to exist is more real? This question is literalized on opening night, when Riggan tries to end his existence by shooting himself with a *real* loaded gun he has substituted for the play's prop gun. Ironically, due to the realism of the suicide attempt, the critic Tabitha responds with rave reviews for the play, implying that the "real art" she desires has been achieved. But how is this real art? Rather than becoming indistinguishable from reality, doesn't real art inculcate appreciation for stigmata of the craft, for the power of fiction to mediate truth? This question drives *Birdman*, which calls attention to montage and mise-en-scène in a way that challenges classical-style cinema.

## Classical Birdman Versus Postclassical *Birdman*

Films made in the so-called classical style encourage viewers to forget the camera, such that the screen seems like a plate-glass window—the fourth wall—through which one watches "real" actions, whether of romantic comedy lovers or of Birdman superheroes. In contrast, as film scholar Eleftheria Thanouli explains, postclassical style foregrounds "filmic signifiers," forcing viewers to think about stigmata of the medium itself: odd cuts, baffling inserts, provocative camera movements, ambiguous voiceovers.[34] In these terms *Birdman* qualifies as postclassical, forcing viewers to consider its sensuous filmic artistry through several distinctive devices.

First, and most obviously, Iñárritu films the action as though it were one long take, the camera continuously running as it follows characters through hallways, up stairs, onto a theater stage, outdoors, even up in the air, changing mise-en-scène without seeming to cut or dissolve from one shot to another. Sometimes the shot looks like Riggan's point of view as he rushes from one place to another (a traveling point-of-view shot); sometimes we see his progress over his shoulder (a traveling over-the-shoulder shot); sometimes we watch his body from the side as he marches down a sidewalk (a tracking shot). The camera even tilts up to linger on a night sky, which slowly brightens before it tilts down to a new scene, thus signaling the passage of time as in time-lapse photography. When filming performances of Riggan's play, the camera several times circles around actors on the stage (circular dolly shots), everything appearing—through visual trickery—to be part of one continuous take.

By creating this illusion, the filmmakers emphasize insertions reminiscent of Eisenstein's "collisions" of montage. When Riggan shoots himself "for real" on stage, the camera moves from a close-up behind his head to a long shot showing the theater audience standing in ovation, and then tilts up to the ceiling. Suddenly the shot cuts to a montage of short takes, including the image of a tree, followed by a marching band, with someone in a cheap Spiderman costume weaving through the instrumentalists. The montage ends with two images that began the film, albeit in reverse order, like a symmetrical framing device.

---

[34]Eleftheria Thanouli, *Post-classical Cinema: An International Poetics of Film Narration* (London: Wallflower, 2009), 72, 141. Thanouli borrows the term "filmic signifiers" from theorist Thomas Elsaesser.

The movie's initial shot is so brief that it barely registers on the brain. Richard Brody incorrectly identifies it as the sky before the shot cuts to a meteor burning through the atmosphere.[35] When the shot is repeated after Riggan's suicide attempt, this time with a much longer take, we finally understand what we first saw: a beach covered with slimy jellyfish as birds sweep down to the sand. The image makes sense in light of something Riggan tells his ex-wife during his play's opening-night intermission: years earlier, after she had caught him in bed with another actress and threw him out of the house, Riggan had waded into the ocean planning to drown himself. In the process, he disturbed a school of jellyfish, whose stings created so much pain that he rushed out of the water seeking relief.

In an Eisenstein-like move, then, the filmmakers juxtapose discontinuous shots of beached jellyfish and a meteor falling from the sky to symbolize Riggan's psyche at the moment of his second suicide attempt. Reversing the cliché of a "meteoric rise to fame," a meteor falls to earth—like Riggan's post-Birdman reputation. Then, after the insert of birds hovering over jellyfish, as though alluding to the way the Birdman character hovers over Riggan's stinging past, the camera returns viewers to the illusion of one continuous take. Whereas before the suicide montage the camera had tilted up to the theater ceiling, afterwards it tilts down from a hospital ceiling, where we eventually see Riggan in bed with a bandage over his face, having shot off his nose rather than succeeding to commit suicide—another failure.

Ironically, people come into Riggan's hospital room with reports that his play was an overwhelming success. Tabitha, who had intended to kill the play with a scathing review, praises it for "giving birth to superrealism." In other words, her decision to kill the play was displaced by Riggan's decision to kill himself. Which killing has more power to affect people's understanding of real art?

### Diegetic Versus Nondiegetic Sound

The *Birdman* filmmakers foreground competing definitions of "real art" by also playing with diegetic versus nondiegetic sound. *Diegesis*, borrowed from the Greek word for "narration," refers to the world of the film story, its era and

---

[35]Brody, "Birdman Never Achieves Flight."

location, as well as the characters that populate it. Diegetic sound, then, is part of that world, not only in character dialogue but also through environmental noises such as ticking clocks and exploding bombs. Nondiegetic sound comes from outside the world of the film, as in the musical score that accompanies most movies. In a postclassical move, however, the film plays tricks on its audiences, drawing attention to the artifice of cinematic sound. Several times drumbeats accompany Riggan's movements, a common nondiegetic device. But as the camera follows Riggan, it suddenly captures someone playing drums in a narrow hallway of the theater building, showing that sound we assumed to be nondiegetic is actually diegetic. Turning out to be "real" sound in the diegesis, the drumming, however, is so farcically located that the situation seems unreal. This happens several times with drumming and music in the film, thus drawing attention to the *agōn* between real and unreal in the film's form as well as its content.

In fact, the very first words of the film allude to the distinction between diegetic and nondiegetic sound. As the camera shoots Riggan from behind, sitting in lotus position, a gravelly voice states, "How did we end up here? This place is horrible!" First-time viewers do not know whether the voice is from a *real* person standing behind Riggan or expresses, in voiceover, Riggan's thoughts. Cinema conventions have trained us to consider both possibilities, but the use of "we" clearly implies someone else in the room; it therefore seems to be diegetic sound. If externalizing his thought process, the speech hovers between the nondiegetic and diegetic. Is character dialogue more real than inner monologue? But if it is part of Riggan's inner world, to whom does the "we" refer?

The questioning continues as a beep sends Riggan over to his dressing table, where he hits a key on his laptop to access his daughter Sam on Skype. The scene is shot so that the oblong laptop screen is framed by the dressing-room mirror, reflecting Riggan's body. The camera slowly pulls back as Riggan closes the laptop, such that we see his face in the mirror, with a poster of his Birdman character above and to his right on the wall behind him. Hovering over Riggan's shoulder in a stage dressing room, Birdman seems to fulfill the words of Val Gielgud: "Over all brooded the shadow of Hollywood."

### MIRRORING TRUTH OR ART?

After Riggan closes the laptop, we also see reflected under the Birdman poster an empty suit conforming to the contours of a couch, as though a seated body had evaporated from inside it. Soon another voice is heard inside the room, presumably of a stage manager, announcing, "They're ready for you." As Riggan turns from the mirror to take up the suit for his role in the play, we now see the image of Birdman directly. No longer reflected in Riggan's makeup mirror, the Birdman poster contains its own reflection; a bright rectangle from sun through an adjacent window lights up the lower left hand of the poster, the "real world" outside the theater superimposed on the Birdman image. Which is most real to Riggan's identity? The reality of his Birdman celebrity? Or the light of something more real that exceeds the frames of poster, laptop, mirror, and window?

Generating numerous questions, *Birdman*'s opening scene thus functions as a synecdoche (a part standing for the whole) of the entire film. Overshadowed by his Birdman character (in the fictional sense of *character*), Riggan feels like his real character (defined in terms of talent and ability) has evaporated. He therefore puts on theatrical clothes to prove he has substance to the world beyond his window. The movie's *agōn*, then, is between these two types of character, referenced by the "we" of its first sentence: Riggan as *Birdman* movie star versus Riggan trying to perform "real art" on stage. Indeed, after we see him rehearse on stage, he returns to his seedy dressing room only to hear the gravelly voice of his Birdman past say, "We were *the real thing*, Riggan. . . . We had it all." Later the Birdman voice complains, "We should've done that *reality* show they offered us. . . . Denounce this play." What is "the real thing"? How do we define reality? According to Bazin, "The cinematographic image can be emptied of all reality save one—the reality of space" as displayed on the screen.[36]

Continuing to play tricks with diegetic versus nondiegetic sound, Iñárritu encourages viewers to question even the reality of space. As Riggan leaves a bar in frustration over his play, we hear a famous Shakespeare soliloquy:

> To-morrow and to-morrow, and to-morrow,
> Creeps in this petty pace from day to day,
> To the last syllable of recorded time;

[36]Brody, "Birdman Never Achieves Flight."

And all our yesterdays have lighted fools
The way to dusty death. Out, out, brief candle!
Life's but a walking shadow, a poor player,
That struts and frets his hour upon the stage,
And then is heard no more. It is a tale
Told by an idiot, full of sound and fury,
Signifying nothing. (*Macbeth*, act 5, scene 5, lines 19-28)

Macbeth's words capture perfectly Riggan's sense of futility. He worries that all his yesterdays as Birdman have lighted his way to dusty death as an actor, that his hour on the stage will not achieve for him the fame he desires, that his life, though full of comic book sound and fury, signifies nothing. The speech seems like a nondiegetic commentary on Riggan's emotion—despair over his failure to achieve "real art" like that of Shakespeare. However, Riggan comes upon an actor hanging like a monkey onto scaffolding while powerfully reciting Shakespeare's famous lines. Upon seeing Riggan, the actor breaks character, asking in a wimpy voice, "Was that too much?" Apparently diegetic, the speech seems told by an idiot, signifying nothing. Or is the *Macbeth* speech merely another externalization of Riggan's internalized agon(y), like the gravelly voice of Birdman, which keeps reminding Riggan about "the real thing" he left behind? One is a diegetic voice representing the artistry of theater, the other an internal diegetic voice representing Riggan's thoughts about the glories of cinematic celebrity. Which is more real?

## Magical Realism: The Power of Cinema

While Tabitha, the theater critic, praises Riggan's play as a form of "superrealism," film reviewers have praised Iñárritu's movie for its "magical realism" due to supernatural elements in the diegesis. Often associated with Latin American authors such as Gabriel García Márquez and Jorge Luis Borges, magical realism places unexplainable events into "realistic" narratives, thus undermining clear definitions of the real. Though obvious to the most unsophisticated viewer, the supernatural elements of *Birdman*—scripted by Latin American screenwriters—reinforce the film's *agōn*.[37]

[37]Of the four writers who won the Oscar for *Birdman*'s screenplay, Iñárritu is from Mexico, while Nicolás Giacobone and his cousin Armando Bó are from Argentina.

When Riggan first appears on screen in lotus position, he is levitating several feet off the floor. Later he periodically moves inanimate objects by merely looking or pointing at them, and he repeatedly engages the invisible Birdman character in lively conversation, as though speaking to a ghost. Then, toward the end of the film, Birdman finally appears as more than a poster image, stalking Riggan on a city street. But since no other pedestrians notice the masked, winged creature, we wonder whether it is really there. Perhaps, along with the levitation and magic projectiles, the Birdman conversations are merely a projection of Riggan's inner fantasy: that he can escape his Birdman reputation with a success on Broadway, that he can rise above the superhero-loving masses to achieve "real art." However, due to problems with the stage production, Riggan tells his daughter, Sam, that the play feels "like a major deformed version of myself that just keeps following me around"—as does the character of Birdman.

After a tracking long shot shows Birdman stalking Riggan, the camera moves in front of Riggan, using a low-angle lens so that when Birdman flaps his wings behind Riggan, it looks like they have sprouted from Riggan's shoulders, implying the Birdman character gave Riggan more power than theater ever will. Indeed, after the wing flap, Riggan snaps his fingers, turning the street into a movie set, with multiple explosions and a cheesy monster perched on top of a building. Soon we see Riggan rising above the masses by floating up to the top of a building, where he stands alone. Once Birdman is out of the mise-en-scène, people acknowledge Riggan's presence, a woman on the street yelling, "Is this for *real* or are you shooting a film?" After Riggan replies, "Film," he yells, "Music!" and then jumps off the roof. As he flies above the street, Birdman's voice states, "You see! This is where you belong: above them all," as though to suggest Riggan can achieve a meteoric rise to fame through the illusions of cinema more than on the stage.

Problematically, the Birdman voice endorses what film theorists reject, that is, cinema as mere fantasy entertainment. "Amusement-art," as Sayers puts it, "does not reveal us to ourselves: it merely projects on to a mental screen a picture of ourselves as we already fancy ourselves to be—only bigger and brighter."[38] Viewers don't question the bigger and brighter feats of superheroes because in the world of the film—the diegesis—most other characters accept them.

[38]Dorothy L. Sayers, "Towards a Christian Aesthetic," in *Unpopular Opinions: Twenty-One Essays* (London: Gollancz, 1946), 40.

*Birdman*, however, subverts viewer confidence in its supernatural elements. Because other characters don't hear Birdman's voice or witness Riggan's magic, his powers seem to be projections of his imagination. Indeed, after Riggan flies above yellow taxicabs, following them toward his theater, something odd occurs that undermines any sense of magical realism. He lands on the street in front of his theater, saying, "Stop the music," as he runs into the building, as though to say the cinema magic has ended. Indeed, the camera returns to the street where we now see a yellow cab in the exact spot where Riggan landed, the driver yelling, "You did not pay me." This, of course, implies that Riggan merely imagined flying above the cab while sitting inside it on his way to the theater. The incident goes by so quickly, however, that those who want to believe in Riggan's magic will continue to do so. Either way, Riggan desires mythic superpowers that might elevate him above the stigma of superhero cinema to achieve celebrity in the "real art" of theater. In other words, he simply seeks to replace one myth with another.

## Mythologies and the Greeks

Myth, according to French philosopher Roland Barthes, "abolishes the complexity of human acts, it gives them the simplicity of essences."[39] Influencing film theory in the 1960s, Barthes illuminates Riggan's frustration. In his arduous effort to explore "the complexity of human acts" on a Broadway stage, Riggan becomes increasingly attracted to the simplicity of Birdman, a mythological character that can transcend, quite literally, the "poor player" who "struts and frets" on the Broadway stage. Indeed, right before we see Riggan magically rise to a rooftop, Birdman tells him, "You are a god. . . . Gravity doesn't even apply to you."

Not coincidentally, Barthes, who discusses multiple movies in his famous book *Mythologies* (1957), is mentioned early in *Birdman*. During a press conference, one interviewer, asking Riggan why he gave up the Birdman role, pompously proclaims, "Barthes said cultural work done in the past by gods and epic sagas is now being done by laundry detergent commercials and comic strip characters." In response, Riggan quickly mentions Icarus before another interviewer interrupts. Icarus, of course, is the boy from Greek mythology who, flying too close to the sun with artificial wings, falls into the sea

---

[39]Roland Barthes, *Mythologies*, trans. Annette Lavers (New York: Hill & Wang, 1972), 147.

when the wax in his wings melts. By alluding to Icarus, Riggan implies that, in his artificial Birdman wings, the heat of Hollywood stardom landed him in the sea, quite literally when he considered drowning himself.

The critic's reference to "gods and epic sagas," followed by Riggan's mention of Icarus, resonates with another important motif in *Birdman*. As though alluding to ancient Greek and Roman drama, in which actors wore masks, the filmmakers repeatedly place masks in the mise-en-scène. Birdman, of course, both on the poster and as a character stalking Riggan, always wears a mask. Equally significant is the recurring image of the iconic white mask from *Phantom of the Opera*, placed on a billboard across from Riggan's theater. Appearing in the background during conversations between Sam and Mike, it alludes to ways both are masking their real intentions. Later, after Riggan flies above the taxis to the opening of his play, we see the *Phantom* mask reflected on glass doors of his theater after he walks through them, a long take on the *Phantom* mask indicating the passage of time before audience members exit during intermission. Then, at the end of the film, the hospitalized Riggan wears a mask of bandages on his face, its white color reminding us of the *Phantom* mask, its point over his nose looking remarkably like the Birdman mask. Alluding to two masks at once, the hospital bandage thus captures the two sides of Riggan: his desire to make a mark on Broadway, as did *Phantom of the Opera*, and his inability to escape his *Birdman* past.

### *The Birds* and *Birdman*: From Theater to Film

With the reference to "gods and epic sagas" near the start of the film, Birdman's screenwriters most likely allude to an actual precedent for *Birdman* in Greek theater, which, as we have seen, used masks. In 414 BCE, Aristophanes premiered *The Birds*, in which a character persuades all the birds in the world to form a problem-free realm in the sky called Nephelokokkygia, usually translated as "cloud cuckoo land." To this day, pundits often use the term *cloud cuckoo land* to describe unrealistic, naively optimistic ideas. Val Gielgud, after describing "the shadow of Hollywood" that "broods" over Broadway theater, remarked, "A previous visit to Hollywood had convinced me that life in that singular province of Cloud-Cuckoo Land held no attractions for me."[40]

---

[40]Gielgud, *One Year of Grace*, 75.

Clearly, the cloud cuckoo land of Hollywood no longer attracts Riggan as well. Seeking a more respectable Nephelokokkygia on Broadway, he wants to rise above—quite literally—his cheesy superhero reputation. Parallels between *Birdman* and *The Birds* are in fact quite pronounced. Most obvious are explicit echoes of old comedy conventions employed by Aristophanes. In what is known as the parabasis proper—the ancient precedent for breaking the fourth wall—either an actor or the chorus speaks to the audience from the stage, denouncing viewers for not appreciating artful theater, as does Mike during a preview performance of Riggan's play. Old comedy also placed on stage actors in tights, underneath which excess padding created the illusion of an erect phallus, something *Birdman* echoes. During an adultery scene in Riggan's play, Mike jumps out of bed when Riggan, playing the husband, walks in on them. But, to the horror of the actress playing Riggan's wife, Mike clearly has an erection under his long underwear. Furthermore, old comedy scripts not only quoted from famous playwrights, like *Birdman* quoting from Shakespeare, but they made references to current issues and famous personalities in Greek culture, much as *Birdman* mentions current American actors and films.

Even the plot of *The Birds* seems to influence elements in *Birdman*. *The Birds* begins with two middle-aged men looking for Tereus, a king who was transformed into a bird, because they are fed up with their horrible life in Athens; similarly, *Birdman* begins with the middle-aged Riggan and his middle-aged alter ego, who says, "How did we end up here? This place is horrible!" repeatedly suggesting Riggan was king as Birdman.

Next in Aristophanes's play, a dauntingly powerful bird, servant to Tereus, appears to the men, as does the image of Birdman in the poster behind Riggan. Only then in *The Birds* does the molting Tereus show himself to the men, one of whom, Pisthetaerus, comes up with the idea of creating Nephelokokkygia, where the birds can transcend earth and compete with the gods—much as Riggan wants to transcend his earthbound comic book identity and become a god of Broadway.

The ensuing Broadway production, which makes Riggan feel like "a walking shadow, a poor player, / That struts and frets his hour upon the stage," echoes what Aristophanes's chorus of birds says to humans: "You enfeebled and powerless creatures of earth always haunting a world of mere shadows, / Entities without wings, insubstantial as dreams, you ephemeral things, you human beings: / Turn your minds to our words, our etherial words, for the words of the birds last forever!" (lines 686-88). Soon, of course, we will see Riggan turn his mind to Birdman's words, the camera angle making him appear to sprout wings, followed soon after by his rising in the air as Birdman pronounces, "You are a god."

These parallels help explain the final scene of the film, when Riggan, lying in a hospital bed, is told by visitors that his play achieved rave reviews. "This play is going to last forever," states one. Like Pisthetaerus overseeing the building of cloud cuckoo land, which historian Arnold Toynbee aligns with heaven, Riggan has directed the construction of something everlasting. After his visitors leave, Riggan therefore crawls out of his hospital bed, removes his mask-like bandage, and goes to the window, where we see his reflection on the glass until the shot moves to what he sees: birds singing as they swirl through the air. As Riggan opens the window, we hear symphonic music as he climbs out onto the ledge, but the camera turns from him to the entrance of Sam through the hospital door. Noticing the empty room, Sam rushes to the open window, expecting to see her father dead on the pavement below. After looking down she looks up into the sky, a high-angle shot (the lens looking down on her from above) capturing amazed delight on her face before the screen cuts to black—and we hear her laugh, followed by a birdlike caw in a gravelly voice.

The baffling ending annoyed many viewers, who wanted the closure provided by films in the classical Hollywood style. But *Birdman* follows the classical Greek style, suggesting the existence of a "real" that transcends life as we know it. The ancient Greeks, of course, believed that transcendent gods once came to earth to rescue humans, an assumption visualized by the deus ex machina convention on their stages. Iñárritu, however, refuses to show us the machina that enables Riggan to float up and away to the gods. All we perceive is the beaming face and delighted laugh of Sam. Might this be the real thing for which Riggan has been searching? As C. S. Lewis suggests in *The Pilgrim's Regress*, "sweet desire"—what the Germans call *Sehnsucht*—points to a real that transcends all human constructions.[41]

---

[41]C. S. Lewis, *The Pilgrim's Regress: An Allegorical Apology for Christianity, Reason, and Romanticism* (Grand Rapids, MI: Eerdmans, 1958), 196.

3

# The Theater of War

## *Effects on Film and Faith*

In the 1940s a different kind of theater contributed to the stigma of cinema: the theater of war. Coming from *thea,* a Greek word meaning "a sight," *theater* is related to the Greek term *thauma,* "a thing compelling the gaze, a wonder."[1] Usually defined as an area or place in which important military events happen, the theater of war compels the gaze in a radically different way from other theaters. This chapter integrates the multiple definitions of *theater* to compel the gaze toward war movies in which visual artistry communicates Christian theology more powerfully than character dialogue does. Discussing the varied ways filmmakers respond to horrific historical events, it moves on to illustrate cinematic techniques employed in two films about World War II, one film made by people who lived through the war, the other made long afterward. Assessing how the waging of war contributes to the wages of cinema, discussion is guided by Dorothy L. Sayers, who was accused of causing a major Allied defeat in 1942. Her experiences can help Christians understand not only the attraction of war films but also how to adjudicate the difference between gratuitous violence and genuine art.

### Watching During Wartime

Two years after the start of World War II, a reviewer for the *New York Times* described *Haunted Honeymoon,* the newly released film adaptation of Sayers's *Busman's Honeymoon,* as "an agreeable change . . . from the multiple-corpse detective fiction which some Americans produce." Nevertheless, in addition

---

[1]See Eric Partridge, *Origins: A Short Etymological Dictionary of Modern English* (New York: Greenwich House, 1983), 710. William Bayer notes, "More movies have been made about war than about any other subject." Bayer, *The Great Movies* (New York: Grosset & Dunlap, 1973), 104.

to disparaging the "obvious Americanism" in the Hollywood star playing the British Lord Peter Wimsey, the reviewer denounces the movie's insensitivity to historical contexts: "The most surprising thing about this picture is that it was ever made. Imagine Englishmen trifling with such stuff as a musty mystery film while Norway was being invaded and the low Countries overrun!"[2] The theater of war, he implies, deserves far more attention than cinemas offering escapist entertainment. And they did indeed provide escapism. Jonathan Croall notes that the British "public's imagination was caught during the war not so much by theatre as by film. People went on average once a week, with some cinemas during the worst of the raids offering shelter for the night and five films."[3] People escaped from the theater of war by going to cinema theaters.

## The Attraction of War: Heroes and Villains

War almost literally became a theater for Sayers, who witnessed whirlwind activities in France at the start of World War I. After her second year as an Oxford University student, the twenty-one-year-old and a college friend decided to spend their summer break in Tours, arriving on July 31, 1914—the day before Germany declared war on Russia. On August 2, when the Germans invaded Luxembourg, Sayers wrote home describing shops refusing to sell food, streets clouded in dust from speeding automobiles, and restaurants with umbrella stands "stuck full of swords." Rather than registering terror, however, she asserts, "It is so fearfully thrilling," saying, "I am . . . beginning to enjoy myself immensely, if only we can stay."[4]

Sayers's giddy excitement helps explain consumer thirst for war movies. From historical battles to explosive confrontations among comic book superheroes, viewers consider fighting on screen so "fearfully thrilling" that they enjoy themselves "immensely." Part of the thrill arises from the dramatic contrast with everyday life, conjoined with the ability to view the action from a position of safety. In addition, most moviegoers, like Sayers, enjoy witnessing a struggle between heroes and villains, pleasure arising from the emotional,

---

[2]Bosley Crowther, "THE SCREEN; 'Haunted Honeymoon,' a Leisurely English Mystery Film, at Loew's Criterion," *New York Times*, October 31, 1940, www.nytimes.com/1940/10/31/archives/the-screen-haunted-honeymoon-a-leisurely-english-mystery-film-at.html.

[3]Jonathan Croall, *Sybil Thorndike: A Star of Life* (London: Haus Books, 2008), 306.

[4]*Letters* 1:91-93.

often patriotic, endorsement of a worthy cause. In another letter from Tours, Sayers proudly quotes the proprietor of her French lodgings, who had told her the day before Britain entered the war, "If only we can count on England, we'll give the Germans a good old dressing down," ending her letter with, "One feels rather glad to be English."[5]

Hollywood, of course, often panders to such patriotism, encouraging easy distinctions between good and evil, as did Sayers in France. During the mobilization she describes an incident that would make good movie material: "They shot two men, supposed to be spies, Germans, this morning, and they are going to shoot the *curé* [priest] of a little village near here, who was found to have in the *pneu* [tire] of his bicycle, plans of the surrounding country, marked to show the best spots for dropping bombs from aeroplanes. Anyway, I'm sure traitors *ought* to be shot."[6] Even though her own father was a clergyman, Sayers endorses the murder of a French cleric without question. Most war movies manipulate us to feel the same way, thrilling us with death. When Steven Spielberg's *Raiders of the Lost Ark* premiered in 1981, many audiences cheered when Indiana Jones (Harrison Ford), daunted by the deft sword work of an Egyptian warrior, awkwardly whipped out his pistol and gunned him down. After all, the Egyptian was anonymous to viewers, whereas the movie had given them background on Jones, causing most to identify with his point of view, quite literally through point-of-view shots. Furthermore, the film establishes that Indiana Jones's ultimate enemy was Hitler and his Nazis, easy targets for both bombast and bullets. Hollywood thrives on such clear-cut targets, from the simplistic cowboys-versus-Indians movies of the mid-twentieth century to the plethora of comic book movies in the twenty-first century.

### *Lone Survivor*

The marvel over Marvel heroism taints even historical movies. *Lone Survivor* (Peter Berg, 2013), based on an actual Navy SEALs operation during the war in Afghanistan, shows four SEALs throwing themselves over a cliff, where they bounce off boulders during a one-hundred-foot fall, one body crashing into a tree with a thunderous thud. At the bottom of the drop, however, not a

---

[5]*Letters* 1:95-96.

[6]*Letters* 1:96, emphasis original.

single SEAL appears to have broken a bone. Ironically, while shooting the scene, stunt doubles were injured by a fall of only fifteen to twenty feet, one with broken ribs, another suffering a punctured lung, some having concussions.[7] Nevertheless, on screen, the SEALs walk away after a drop five times more harrowing. Meanwhile, their Taliban enemies climb down the cliff to their level in a matter of minutes, making the jump seem totally gratuitous—except for its cinematic effect. Indeed, we see lots of blood from scrapes and bullet wounds on the heroes, because gore is more visually stimulating than internal injuries. We are even given close-ups of a hideous wound in which shrapnel protrudes from the protagonist's leg; however, while the actual historical figure could no longer walk due to the wound, in the movie he (Mark Wahlberg) limps away to safety. By thus elevating, or perhaps reducing, historical figures to superhero status, the film sullies the heart-rending authenticity of a true story.

Like many war films, *Lone Survivor* inserts gratuitous human-interest stories at its start, ostensibly to generate sympathy for the soldiers before focusing on high-energy combat and bloody injuries. Far more worthy of attention are war films that primarily focus on human psychology tested by battles "that try men's souls," as Thomas Paine famously put it. This is what attracts thousands to the *Chronicles of Narnia* and the *Lord of the Rings* novels, wherein C. S. Lewis and J. R. R. Tolkien echo their own experience of the Great War through battle scenes. More importantly, Lewis and Tolkien develop distinctive characters whose internal moral battles outweigh physical combat. Both authors' novels, which have been made into multiple movies, might encourage Christians to assess their attraction to films about war: Are we more interested in superheroics that can destroy our enemies, or do we value films that destabilize clear-cut distinctions between good and evil? How might war movies help us recognize not only the image of God in our enemies but also visual artistry that explores the *agōn* of battle? How might Sayers guide us through cinematic depictions of military infernos?

[7]See Oliver Gettel, "*Lone Survivor*: Navy SEALs, Stuntmen and a Five-Story Jump," *Los Angeles Times*, November 21, 2013, www.latimes.com/entertainment/movies/moviesnow/la-et-mn-lone-survivor-envelope-screening-series-five-story-jump-20131121-story.html; Perri Nemiroff, "Peter Berg and Marcus Luttrell Talk LONE SURVIVOR, Cast and Crew Dedication, Making the Movie for the Right Reasons, Honoring Lives Lost, and More," Collider, December 19, 2013, https://collider.com/peter-berg-marcus-luttrell-lone-survivor-interview/.

## Sayers, Cinema, and World War II

Forty-six years old when World War II began, Sayers demonstrated as much patriotism as during the Great War. However, rather than echoing the jingoistic platitudes of her youth, this time she committed herself to "good work well done," a phrase she coined during the war to encapsulate her sense of "Christian work."[8] As biographer Barbara Reynolds notes, Sayers's "sense of responsibility" during World War II was "titanic": "She took part in conferences, she gave talks to the Forces, she broadcast, she wrote letters to the press, she wrote articles, she formed a group for knitting socks and sweaters, . . . she became an air-raid warden and took her share of fire-watching."[9]

Several of her patriotic publishing efforts were made in collaboration with Helen Simpson, who wrote dialogue for Alfred Hitchcock. This may explain why Sayers regarded cinema as a creative way to surmount the "boredom and discontent" generated by the disruption of life for those not on the front lines. As she told Sir Richard Acland, a member of Parliament, in April 1940, she worried about people who "are too old or too timid to venture out in the blackout to visit their friends or the cinema." However, rather as than escapist entertainment, she wanted the war-weary British to watch movies to become "much more useful citizens." Unless the British "learn to think," as she puts it, "they will remain a passive nation, ready to fall for the next Hitler."[10] Clearly, Sayers believes that well-crafted movies can generate active reflection.

Sayers makes much the same argument to another correspondent in August 1941. Because the war has "given everybody a nasty jolt" about "our sense of values," she advocates the need for citizens to contemplate new ideas, "especially about the value of work" and "intellectual integrity." To inculcate such thoughts, she suggests "admiring a film for good dialogue and good photography, rather than for the dresses worn by the star and the amount spent on production."[11] She would certainly argue the same for films *about* World War II, as would two of her filmmaking contemporaries whose lives intersect with hers in unexpected ways.

---

[8]The phrase comes from "Why Work?," a talk Sayers presented at Eastbourne, UK, April 23, 1942. She had given an earlier speech at Brighton in March 1941, which included many of the same topics. See Dorothy L. Sayers, "Why Work?," in *Creed or Chaos?* (Manchester, NH: Sophia Institute, 1974), 78, 63n56.

[9]Barbara Reynolds, *Dorothy L. Sayers: Her Life and Soul* (New York: St. Martin's, 1993), 296.

[10]*Letters* 2:161.

[11]*Letters* 2:286-87.

## FROM THEATER TO FILM: NOËL COWARD

By the start of World War II, Noël Coward (1899–1973) was famous throughout the English-speaking world for writing, directing, and performing for the stage, leading Sayers to compare him with Aeschylus.[12] Early in his career, he allowed three of his plays to be made into silent movies, one of which Alfred Hitchcock adapted in 1927. Called *Easy Virtue*, the film was a box-office failure, illuminating what Barry Day calls "the crucial problem of translating Coward's articulate—and at this stage often melodramatic—plays into an essentially nonverbal medium."[13] Coward himself perpetuated the stigma of cinema when comparing film adaptations to staged drama: "Of all my plays only one, *Cavalcade* [1932] had been filmed with taste and integrity. The rest, with the possible exception of *Private Lives*, which was passable, had been re-written by incompetent hacks, vulgarised by incompetent directors and reduced to common fatuity."[14] Produced by MGM in 1931, *Private Lives* opens with Robert Montgomery on his honeymoon, perhaps explaining why MGM cast Montgomery as the newlywed Lord Peter in its 1940 adaptation of Sayers's novel *Busman's Honeymoon*.

World War II changed Coward's perspective on cinema. In 1941, several studio heads asked him to write and direct "a war propaganda film," his first attempt at filmmaking. Deciding to dramatize the 1941 sinking of a British Navy ship during the Battle of Crete, Coward starred in the film he created, *In Which We Serve* (1942), a smash hit in both England and the United States.[15] To develop a scenario for *In Which We Serve*, Coward collaborated with his "old friend" Clemence Dane: a member, like Sayers, of London's Detection Club since 1930, and coauthor of three detective novels with Sayers's close friend Helen Simpson.[16] Having socialized with Dane for years and attended live theater for decades, Sayers was well acquainted with Noël Coward's work. More surprising is Coward's knowledge of Sayers. In November 1944 Coward

[12]Dorothy L. Sayers, *The Mind of the Maker* (San Francisco: HarperCollins, 1979), 165.

[13]Barry Day, *Coward on Film: The Cinema of Noël Coward* (Lanham, MD: Scarecrow, 2005), 8.

[14]Quoted in Day, *Coward on Film*, 13.

[15]Barry Day, ed., *The Letters of Noël Coward* (New York: Knopf, 2007), 462.

[16]Day, *Coward on Film*, 71. Online sources disagree about the starting date of the Detection Club. Some say 1928, others 1930. All agree that records, begun in 1930, establish Sayers, Helen Simpson, and Clemence Dane (the pseudonym of Winifred Ashton [1888–1965]) as members in 1930. Dane won an Academy Award in 1946 for her contributions to *Perfect Strangers*, a 1945 film directed by Alexander Korda, who helped raise money for Coward's film *In Which We Serve*. Dane wrote the story and collaborated on the screenplay for Korda's film.

recited one of Sayers's war poems to British forces stationed in India. Called "The English War," Sayers's poem first appeared in *The Times Literary Supplement* (September 7, 1940), only to be anthologized in *The Best Poems of 1941*, where Coward first encountered it.[17]

Over two decades later, Sayers was still providing Coward with material. Having gone to Australia in 1963, for the opening of his play *Sail Away* Coward helped an "insecure" actress better perform her role on stage by telling her to model her character after the famous Dorothy L. Sayers: "I had [the actress] in slacks, drill coats, and slapping her thighs and smoking a cigar! I pretended to base the whole thing on Dorothy Sayers," resulting in "rounds of applause and good notices!"[18] Clearly, the persona of Sayers was still famous enough five and half years after her death to guide an actress halfway around the world to achieve her best work.

## Noël Coward and David Lean

During World War II, Coward helped someone else achieve his best work. Wanting *In Which We Serve* to have the highest possible quality, Coward recruited film crew from Michael Powell, the director who later discussed film rights with Sayers. Included in the crew was Powell's current editor, David Lean (1908–1991). Considering him "the best cutter in the business," Coward honored Lean's request to help direct the film.[19] After *In Which We Serve* garnered rave reviews, Coward had Lean take over full direction for three adaptations of his plays: *This Happy Breed* (1943), *Blithe Spirit* (1944), and *Brief Encounter* (1945).

Aided by early support from Michael Powell and Noël Coward, Lean has been rated by both the British Film Institute and the American Film Institute as one of the greatest filmmakers in history. He is the only director to have more than one film on the British Film Institute's list of the top ten best British films of the twentieth century: *Brief Encounter* (1945), *Great Expectations* (1946), and *Lawrence of Arabia* (1962).[20] Three more David Lean films

---

[17]See *Letters* 2:231; *Letters* 3:113, 120-21. For the poem and details about it, see Dorothy L. Sayers, *Poetry of Dorothy L. Sayers*, ed. Ralph E. Hone (Cambridge: Dorothy L Sayers Society, 1996), 120-21.

[18]Day, *Letters of Noël Coward*, 683.

[19]Day, *Letters of Noel Coward*, 446. See also Michael Powell, *A Life in Movies: An Autobiography* (New York: Knopf, 1987), 397.

[20]The list is based on a 1999 survey of one thousand cinephiles by the British Film Institute. See "BFI Top 100 British Films," Wikipedia, https://en.wikipedia.org/wiki/BFI_Top_100_British_films.

appear on the top one hundred list: *Oliver Twist* (1948), *Doctor Zhivago* (1965), and *The Bridge on the River Kwai* (1957). The latter grapples with a World War II crisis that Sayers was accused of causing, the fall of Singapore to Japan in February 1942.

### Sayers and the Fall of Singapore

In February 1940, five months after England had declared war on Germany, the BBC asked Sayers whether she would consider writing the series of radio plays about Jesus mentioned in chapter one. She agreed to take on the task only if she could use contemporary language for the characters, including terminology made familiar by the current war.

On December 10, 1941, three days after Japan bombed Pearl Harbor, Sayers read sample dialogue from her plays during a London press conference. Journalists on the prowl for juicy copy stoked war-weary fears by emphasizing that Sayers had replaced King James English with, significantly enough, "the language of Hollywood."[21] Protests were mounted by members of the Protestant Truth Society and the Lord's Day Observance Society, outraged Christians writing letters to Winston Churchill and the archbishop of Canterbury demanding that the plays be taken off the air. Refusing to capitulate to nationwide demands for censorship, the BBC proceeded with the broadcasts, the third play airing on February 8, 1942—the day Japanese troops invaded Singapore, Britain's largest military base in Southeast Asia. After Japan conquered the British stronghold a week later, the press published proclamations that the disaster was God's retribution for "blasphemy" in Sayers's plays.[22]

The fall of Singapore was indeed devastating, turning eighty thousand Allied troops into POWs, many forced into backbreaking construction of a railway through Thailand to Burma. The experience of these prisoners provides the setting for David Lean's *The Bridge on the River Kwai*. Premiering in England on October 2, 1957, the film certainly attracted Sayers's attention, if not her attendance. Remaining intellectually and physically active until her heart gave out following a day of shopping in London (December 17, 1957),

---

[21]Dorothy L. Sayers, introduction to *The Man Born to Be King: A Play-Cycle on the Life of Our Lord and Saviour Jesus Christ* (Grand Rapids, MI: Eerdmans, 1943), 8.

[22]Reynolds, *Dorothy L. Sayers*, 322.

Sayers would have valued how *The Bridge on the River Kwai* not only illustrates but also challenges the meaning of "good work well done."

## *The Bridge on the River Kwai:* Historical Accuracy

Though considered a film classic today, *The Bridge on the River Kwai,* like Sayers's radio plays, generated considerable controversy when released, one viewer calling it "a load of high-toned codswallop."[23] In 1957, British prisoners who had suffered appalling conditions in Japanese camps were still alive and could testify to the film's sanitized version of camp conditions. One of those prisoners, Ian Watt, whose famous work *The Rise of the Novel* also appeared in 1957, lamented, "To the survivors of the real Kwai story the movie version naturally seemed a gross insult." He despaired that, even though the film was "pure fiction," based on a 1952 French novel, viewers assumed "they were seeing the real thing."[24] Watt therefore indicts the movie for its inaccuracies and contradictions.

Sayers, in contrast, indicted protesters for simplistic viewing practices. In letters she sent to the director of religious broadcasting while composing her radio plays about Jesus, she advocates "techniques appropriate" for the "chosen medium" rather than leaden attention to biblical material. Instead of writing "something intended to improve the minds of the young," she asserts that the addition of nonbiblical elements could make the gospel message more relevant for her listeners.[25] And she was right. As she later recounted to C. S. Lewis, "thousands of people write to say that they have been 'brought back to God'" due to the power of the medium.[26] The same, then, might be said of the medium for *The Bridge on the River Kwai,* making its historical inaccuracies not as important as its visual power.

## Good Work Well Done

The film starts in silence—like cinema itself—the camera focused on an isolated bird circling the sky. The shot then cuts to densely forested land from the

---

23Quoted in Laura Noszlopy, introduction to *Railroad of Death,* by John Coast (Newcastle upon Tyne, UK: Myrmidon, 2014), xxix.

24Ian Watt, "The Humanities on the River Kwai," in *The Literal Imagination,* ed. Bruce Thompson (Stanford, CA: Stanford Humanities Center, 2002), 240-42. Watt seems to have a dismissive attitude toward electronic media in general, expressing disdain for "the perpetual hubbub of the phonograph, the radio, and the television" (231).

25*Letters* 2:226, 303.

26*Letters* 3:258.

perspective of the bird while including faint bird calls, as though literalizing what is called a bird's-eye-view shot. In this case, a bird's-eye view of the Thai jungle fails to capture the death and destruction under the dense foliage. The next shot, however, takes the opposite perspective, looking up through jungle foliage to the blue sky above. Then the camera slowly tilts down and pans right until rude wooden crosses appear at the foot of the trees, almost blending in with the trees from which they were made. As bird sounds get louder, the camera continues to pan right, revealing railroad tracks adjacent to more crosses, implying a connection between them. Suddenly, a train whistle invades the bird whistles, followed by a low-angle shot at the level of the tracks, which captures the undercarriage of a train as it screeches by. Darkness thus overwhelms the screen, punctuated by glimmers of light between the moving cars as the train rushes across the screen. Using no words, this entire opening sequence functions as a visual synecdoche for the film to follow, where opposite perspectives provide glimmers of hope in the midst of war's oppressive darkness.

The next shot explains the crosses and tracks. We see a Japanese gunner on top of a moving train, an over-the-shoulder shot capturing, from behind his back, what he aims his gun toward: a crowd of humans in an open railroad car, packed together almost as densely as the trees in the opening bird's-eye-view shot. When the train stops, the indistinguishable masses climb out of the car to join gaunt, sweaty men working on the tracks. Needing no words, the medium has communicated that the trees, like Japanese guards beneath them, oversee hundreds of beleaguered laborers, and, like workers forced to contribute limbs for the Japanese cause, the trees contribute limbs for crosses when the laborers die.

As in most good cinema, the medium thus speaks its own powerful language, the first words in *The Bridge on the River Kwai* not spoken until the camera takes us inside a POW camp, where we see and hear a well-muscled, sweaty American (William Holden) comment on the crosses he makes for graves, wondering how the new POWs might respond to them. Their arrival is accompanied by whistling that contrasts with the bird and train whistles that start the film. Scores of British soldiers—recent POWs from the fall of Singapore—whistle "The Colonel Bogie March," composed by a British Army bandmaster in 1914. Hearing the upbeat tune, Camp Commandant

Saito (Sessue Hayakawa) stands up to look out his window, which frames his vision of the entering Brits much as the film screen frames our vision of the action. From the bird's-eye view that opens the film to this framed image, Lean self-referentially alludes to techniques of the craft itself. Furthermore, as we view Saito watching the commander of the whistling troops, we get an image of the film's initial *agōn*, the conflict of wills between a Japanese and a British colonel.

Their antagonism intensifies when Nicholson, appealing to rules of the Geneva Convention, protects his officers from manual labor on the Burmese railroad. Proving that his defiance of Saito reflects military law and not cowardice, Nicholson submits to solitary confinement in a tiny metal pen, with no standing room or fresh air. After several days Saito releases Nicholson, but only because he needs help building a bridge over the River Kwai in time for a Japanese train's safe crossing. Nicholson becomes fully committed to the project, motivated primarily by belief in what Sayers calls "the integrity of the work."[27] Recruiting an engineer among his officers to design a viable bridge, Nicholson solicits the help of another officer to organize the enlisted men, who have been doing shoddy, undisciplined work on the railroad. Realizing that unfruitful labor is dehumanizing, Nicholson believes "our task is to rebuild the battalion" by constructing a "proper bridge." Knowing that "it's essential that they take pride in their job," he confirms Sayers's assertion, written at the start of World War II, that "man is never truly himself except when he is actively creating something."[28] Indeed, as Nicholson's men collaboratively construct the bridge over the River Kwai, their morale as well as their physical health improves.

The film, however, complicates the idea of collaboration. The Allied POWs are not just working together to make a viable bridge; they are collaborating with their Japanese captors to build a device that aids the Axis powers. When a British POW medic (James Donald) questions this collaboration, Nicholson asks him a hypothetical question: If asked to operate on Saito, "Would you do your best or let him die?" The medic's silent response suggests the true *agōn* of the film: agony over defining what Sayers calls "good work well done." Nicholson's collaborative project may be "well done," but does it serve a "good"

[27]Sayers, *Mind of the Maker*, 223.

[28]Dorothy L. Sayers, *Begin Here: A War-time Essay* (London: Gollancz, 1940), 23.

cause? Like the two definitions of work—both an object and an action—there are multiple ways to understand *good*.

## The Agony of Collaboration

As former antagonists Nicholson and Saito collaborate to get a "good" bridge built in time for a Japanese train to cross, a British officer in Ceylon recruits an escapee from Saito's camp to collaborate on a "good" cause: a project that will demolish the bridge and thus help undermine the Japanese war effort. The tension between these two definitions of *good* is visualized through the medium rather than arising from dialogue. As the demolition team advances toward the Kwai, they see Japanese soldiers through the trees. Launching a grenade, they kill most of the soldiers, but the film refuses to focus on the dead bodies. Instead, it offers a montage of related images. We see native women guides draw back in horror, as well as hundreds of birds rising to the air, darkening the sky with chaos, much as the rushing train darkens the screen near the start of the film. Echoing the screeching train, the screeching birds are initially shot with a low-angle lens, creating a contrasting parallel with the silent, soaring bird in the film's opening shot. Then, as the demolition crew proceeds through the jungle, one member tracking the lone Japanese survivor of their attack, we see distinct shadows cast by the careening birds, not only over the vegetation but also crossing the faces of the advancing team. The long and repeated takes of birds above and their shadows below speak louder than words: the "good" of the demolition project is overshadowed by the necessary killing of other human beings.

The mise-en-scène then makes a sudden shift to illustrate the other definition of *good*. A sunshine-filled close-up focuses on someone hammering onto the bridge a wooden sign announcing the bridge "designed and constructed" by soldiers of the British army led by Colonel Nicholson. Soon we see Nicholson walking with pride to the middle of the bridge, where he is joined by Saito. Leaning over the railing to look at the water, Nicholson hears Saito, behind him, say, "Beautiful," and he responds with, "First-rate job." The medium, however, creates ambiguity by inserting a shot of a sunset immediately before the interaction, causing attentive viewers to wonder whether Saito's "beautiful" refers to the bridge or the sunset. Nicholson sees only the beauty and goodness of the job itself, which, the medium implies, is part of his problem. The work of war is never unambiguously good; shadows of death and destruction inevitably block out the light.

The medium intensifies the contrast between competing definitions of the good in the next scene, through crosscutting. The shot cuts back and forth between the demolition crew sneaking up on the finished bridge in the dark and Nicholson's building crew celebrating the completion of their good work well done. On the most obvious level, crosscutting signals simultaneity of action, but it can also function symbolically. Lean makes the symbolism obvious by having the POWs perform silly skits on a stage that contains a three-foot-high model of the bridge they just completed. At the end of the show, Nicholson addresses the prisoners from the stage, telling them that they may feel "let down" now that "the work here is finished." But the constructed work, which we see in miniature behind him, stands as a testimony that "you're going to feel very proud of what you have achieved here in the face of great adversity." Then, as the Allied POWs sing "God Save the King," the shot cuts to Allied forces attaching explosives to the foundations of the newly constructed bridge. The crosscutting thus moves back and forth between different interpretations of the good.

Original viewers of *The Bridge on the River Kwai*, most of whom lived through World War II, probably saw only one good. For them and most audiences in 1957, members of the demolition crew were the film's true heroes, for they sacrificed their lives to destroy the enemy. Looking through the lens of Dorothy L. Sayers, however, we might see how the film refuses simple answers about the sacrifices of war. In *The Mind of the Maker* (1941), written during the Battle of Britain, Sayers argues,

> To feel sacrifice consciously as self-sacrifice argues a failure in love. When a job is undertaken from necessity, or from a grim sense of disagreeable duty, the worker is self-consciously aware of the toils and pains he undergoes, and will say: "I have made such and such sacrifices for this." But when the job is a labor of love, the sacrifices will present themselves to the worker—strange as it may seem—in the guise of enjoyment.[29]

Though not talking about military service, Sayers's words nevertheless explain the motivation of Nicholson, who revels—strange as it may seem—in the beauty of what he and his men have accomplished. Walking with admiration

[29] Sayers, *Mind of the Maker*, 134.

over the finished bridge while waiting for the first Japanese train to cross it, he picks up a stone from the tracks, tossing it aside like a gardener tossing away a weed that invades a beautiful flower bed. Adding complexity to this loving gesture, however, the filmmakers place it between two shots of Clipton, the medic who could not answer whether he would save Saito's life. First we see Clipton tell Nicholson, "I'd rather not be a part of it," before he scrambles up a hill. Then, after Nicholson tosses the stone, we see Clipton on the hillside throwing a stone in the exact same direction on the screen, creating a graphic match. The similar actions, one done with loving care, the other with angry frustration, visualize opposite responses to the good. The message needs no words.

When the camera cuts back to Nicholson on the bridge, we see him lean over the railing in the same location and with the same body gesture as earlier, when he responded to Saito's word "beautiful." This time, however, he notices something sullying the beauty of the construction: wires attached to the bridge supports. He calls Saito over to help him figure out what the wires mean while members of the demolition crew watch in dismay from their hiding places. After Saito and Nicholson go down to the water to inspect the anomaly, shots ring out from both sides, killing Allied and Axis soldiers alike. Only then does Nicholson stop to groan in anguish, "What have I done?" The obvious answer is that of the medic: "collaboration" with a vicious enemy. The medium, however, offers another perspective by filming Nicholson with a low-angle lens as he asks the question, such that we see his head exactly framed by the arches of the bridge above and behind him. The shot thus provides a second answer to what he has done: he has built a beautiful bridge, a work that sustained the physical and mental health of numerous men. Nevertheless, the medium sustains ambiguity over the goodness of Nicholson's actions by having him stumble toward the explosion detonator until a bullet penetrates his body, causing him to fall onto the trigger. Though this fall ignites the explosion, sending a train and all its Japanese dignitaries and soldiers to certain death, his actual intentions are left in the dark: light and dark together, like the shadows of birds flying over men's faces.

## THE MADNESS OF WAR

The ambiguity continues with a shot of the medic as he yells the final words of the film: "Madness, madness!" Attentive viewers are forced to ask which action demonstrated the greatest madness, building the bridge or destroying it? Or does the repeated word imply that both actions are mad, capturing the conundrum of war itself? As Clifton walks toward the demolished bridge, the shot pulls back and up, the camera getting farther and farther away from the scene, such that Clifton's body becomes smaller and smaller on screen, as though to say he cannot rise above the action to get a bird's-eye—or God's-eye—view of madness. The film then ends as it began: with a shot of a bird in the air. This time, however, the bird is joined by another bird soaring through the air, as though alluding to the idea of collaboration. For, if Nicholson had not collaborated with Saito to build a viable bridge, the train carrying enemy forces would not have attempted a crossing that, with the collaboration of the demolition team, killed all on board. Both collaborations were necessary for the Allied cause: madness, madness!

Winning seven Academy Awards, including Best Picture, *The Bridge on the River Kwai* thus fulfills the definition of great war movies offered by novelist/screenwriter William Bayer: "To be great, a war film must view the madness that is war in the context of characters in conflict; then it must probe that madness, take its measure, and render it convincingly on the screen."[30] *The Bridge on the River Kwai* thus suggests both/and thinking consonant with Christianity. Indeed, throughout the history of the church, Christians have disagreed about the good of war. Rejecting the just war theory suggested by Augustine (354–430) and elaborated by Aquinas (1225–1274), Christian pacifists privilege Christ's words about turning the other cheek and loving one's enemies (Mt 5:39, 44). Both positions are necessary. We need Christian proponents of just war to stop tyrants like Hitler, but we also need Christian pacifists committed to building bridges with the enemy to get us questioning our definitions of *just* and *good*.

## Sayers and Bridge Building

Sayers herself reflected both/and thinking during World War II, rejecting pacifism due to the outrages of Hitler but also arguing that "peace had to be actively constructed." These words appear in *Begin Here*, an essay commissioned early in the war as "a Christmas message to the nation."[31] Sayers's

[30]Bayer, *Great Movies*, 104.

[31]Reynolds, *Dorothy L. Sayers*, 295.

message encourages readers to consider life as "perpetual activity," with "peace conceived as the energetic balance of liberty and equality, mercy and justice, truth and charity": both/and activity rather than either-or thinking.[32]

Practicing what she preached, Sayers's "perpetual activity" led her to collaborate on a peace-construction project with two friends: Muriel St Clare Byrne, who taught her how to write for the stage (they cowrote *Busman's Honeymoon*), and Helen Simpson, whose work with Alfred Hitchcock taught Sayers what good film dialogue looked like. Together, the three conceptualized a series of books about "social reconstruction," using a military term to title their project, *Bridgeheads*. Anticipating the spirit of Nicholson in *Bridge on the River Kwai*, their statement of aims, written by Sayers, encourages "self-discipline in a self-disciplined community": "We shall try to quicken the creative spirit which enables man to build . . . in the light of his spiritual, intellectual and social needs."[33]

The bridge metaphor gets more explicit in Sayers's description of the project to Lord David Cecil, a professor of English at Oxford University: "Our job is rather to build our 'bridge' between one set of thinkers and another than to attempt reconstruction inside any particular sphere of thought."[34] In other words, like enemies employing self-discipline and creativity to collaboratively build a bridge over the Kwai, people espousing different political and economic philosophies must work together to rebuild the peace. As stated in the *Bridgeheads* aims, "Nationalism must not be 'deified.'"[35]

One could argue, in fact, that the deification of nationalism generated the artistic flaws in *The Bridge on the River Kwai*. The American escapee from Saito's POW camp, who leads the demolition crew in the film, is played with wooden, feckless machismo by William Holden. The filmmakers obviously felt the need to insert a character not in the original novel, one that might appeal to the patriotism—and thus pocketbooks—of American audiences. Concerning Holden's character, Ian Watt cynically comments, "On the Kwai, hundreds tried to escape; most of them were killed; not one succeeded; but

---

[32]Sayers, *Begin Here*, 134, 136.

[33]Dorothy L. Sayers, "Statement of Aims for the Proposed Bridgehead Series of Books," in *Dorothy L. Sayers: A Biography*, by James Brabazon (New York: Scribner's, 1981), 279. During World War II, *bridgehead* was commonly used to describe the area an army controlled near a bridge terminus.

[34]Quoted in Reynolds, *Dorothy L. Sayers*, 309.

[35]Sayers, "Statement of Aims," 281.

for Bill Holden it was a breeze." Watt also critiques depictions of Asians in the film. As though pandering to nationalist pride, the film has British POWs do all the intellectual work—engineering the bridge as well as organizing the workers—when, in actuality, the Japanese designed all bridges over the Kwai. As Watt acerbically notes, "To present the Japanese as comically inept bridge-builders gratified the self-flattering myth of white superiority."[36] Though few today would find the film's depictions of Japanese soldiers comical, Watt has a point.

Had he lived long enough, Watt would have found far more satisfying a 2013 movie also inspired by World War II, *The Railway Man.* Containing shots reminiscent of *The Bridge on the River Kwai,* the film depicts the horrific suffering of POWs forced to build the Thai-Burmese railroad, cutting back and forth between brutal depictions and scenes of their lives forty years later. Creatively employing cinematic devices to visualize rather than verbalize how horrors of the past remain present in a victim's psyche, *The Railway Man* verifies Sayers's wartime argument that only by building bridges can we guarantee peace.

## Building a Bridge: *The Railway Man*

With its very first image, *The Railway Man* (Jonathan Teplitzky, 2013) indicates its focus will be on bridges. A low-angle shot fills the screen with the Forth Bridge, which carries trains over Scotland's Firth of Forth, the location of the first German air attack on Great Britain during World War II. Built of iron in the 1880s, the Forth Bridge looks remarkably like the wooden bridge constructed in *The Bridge on the River Kwai,* a likeness reinforced by the original movie poster for the 1957 film.[37] By reminding astute viewers of both famous bridges, the first image in *The Railway Man* hints at its subject matter, especially when a uniformed soldier enters the shot on the bottom right of the screen. He stops at the center of the screen, such that the famous arches of the Forth Bridge frame his body, much as the similar-looking arches of the Kwai bridge had framed Nicholson's head at the end of David Lean's film. The brief,

---

36Watt, "Humanities on the River Kwai," 243, 236.

37To view the poster, see "'Style A' Poster for the US Theatrical Release of the 1957 Film *The Bridge on the River Kwai,*" Wikipedia, https://en.wikipedia.org/wiki/The_Bridge_on_the_River_Kwai#/media/File:The_Bridge_on_the_River_Kwai_(1958_US_poster_-_Style_A).jpg.

wordless shot establishes location, era, and symbolism, implying that the film to follow, like *The Bridge on the River Kwai*, will grapple with bridge building.

Indeed, viewers soon discover that *The Railway Man* addresses the same historical trauma as the earlier film. However, while *The Bridge on the River Kwai* was adapted from a novel about fictional characters, Teplitzky's film is based on the 1995 memoir of an actual veteran, Eric Lomax (1919–2012), a British officer stationed in Singapore when it fell to the Japanese. Eric and his comrades were marched through the jungle to help build the infamous railroad. When Japanese officers discovered that some prisoners had secretly put together a radio, they beat to death one of the collaborators until Eric confessed to initiating the radio assemblage. In retribution, Eric was stuffed into a sheep-sized bamboo cage between bouts of dehumanizing torture.

The film captures these historical incidents with disturbing imagery that dramatically contrasts with the depictions of POW life in *Bridge on the River Kwai*. Nevertheless, like the earlier film, *The Railway Man* explores an *agōn* that far transcends documentary accuracy. In fact, without attention to visual details, people used to the classical Hollywood style might consider *The Railway Man* a deficient movie. As with many postclassical films, *The Railway Man* necessitates repeat viewings, its early images making more sense once one sees the whole picture, both literally and figuratively.

### CINEMA TRADITIONS: BRIEF ENCOUNTERS IN *THE RAILWAY MAN*

Before the opening shot of the Forth Bridge, *The Railway Man* begins with white credits against a dark screen, the faint gong of a church bell soon invaded by the sound of a train engine. Traditionally, of course, church bells signal the hope for new life after the despair of death, rung not only when a parishioner dies but also every time a priest blesses the Eucharist bread and wine. Hence, by starting with the overlapping sounds of train engines and church bells, *The Railway Man* adumbrates its topic: the overlap of death and life, despair and hope. This is confirmed later in the film when a flashback shows Eric and other POWs in a tent, surreptitiously listening to BBC reports about British advances against the Japanese, one commenting, "They rang the church bells at home for the first time since the beginning of the war." After Eric leaves the tent, the camera immediately cuts to a close-up of him in Edinburgh after the war, with bells and a train in the background. Sights and sounds of the past thus continue to invade the diegesis, much as disturbing memories continue to invade Eric's psyche.

Soon after we see Lomax framed by the Forth Bridge, the film cuts to close-ups on a military medal behind glass and a photograph of a military squadron, a common cinematic device indicating that the protagonist was a soldier. Next the title "Veteran's Club / Berwick-upon-Tweed, England 1980" appears over a sterile lunchroom, until the shot cuts to an extreme close-up on pages of a railway timetable book. Only then does the camera focus on the middle-aged Eric Lomax (Colin Firth), who sits by himself with the book, after which the shot cuts to a line of men watching him. One of them, Finlay (Stellan Skarsgård), mocks Eric's obsession with timetables until Eric says, "I have a small problem. Last Thursday . . ." The movie then shows us what we now hear in voiceover, Eric running to board a train. As usually happens with such a convention, the voiceover stops as the action takes over.

Inside the train, Eric converses with a charming younger woman, Patti (Nicole Kidman), until he must debark at his station. On the station platform, the voiceover resumes to explain Eric's "small problem": "I've fallen in love." Only then does the shot cut back to Berwick-on-Tweed and a close-up on the veterans' faces listening to Eric's narrative. The earlier close-up on train timetable pages is now explained. Eric has figured out what train will get him to Patti's destination, enabling him to show up just in time to pleasantly surprise her on the railroad platform. Their rendezvous delivers such stuff as movie dreams are made on. Indeed, *The Railway Man* implies as much by explicitly alluding to a famous British love story made during World War II, *Brief Encounter* (1945), which was the third collaboration between Noël Coward and David Lean after *In Which We Serve*.

As Eric and Patti converse on the train during their first encounter, he points out the location where David Lean filmed *Brief Encounter* during World War II. Significantly, the 1945 film opens with a high-angle shot of trains chugging through a station before introducing Laura (Celia Johnson) and Alec (Trevor Howard), who fall in love while waiting for their trains in the station. The allusions continue as Eric runs down a ramp to catch the train on which he will meet Patti, echoing scenes when Laura runs down station ramps to meet Alec. Furthermore, narrators in both movies using the exact same phrase in their initial voiceovers, "I've fallen in love," and a railway timetable also "rules the lovers' lives" in *Brief Encounter*, as film scholar Richard Dyer explains. Listing the many references to watches, clocks, and time in Lean's 1945 film, Dyer passes over the most obvious one: a high-angle shot shows Laura on a railway station ramp with a huge clock filling the top right-hand quarter of the screen as she runs underneath it. Laura and Alec feel the overbearing presence of time, "its pressure, its fleetingness," as Dyer puts it.[38]

By explicitly invoking two radically different David Lean films, *Brief Encounter* and *The Bridge on the River Kwai*, then, *The Railway Man* brilliantly encapsulates its subject matter: the radical difference between Eric's current love life, based on a brief encounter, and his horrific experience working on the Burmese railroad near the River Kwai.

## Conventional Bridge Building

Like Laura and Alec in *Brief Encounter*, Eric and Patti spend more and more time together. After he successfully surprises her at the train station, their first kiss takes place in his Edinburgh kitchen, followed by a return to Berwick-on-Tweed, where the two walk with Finlay under the Royal Border Bridge, a famous railway viaduct. Built in the mid-1850s to carry trains over the River Tweed, the bridge's twenty-eight arches leap into and over the town, much as memories of the Burmese railroad leap into Eric's psyche, always hovering over his thoughts—just as the Forth Bridge hovers over the young Eric in the film's opening shot.

As the three walk under the Royal Border Bridge, Patti tells Finlay about her first encounter with Eric on the train, "He was more interested in my timetable." But then the shot suddenly cuts back in time to the Veteran's Club, where we see a close-up on Finlay's concerned face after Eric, flipping through timetables, announces he's in love. Before we can figure out why, the scene cuts just as quickly to another conventional romantic scene, an extreme long shot of the couple walking on a beach in the rain. We next see them nestled together in a car where Eric talks of a Viking invasion that happened nearby, despairing over the psychological ravages of war. When he states, "I don't think I can be put back together," Patti responds, "Why don't we try. Together." The sappy Hollywood dialogue is challenged, however, by the ominous sound

38Richard Dyer, *Brief Encounter* (London: British Film Institute, 1993), 44-45.

of a train in the background, implying that, in real life, the devastation of war on veterans' mental health can undermine even the most idealized romantic scenarios. This would also explain the insertion of the concerned face of Finlay—an image from the past of the film—in the middle of a generic romantic sequence. After all, Finlay was part of Eric's disturbing past as a POW.

An insert also destabilizes the scene in which Eric and Patti first kiss. As he makes lunch, Eric brusquely stops Patti from looking into a pot on the stove, setting an oven timer instead. An extreme close-up on the timer, along with the enhanced sound of its ticking, suggests that time "rules the lovers' lives," as in *Brief Encounter*. Just as Eric does not allow Patti to look into the pan on his stove, he does not allow her to look into his past: the time is not ripe. When she tells him that she wants to get a Brillo pad to clean burn marks off the bottom of the pan, Eric responds with a gruffly angry, "No!" right before the timer goes off. No one can scrub away the scars that still burn his psyche.

## Subverting Cinematic Conventions: Marriage to a Traumatized Veteran

Disjunction between Eric's tortuous past and his hopeful present is thus communicated through disjunctions in the film medium itself, beginning with a disturbing insert that follows the opening image of the Forth Bridge. Blackness once again fills the screen until we hear Colin Firth's voice state, "At the beginning of time, the clock struck one." The screen lightens only enough to show the feet of a body lying on a floor, the camera panning from right to left along the supine form as Firth continues to recite the poem about a striking clock. By mid-torso we see the body is breathing, just as the voiceover states, "The man came alive and the clock struck five." When the panning camera finally arrives at the body's head, we discover the supine man is reciting the poem, finishing with "Hours on the clock. Behold I stand at the door and knock." Only later do we recognize this famous Bible verse as a clue to Eric's future redemption, his salvation dependent on time, as are church bells and railway timetables. Later in the film we will see the young Eric (Jeremy Irvine) recite the same poem as he undergoes excruciating torture. It is an experience that the older Eric refuses to share with Patti, who stands at the door of Eric's past, knocking for entrance with the hope of saving him from his psychological wounds.

This interplay of past and present is confirmed by the film's wedding sequence. Films in classical Hollywood style often use a montage of quick takes to capture key moments in a wedding: the bride going down the aisle, the "I do" of the groom, the best man's toast, the cutting of the wedding cake, and so on. But *The Railway Man* subverts such conventional montage with confusing temporal discontinuities, preparing us for the confusion Patti will experience in her marriage. The shots appear in this order:

A fully clothed Patti and Eric, who wears a boutonnière, on a bed

A close-up on Eric, with his boutonnière, standing in front of a church

A medium shot of Patti with a river behind her

People entering a church

Eric on the bed with Patti

A different angle of people entering a church

Eric and Patti starting to take off their clothes on the bed

Eric and Patti enter the church together

A line of men saluting Eric as he walks up to the church

An unclothed Eric on the bed alone, with shower sounds in background

These discontinuities culminate in a surreal scene. The camera pans left along Eric's unclothed body lying alone on the bed, then turns to show the top of his head, where it remains as Eric props himself up, giving us an over-the-shoulder shot of a Japanese soldier standing at the foot of the bed. By showing the back of Eric's head along with what he faces, the shot tells us we are seeing Eric's perspective. This prepares us for the next over-the-shoulder shot, when a disheveled Eric walks with the soldier out of the honeymooners' hotel directly into a jungle. Then, as the soldier attempts to force Eric into an isolated chamber in a prison camp, Eric resists, until the camera cuts back to his hotel room, with Eric screaming and writhing on the floor.

Written out like this, the point seems obvious: Eric's view of existence has been warped by a devastating personal history that he feels unable to share with his newlywed wife. However, each shot appears so quickly that viewers are baffled—as is Patti when she views Eric writhing on the floor. From that moment, the film intercuts extended scenes of Eric's horrific POW past with much briefer scenes of his present life with Patti. For example, after showing

Eric's capture in Singapore, the camera cuts back to Eric's married life as he angrily creates a mess in his house after Patti has straightened things up. The scene, of course, suggests that Patti cannot straighten out the messiness of Eric's past. He, in fact, becomes increasingly, almost abusively, frigid toward Patti, refusing to tell her what happened during the war, despite her pleading.

Viewers mollified by the heartwarming early scenes of Hollywood romance will think that Eric's change in personality is too unbelievably sudden and/or that the myopic Patti made a clueless choice in husbands. But those attentive to the artistry of cinema will see the clues, and those familiar with the life of Sayers will sympathize. Like Patti in *The Railway Man*, Sayers married a veteran "damaged psychologically" by war, with children from a previous marriage.[39] Though the film eliminates references to Eric Lomax's first family, the cinematic medium makes his marriage to Patti seem sudden.

Whereas Sayers escaped her husband's truculence by immersing herself in work, Patti seeks answers from his best friend. Brief takes of meetings between Patti and Finlay are intercut with much longer depictions of life in the POW camp: visualizations, we assume, of Finlay's explanations of Eric's past. Later, as Finlay meets with Eric in his study, we see a close-up of Patti's concerned face on the other side of glass, as though she were looking through a window at the two friends conversing. But as Patti turns away, a rack focus (change in camera focus from a subject in the foreground to one in the background, or vice versa, thus highlighting something blurred out before) reveals that her image was a reflection in glass covering a photograph of a train that she was contemplating. Eric's experience with the Burmese railway, the rack focus implies, impedes Patti's window onto the real Eric. In fact, during the conversation in the study, Finlay not only rebukes Eric for how he treats Patti but also asks him about his torture: "What happened in that room? What did they do to you?" Clearly, Eric's experience was so dehumanizing that he cannot bear to share details even with a fellow POW. Encouraging Eric to take revenge, Finlay shows him a newspaper article about one of the torturers, who now earns money by giving tours of the prison camp—horrors of the past turned into paid entertainment. Finlay's angry comment, "Bridge over the Bloody River Kwai Holidays," alludes, of course, to discomfort over *The Bridge on the*

---

[39]Reynolds, *Dorothy L. Sayers*, 154. Born 1881, Oswald Arthur "Mac" Fleming was increasingly wracked by physical and emotional problems, becoming abusive enough that Sayers considered divorcing him in 1933.

*River Kwai,* a film that eliminated, for veterans like Ian Watt, burn marks from a despicable past.

### SEEKING REDEMPTION

Only by facing his past, quite literally, can Eric begin to heal. Motivated by Finlay, he returns to the Japanese prison camp, where he confronts his past torturer, the current tour guide, Takashi Nagase (Hiroyuki Sanada). At first, Eric merely imitates his torturer, brutally spitting out statements that echo language used by Nagase forty years earlier, a parallel established as the film once again cuts back and forth between past and present. We see Nagase forced to sit at the same table where Eric sat under interrogation decades before, Eric placing the past torturer in a position, both literally and figuratively, of present victim, a clear image of retributive justice. Such, Eric implies, are the wages of sin.

When Eric tries to get his former torturer to confess his sin, Nagase peacefully explains that he now works for "reconciliation," saying, "I tried to make amends." Not palliated, Eric places the arm of the unresisting Nagase on blocks, getting ready to smash it with a metal pipe. Pulling his blow at the last minute, Eric instead pushes his former torturer into a wicker cage, mirroring what was done to him. These multiple mirroring scenes imply that the past continues to control the present. Eric is still suffering from being tortured forty years ago, and Nagase still passively complies with retributive brutality, as he did when his Japanese superiors made him torture Eric decades earlier. Mirroring each other, both mirror the dehumanization of war.

And both mirror an economic model of redemption, what famous philosopher Jacques Derrida called an "economy of exchange."[40] Eric wants to punish Nagase *in exchange for* torture he suffered, even as Nagase attempts to do good works *in exchange for* his complicity with that torture. This concept of sacrificial exchange, key to multiple religions, is reinforced when the film gives us an extreme close-up on a knife, which Eric takes to the sheep-sized cage where he has interred Nagase—implying that the blood of animals like Nagase must be shed in exchange for their sin. However, rather than showing us his knife-wielding act, the shot immediately cuts to Eric walking along a

---

[40]For a more detailed discussion of Derrida's "economy of exchange," see Crystal Downing, *Salvation from Cinema: The Medium Is the Message* (New York: Routledge, 2016), chap. 6.

railroad bridge over a river. As he throws the knife into the water, we hear the knoll of a bell and a train rumbling behind him on the tracks. At the start of the film, of course, we heard the same two sounds, succeeded by a long shot of the younger Eric walking from right to left across the screen with a railroad bridge behind him. This time, however, the train and bell sounds are followed by a long shot of the older Eric walking home from left to right across the screen, as though to say he has reversed the trajectory of his life. He has killed his torturer and thrown away the knife.

The medium, however, offers a different message, one consonant with Christian orthodoxy. After a short take of the older Eric walking toward his flat in Edinburgh, left to right, the shot immediately cuts back to Nagase in the cage as Eric approaches with the knife. Rather than killing Nagase, Eric instead cuts the rope holding the door closed, the shot immediately cutting back to Eric entering his Edinburgh house and embracing Patti. By intercutting these non-simultaneous actions, the film subverts an economic model of redemption, implying that salvation is a gift that cuts imprisoning ties to the past. Indeed, Eric cannot fully embrace love until he cuts the rope that binds his psyche to hatred of Nagase. Forgiveness, then, is the bridge to new life, the place where one discards the knife of retribution. It is the radical act that surmounts an economy of exchange.

The bridge of forgiveness finally enables Eric to accept Patti's love, and the film ends with his return to the location of his imprisonment, this time with Patti by his side. The two enter a cavernous scar cut out of rock, excavated by 1940s POWs for the Burmese railway. As the couple stands at one end of the manmade ravine, a long shot shows Nagase entering from the other end. While Patti remains at one entrance, the two enemies meet in the middle of the scar, the medium suggesting that both, embedded in scarring wounds of war, must meet halfway. Indeed, Nagase finally says, "I am sorry," and Eric says, "I know you have suffered too. . . . I assure you of my total forgiveness. Sometime the hating has to stop." The film, however, does not have Eric speak these words; instead, he hands a letter to Nagase, the contents of which we hear in voiceover. Though striking many people as odd, this may be the most theologically brilliant moment of *The Railway Man*. If Eric were to forgive only because a weeping Nagase says, "I am sorry," he would still be caged within an economic model of salvation, offering forgiveness only in exchange for apologetic groveling. However, by having Eric write down his forgiveness in advance, before any apology has been offered, the film establishes salvation as a gift. The time of torture has been redeemed, not because of works, lest either man should boast. Consonant with the gospel message, *The Railway Man* thus suggests that salvation from the wages of sin is an unmerited gift of forgiveness that must be accepted with humility.

## TRANSFORMING THE FALL: THE GIFT OF FORGIVENESS

Convinced that the wages of sin is death, Sayers not only celebrated the gift of salvation made possible through Christ but also repudiated "disgusting ideas about 'satisfaction' and 'paying-off'"—an economy of exchange—that have sullied Christianity through the ages.[41] For her, the heart of the gospel is forgiveness, a truth no less applicable during times of war. Therefore, in April 1941, Sayers published an essay titled "Forgiveness and the Enemy," arguing, "Forgiveness has no necessary concern with payment or non-payment of reparations; its aim is the establishment of a free relationship," reminding us of Eric and Nagase in *The Railway Man*.[42]

When "Forgiveness and the Enemy" appeared in *The Fortnightly*, Sayers had already started composing her BBC radio plays about Jesus, in which she repeatedly distinguishes between the gift of salvation and an economy of exchange, the latter employed by Satan in the temptation of Jesus: "Son of God, I will *give* you all these for your own, *if* you will serve me." For her fifth radio play, broadcast two months after the fall of Singapore, she explicitly states that she wanted "to get rid of the 'reward and punishment' notion" that has marred understanding of Christ's Beatitudes.[43] Ironically, Christians followed a "reward and punishment" notion when they proclaimed the fall of Singapore to be God's retribution for blasphemy in the BBC broadcasts.[44] Sayers, in contrast, fulfilled the gospel message by communicating the gift of salvation through her "chosen medium." In addition to hundreds of listeners writing her to say they finally understood the relevance of Christ's sacrifice for their lives, C. S. Lewis was so profoundly moved by the plays that he read a printed

---

[41]*Letters* 2:54.

[42]Dorothy L. Sayers, "Forgiveness and the Enemy," *The Fortnightly* NS 149, no. 892 (April 1941): 381.

[43]Sayers, *Man Born to Be King*, 70, 124.

[44]In Reynolds's words, Singapore was "a sign of God's judgment on Britain" (*Dorothy L. Sayers*, 322).

version of the broadcasts, *The Man Born to Be King* (1943), every year for his Lenten devotions until he died.[45]

## A Concluding Gift

Two years after the fall of Singapore, Sayers was grappling with the gift of forgiveness on another front. In March 1944 she published a poem in the *Fortnightly* and the *Atlantic Monthly* about a recent Allied bombing of Frankfurt. Called "Target Area," the 138-line poem talks about a Frankfurt resident, Fräulein Fehmer, who had taught piano at the British boarding school Sayers attended thirty-five years earlier. Describing Fehmer's pedagogical precision and musical power, Sayers wonders whether the "exchange" of bombs between Germany and Britain killed her former piano teacher. She ends the poem emphasizing the collaborative guilt of war rather than an economy of exchange: "The solidarity of mankind is a solidarity in guilt, / and all our virtues stand in need of forgiveness." In addition to summarizing the Christian implications of *Bridge on the River Kwai* and *Railway Man*, these lines show Sayers practicing what she preached. For, at the center of her poem, Sayers quotes from a letter in which Fehmer tells her, "I am an ardent Nazi." Through the poem, then, Sayers establishes "solidarity in guilt" with a Nazi, recognizing that *all* humans "stand in need of forgiveness."[46] This profoundly Christian insight might help us distinguish generic war movies from those plumbing the depths of human nature.

Refusing to reduce the theater of war to clear-cut distinctions between good and evil, *The Bridge on the River Kwai* and *The Railway Man* fulfill a belief foundational to *Bridgeheads*: "The only way to overcome evil is to transform it into a greater good." For Sayers, these words refer not only to the gift of forgiveness modeled after Christ's sacrificial gift on the cross but also to "the importance of the creative arts in the life of the community"—which includes creative films that visualize the ambiguities of war, world without end, Amen.[47]

---

45 C. S. Lewis, *God in the Dock: Essays on Theology and Ethics*, ed. Walter Hooper (Grand Rapids, MI: Eerdmans, 1970), 260.

46 Dorothy L. Sayers, "Target Area," in Hone, *Poetry of Dorothy L. Sayers*, 140-45.

47 Sayers, "Statement of Aims," 279, 281.

4

# From Silent Film to Sound Work

During World War II, Marxist cultural critics Max Horkheimer and Theodor W. Adorno intensified the stigma of cinema by denouncing the consumer culture in which it was embedded. After distributing drafts of their critique to fellow scholars, they published their assessment in 1947, *Dialectic of Enlightenment*. In their famous text, they argue that film generates an escapism that "always means not to think about anything, to forget suffering even where it is shown. . . . It is flight; not, as is asserted, flight from a wretched reality, but from the last remaining thought of resistance." For them, the "culture industry," as represented by cinema, is "a parody of the never-never land."[1] Just as Peter Pan takes flight from the responsibility of growing up by going to Never-Never Land, consumers of cinema take flight from addressing problems in the real world.

Dorothy L. Sayers would agree, despairing over people who consume the conventions and clichés of movies no differently from the popcorn and candy they consume while watching them. In January 1925, she screened *Peter Pan* (Herbert Brenon, 1924), a silent film adaptation of the famous 1904 play by J. M. Barrie, writing a friend soon afterwards and denouncing the escapist "mentality" behind the story.[2] Then, during the same decade in which Horkheimer and Adorno were attacking unreflective consumerism, she mounted her own attack.

Whereas Marxist critics blamed bourgeois capitalism for never-never-land attitudes, Sayers put more responsibility on the individual. For her, life practices, like religious beliefs, reflect God-given free will. Though exercising her

---

[1] Max Horkheimer and Theodor W. Adorno, *Dialectic of Enlightenment*, trans. John Cumming (New York: Continuum, 1972), 144, 155, 134, 156.

[2] *Letters* 1:228.

free will to screen movies, she also intensely promoted "the integrity of work" in all areas of life, bemoaning the fact that all too many people think "the value of all work is to be measured in money—profits and wages and expenditure." And she exemplifies her point with cinema: "People . . . really admire wealth and idleness, and go to see films about idle rich people in America, and wish they could live like that."[3] Furthermore, like her Marxist contemporaries, she believed that the advent of "talkies" had exacerbated the problem with never-never-land desires.

This chapter interweaves the history and theory of sound film with Sayers's own experience, showing how disgust over a talkie inspired her to develop a Christian theory of art that can guide Christian screening practices today.

## Sound Investments

*Dialectic of Enlightenment* asserts that the appearance of talkies in 1927 destabilized any possibility of cinema turning into an art form. "Sound film," for Horkheimer and Adorno, "leaves no room for imagination or reflection on the part of the audience, who is unable to respond within the structure of the film."[4] As late as 1957, the year Sayers died, a specialist in the psychology of visual perception, Rudolf Arnheim, was still arguing that cinema had reached its apex as "an artistic medium" in the late silent period.[5]

Ironically, silent film was rarely silent. Some of the earliest exhibitors provided "explainers" who would stand by the screen to tell viewers what was going on, a practice so common in Japan that explainers developed their own guild.[6] In the West, however, title cards, such as those designed by the young Alfred Hitchcock, soon became the norm. Often called "intertitles," these bits of printed text were edited into a silent film to explain narrative changes (expository intertitles) or what a character was saying (dialogue intertitles). Art historian Erwin Panofsky aligns intertitles with a convention used by artists during the Middle Ages: "The [film] producers employed means of clarification similar to those we find in medieval art. One of these were printed titles

[3]*Letters* 2:286.

[4]Horkheimer and Adorno, *Dialectic of Enlightenment*, 126-27.

[5]Quoted in James Monaco, *How to Read a Film: The Art, Technology, Language, History, and Theory of Film and Media*, rev. ed. (New York: Oxford University Press, 1981), 318.

[6]Peter Wollen, "The Semiology of the Cinema," in *The Film Theory Reader: Debates and Arguments*, ed. Marc Furstenau (New York: Routledge, 2010), 173.

or letters, striking equivalents of the medieval *tituli* and scrolls" that identified the religious significance of the painting.[7]

Even with intertitles, silent cinema was rarely silent. British filmmaker Michael Powell explains in his autobiography that distributors sent sheet music along with their silent features so that live musicians had a pre-established score to play along with each movie. Large cinemas might boast professional orchestras of up to sixty members, leading Powell to effuse, "The only thing silent about them were the actors. It was paradise!"[8] Inadequate musical accompaniment, however, led to paradise lost. Sayers implies as much in her sixth detective novel, *Strong Poison* (1930), when Lord Peter despairs over "third-class musicians" who ruin silent movies by "playing the most ghastly tripe."[9] Synchronized sound, recorded onto to the celluloid itself, made things worse.

Sound conquered the silver screen gradually. The first publicly exhibited sound shorts appeared at the Paris Exposition in 1900, and by 1907 the French-born, American-trained, and British-based Eugene Lauste was awarded the first patent for recording sound directly onto celluloid. But the technology was not commercially viable until the late 1920s. In 1921 D. W. Griffith included brief talking sequences in his film *Dream Street*, but audiences did not respond well to the movie, which many critics consider Griffith's worst film. In 1926, Warner Brothers started using a new sound-on-disk device that coordinated the projection of silent shorts with music and speeches recorded on a phonograph disk. Then, in October 1927, Warner Brothers released *The Jazz Singer*, a feature-length silent film using the device for several singing and brief dialogue sequences, including a line uttered by vaudeville star Al Jolson, "You ain't heard nothin' yet." Famous in film history, Jolson's sentence proved to be prophetic, with *The Jazz Singer* succeeding stunningly at the box office.

Soon all the major Hollywood studios had determined that the expense of equipping their theaters for synchronized sound was a sound investment. By 1928, as Louis Giannetti and Scott Eyman note, "Mediocre films with talking

---

[7]Quoted in Wollen, "Semiology of the Cinema," 172-73.

[8]Michael Powell, *A Life in Movies: An Autobiography* (New York: Knopf, 1987), 181. For orchestra size, see Philip L. Scowcroft, "Dorothy L. Sayers and the Cinema," *Sidelights on Sayers* 4 (April 1984): 21. In a note to his essay, Scowcroft reports that he published a study titled "Live Music in Doncaster Cinemas 1908–34," in the magazine *Vintage Light Music* (22n19).

[9]Dorothy L. Sayers, *Strong Poison*, in *Dorothy L. Sayers: On the Case with Lord Peter Wimsey* (New York: Wings, 1991), 81.

sequences were out-grossing the finest silent films."[10] By 1929, Warner Brothers had released its first all-color talkie, *On with the Show!*, and though reviews identified its many weaknesses, the movie was a box office hit. Michael Powell therefore laments, "All over the world, people were demanding talkies in their own language. An art that spoke a universal language had ceased to exist. Money talked."[11] More concerned about financial profits than artistic prophets, studios were churning out movies with static, uninteresting scenes because they needed the actors to limit their movement so that hidden microphones could catch the dialogue during filming. The 1952 film *Singing in the Rain* (Gene Kelly and Stanley Donan) delightfully showcases these problems. As film historians Kristin Thompson and David Bordwell summarize, "Set during the transition to talkies, the film pokes fun at Hollywood pretension while satirizing the style of early musicals and creating gags with out-of-synch sound"—all while dazzling viewers with the singing and dancing of Gene Kelly and Debbie Reynolds.[12] It remains a movie worth seeing, a prophetic film about film profits—perhaps explaining why it won no Oscars.

## Profits Versus Prophets

Called a prophet later in life, Sayers understood the motivation of profit, having begun her fiction-writing career thinking primarily of wages.[13] When seeking a publisher for her first novel, she told her parents, "Lord Peter is still my chief anxiety, but I am quite sure now that there is money in him." And even after the 1923 publication of *Whose Body?*, she was writing home, "I wish I could write a good detective play—that's where the money is!"[14] Several months after the advent of talkies, however, she told Eustace Barton, a fellow detective fiction author, that she was tired of churning out novels focused on Peter Wimsey, "because his everlasting breeziness does become a bit of a tax at times"—despite the financial profit he provided her.[15]

---

[10]Louis Giannetti and Scott Eyman, *Flashback: A Brief History of Film* (Saddle River, NJ: Prentice Hall, 2001), 78.

[11]Powell, *Life in Movies*, 197.

[12]Kristin Thompson and David Bordwell, *Film History: An Introduction*, 3rd ed. (New York: McGraw-Hill, 2010), 315.

[13]James Welch, the director of religious programming at the BBC, wrote Sayers to say, "We must make you a prophet to this generation and hand you the microphone to use as often as you feel able" (*Letters* 2:364).

[14]*Letters* 1:183, 203.

[15]*Letters* 1:274.

Choosing artistic integrity over a sound investment, Sayers published two novels in 1930 that took her in a financially risky direction. First, she collaborated with Barton to produce a novel in which Lord Peter never appears, *The Documents in the Case*. Second, she planned to "get rid of" Peter altogether by creating a character in her next novel to marry him.[16] Both novels address the topic of artistic integrity, *Documents in the Case* comparing two painters in love with the same woman. The Book Guild named *Documents* "detective story of the year," and Sayers's novel published several months later took artistic integrity to a new level.[17] *Strong Poison* introduces Harriet Vane, a detective novelist committed to intellectual integrity with whom Peter falls in love.

Sayers sustains the tension between art and money in *Strong Poison* by contrasting Lord Peter's despair over "third-rate" music at silent movies with the gleeful celebration of talkies by an uneducated manicurist. "Prepared to sell her honour" for cash, the manicurist echoes film studio bosses who, by paring away visual artistry, were selling out the honor of silent cinema for cash.[18] This may explain why Sayers mentions silent film stars in *Strong Poison*. Wanting to give honor where honor is due, she inserts a character with a "militant High-Church conscience," Miss Climpson, who tells Lord Peter, "I have never greatly cared for George Robey, though Charlie Chaplin always makes me laugh." Having seen Robey perform on stage and mentioning him in an earlier novel as well as a short story, Sayers makes a prescient distinction between the two celebrities.[19]

## The Poison of Talkies Versus the Art of Chaplin

Both born in London, George Robey (1869–1954) and Charlie Chaplin (1889–1977) became similarly famous for their staged comedy and pantomime acts. However, even though Robey appeared in thirty movies, most famously as Falstaff in Laurence Olivier's *Henry V* (1944), his name rarely

---

16Dorothy L. Sayers, "Gaudy Night," in *The Art of the Mystery Story: A Collection of Critical Essays*, ed. Howard Haycraft (New York: Simon & Schuster, 1946), 210.

17Martin Edwards, *The Golden Age of Murder: The Mystery of the Writers Who Invented the Modern Detective Story* (London: HarperCollins, 2015), 126.

18Sayers, *Strong Poison*, 137-38.

19Sayers, *Strong Poison*, 25, 32. In *The Unpleasantness at the Bellona Club* (New York: HarperCollins, 1995), Sayers has Lord Peter quote Robey (182).

appears in books on film history, whereas Chaplin's name always does. Having moved to California to join Mack Sennett's Keystone Studios in 1914, Chaplin had been working in Hollywood for sixteen years by the time *Strong Poison* was published (1930), making it more than likely that Miss Climpson refers to Chaplin's film work and not his vaudeville routines. Furthermore, when biographer Barbara Reynolds established that Sayers enjoyed seeing "Robey at the Holborn Empire," she may not have realized that the Holborn premiered feature-length films as early as 1914.[20] Either way, when Sayers has Miss Climpson value Chaplin over Robey, she reflects a judgment confirmed by film scholars, who often consider Chaplin to be "the grandfather of modern film."[21]

Charlie Chaplin maintains his reputation as one of the most important figures in the history of film not only due to his presence both before and behind the camera but also because "he understood the importance of the medium," as Michael Powell puts it.[22] *The Tramp* (1915), considered Chaplin's first directorial masterpiece, turned his unassuming bowler-topped, cane-swinging character into an iconic figure recognized around the world. Chaplin reprised the tramp persona in his first feature-length film, *The Kid* (1921), which became an international hit.

Significantly, Chaplin worked to uphold the artistic integrity of silent cinema far longer than most others in the industry. Four years after the sound revolution, he released the silent *City Lights* (1931), which focuses on a blind flower seller given sight when Chaplin's tattered tramp, through numerous sacrifices, supplies money for an operation. After serving time in jail, the innocent but poverty-stricken tramp encounters the healed girl by chance, viewing her with delighted adoration. But she does not recognize her benefactor, either by sight or by voice, even though they had conversed multiple times before her operation. Realization comes only when she places a coin into his hand, for, as with many blind people, touch had been her sight. Recognizing the hand that had reached out to her in the past, she finally

[20]Reynolds, *Dorothy L. Sayers*, 163. Sayers ends her 1933 story "The Incredible Elopement of Lord Peter Wimsey" (in *Hangman's Holiday* [New York: HarperCollins, 1961], 61) with Lord Peter suggesting a trip over to the Holborn Empire to see Robey. We don't know but that Sayers intended Peter to see Robey in his first sound film, *The Temperance Fête*, released in 1932, when Sayers was most likely writing her story.

[21]Ron Austin, *In a New Light: Spirituality and the Media Arts* (Grand Rapids, MI: Eerdmans, 2007), 26.

[22]Powell, *Life in Movies*, 180.

apprehends the truth, closing the film with an intertitle presenting her words: "I can see now."[23]

Chaplin asks the same of his viewers: rather than merely listening to the artifice of voice, they need to be touched by mise-en-scène and montage in a way that they can finally see. Through *City Lights,* he suggests that most moviegoers are blind to the gifts of silent filmmakers, a belief he sustained five years later through *Modern Times* (1936). Considered by many to be Chaplin's greatest achievement, *Modern Times* mocks the Hollywood machinery behind third-rate talkies, the film's occasional audible speech produced not by the film's protagonists but by machines visualized in the movie: phonographs, radios, and a public announcement system by which an oppressive boss speaks from a screen to his subordinates. In other words, the screen projects a talking head that does not value human creativity. Not coincidentally, after Chaplin's first completely sound film, *The Great Dictator,* premiered in 1940, Sayers wrote a movie-loving friend to say she didn't think either of them would like Chaplin's film.[24]

## NEW MOV(I)ES: WAGES VERSUS THE INTEGRITY OF WORK

As Chaplin was defying the sound revolution, Sayers was writing another novel that derogates talkies, *Murder Must Advertise* (1933). This, her ninth novel, like her seventh (*Five Red Herrings*), returns the focus to Lord Peter, not because she had given up on artistic integrity but because she had too much integrity to saddle Harriet Vane with the breezy Wimsey. In *Murder Must Advertise,* then, she has Peter learn what it is like to be a wage earner like Harriet, having him go undercover as an advertising copywriter to solve a murder.

Sayers, having worked at an ad agency, recognized that talkies were all too often motivated by the same interests as advertising: the generation of income rather than the creation of beauty and insight. In the last chapter of *Murder Must Advertise,* she has a colleague tell Wimsey, "I've got to get out a new series for Sopo. 'Sopo Day is Cinema Day.' 'Leave the Laundry to ruin itself while you addle your brains at the Talkies.' Muck! Dope! And they pay

---

[23]For a sensitive reading of *City Lights,* see Grant Horner, *Meaning at the Movies: Becoming a Discerning Viewer* (Wheaton, IL: Crossway, 2010), 108-12.

[24]Dorothy L. Sayers to Muriel St Clare Byrne, March 1, 1941 (Wade 187/71).

me £10 a week for that sort of thing."[25] By connecting talkies with advertising and mental dope, Sayers anticipates Horkheimer and Adorno, who despair how "amusement itself becomes an ideal, taking the place of the higher things . . . in a manner even more stereotyped than the slogans paid for by advertising interests."[26]

By 1939, the year Hitchcock left England to make more profitable movies in Hollywood, Sayers had published her last detective story, despite the generous deposits Lord Peter had made to her bank account.[27] In a lecture delivered the same year Hitchcock released his less-than-artful but money-making *Saboteur*, 1942, Sayers emphatically argued that creative work should *not* be done merely to make money; instead, it should be "undertaken for the love of the work itself."[28] When an American studio promised her "big money" to write a screenplay celebrating St. Francis, she responded that, since she disliked St. Francis, it would have been a Judas-like betrayal to "write lies" for money.[29] Perhaps not coincidentally, Sayers developed her theory about "love of the work" through a painful experience with cinema.

## Wages from *The Silent Passenger*

In 1934, a producer at British-based Phoenix Films, Hugh Perceval, asked Sayers whether she would write a twenty-page Lord Peter story that could be turned into a screenplay.[30] As part of the negotiation, Perceval suggested that Sayers see a recent Phoenix talkie, *Death at Broadcasting House* (1934), in order to assess whether one of the film's minor actors, Peter Haddon, might make a good Peter Wimsey. While watching Haddon in *Death at Broadcasting House*,

---

[25] Dorothy L. Sayers, *Murder Must Advertise* (New York: HarperCollins, 1961), 354.

[26] Horkheimer and Adorno, *Dialectic of Enlightenment*, 143-44.

[27] A collection of Sayers short stories, *In the Teeth of the Evidence*, was published by Gollancz in 1939. Other Lord Peter stories were published posthumously, including a barely begun novel called *Thrones, Dominations*, finished by Jill Paton Walsh. Making no effort to publish a 1942 Wimsey story called "Talboys," Sayers was clearly interested in a different kind of work.

[28] Dorothy L. Sayers, "Why Work?," in *Creed or Chaos?* (Manchester, NH: Sophia Institute, 1974), 63. The essay was first delivered as a speech in 1942. But Sayers's transformation occurred years earlier, as the rest of the chapter illustrates.

[29] *Letters* 4:140.

[30] Hugh Perceval was recruited, twenty years after he worked with Sayers, by Sir Laurence Olivier to serve as executive producer for *The Prince and the Showgirl*, a frothy film pairing Olivier with Marilyn Monroe (1957). The 2011 movie *My Week with Marilyn* portrays Perceval, as played by Michael Kitchen of *Foyle's War* fame. Based on memoirs written by Colin Clark, who worked for Perceval during filming of *The Prince and the Showgirl*, *My Week with Marilyn* garnered numerous award nominations.

Sayers also saw Val Gielgud, cowriter of the screenplay, who portrays a drama producer in the film. Little did Sayers know that Gielgud would become her own BBC producer four years later, not only for the radio play *He That Should Come* (broadcast 1938), but also for *The Man Born to Be King*, broadcast 1941–1942.

After screening *Death at Broadcasting House*, Sayers wrote Perceval about the film's photography rather than its plot. Doing so, she reflects the assumptions of many cineastes, such as her contemporary, French filmmaker and film theorist Germaine Dulac (1882–1942), who called the common emphasis on plot a "criminal error."[31] The real crime in *Death at Broadcasting House*, then, was its total disregard for the stigmata of cinema. Indeed, Sayers responded to Perceval with comments on some of the movie's "camera-angles" before she tepidly agreed that the actor Peter Haddon might be able to play Lord Peter, assuming that his hair could be dyed blonde and that they "get the *Dialogue* right."[32]

Sayers was therefore appalled when she received the shooting script for her story, *The Silent Passenger*. In response, she wrote Peter Haddon in March 1935 to say that "under no circumstances" would she allow Phoenix Films to use either Lord Peter's name or hers unless she were allowed to make extensive revisions.[33] When her protestations were ignored, Sayers wrote her literary agent, David Higham, protesting that Phoenix Films led her to believe she would have final say on the script. Though feeling betrayed, she was willing to spend as much time as necessary to "make a workmanlike job of the whole thing," if even at a "financial loss" to herself.[34] In other words, Sayers was more concerned about the quality of the work than about her wages from cinema.

What occurred next is unclear. Sayers biographer Barbara Reynolds writes that Peter Haddon withdrew from the project, but an unpublished letter dated April 7, 1935, has Sayers telling Muriel St Clare Byrne that she telephoned Haddon when shooting began in order "to convey best wishes for the film," and the poorly made movie, with Haddon in the starring role,

---

[31] Quoted in Robert Stam, *Film Theory: An Introduction* (Oxford: Blackwell, 2000), 37.

[32] Dorothy L. Sayers to Muriel St Clare Burne, March 15, 1935 (Wade 185/217), emphasis original.

[33] *Letters* 1:346.

[34] Dorothy L. Sayers to David Higham, March 25, 1935, included as carbon copy enclosure with a letter to Muriel St. Clare Byrne with the same date (Wade 185/234-37).

was released the following July.[35] Whatever happened, perhaps through dicey negotiations between Higham (literary agent) and Perceval (film producer), Sayers agreed to have her name attached to the film, the first title screen announcing,

> PHOENIX FILMS
> *PRESENTS*
> JOHN LODER
> *IN*
> THE SILENT
> PASSENGER
> *BASED ON*
> *AN ORIGINAL STORY*
> *BY*
> *DOROTHY L. SAYERS*

The very next year, John Loder's name similarly appeared on the first title screen for Alfred Hitchcock's *Sabotage* (1936), soon followed by the name of Sayers's dear friend Helen Simpson as Hitchcock's dialogue writer. Sayers and Simpson surely talked about this as well as another coincidence. Years earlier, Sayers had chosen the name Loder for a murderer in her story "The Abominable History of the Man with Copper Fingers." Primarily narrated by a cinema star, the tale was initially published in 1928, a year after John Loder appeared in three silent films produced in Germany, one of which was the studio in which Hitchcock made his directorial debut, *The Pleasure Garden* (1925).[36]

## Transforming Work: Sayers and Erich von Stroheim

While arguing with Phoenix Films about *The Silent Passenger*, Sayers was completing her transformation of Peter Wimsey, composing one novel in which Harriet finally accepts Peter's marriage proposal and another about the

---

[35]Reynolds makes her comment about Haddon in *Letters* 1:347n1. Sayers's comments come from Dorothy L. Sayers to Muriel St Clare Byrne, July 4, 1935, written over several days (Wade 186/22). Haddon's screen debut as Lord Peter may have influenced his being cast as a "Lord Petcliffe" in a film made several years later: *Over the Moon* (1939), starring Merle Oberon and Rex Harrison.

[36]Of Loder's three German films, one, *The Last Waltz*, was made by Universum Film Aktiengesellschaft; another, *The Great Unknown*, was distributed by Bavaria Film, Universum Film Aktiengesellschaft's biggest German competitor, which provided the studio for Hitchcock.

Wimsey honeymoon, based on a play she was constructing with her friend Muriel St Clare Byrne. Significantly, both novels, the former called *Gaudy Night* (1935), the latter called *Busman's Honeymoon* (1937), make substantive references to cinema.

Published the same year that Phoenix Films premiered *The Silent Passenger*, *Gaudy Night* focuses on Harriet Vane's return to her alma mater, Shrewsbury College at Oxford University, where she is called on to discover the perpetrator of mean-spirited threats and destructive pranks. Not coincidentally, the novel explores the integrity of work, the word *integrity* repeatedly appearing in the narrative. As Sayers puts it to Muriel, the "whole theme" of *Gaudy Night* is the "sin against intellectual integrity."[37] Sayers was in the midst of composing chapter seventeen when her disgust with the Phoenix script led her to demand removal of her name, as well as Lord Peter's, from *The Silent Passenger*.[38] In the chapter, Harriet mentions prestigious silent film director Erich von Stroheim (1885–1957), telling Peter, "Like the lovers in that Strohheim [*sic*] film, we'll go and sit on the sewer."[39]

The allusion is intriguing on several levels. First, Stroheim made multiple films about aristocrats pursuing and/or proposing to commoners: *Merry-Go-Round* (1923), *The Merry Widow* (1925), *Wedding March* (1928), and *Queen Kelly* (1929).[40] *Gaudy Night*, of course, is the novel in which Harriet, a commoner, agrees to marry the aristocratic Lord Peter, after turning him down multiple times since she met him five years earlier, as recounted in *Strong Poison*. Second, Stroheim was famously passionate about the integrity of his work. He "lavished infinite care" on the "visual texture" for each film he made, often ignoring his producers' bottom lines—making money.[41] Nowhere is this more evident than in *Greed* (1924), the Stroheim movie to which Harriet alludes in *Gaudy Night*.

---

[37]See *Letters* 1:353.

[38]In her notes to a March 6, 1935, letter from Sayers to Muriel St Clare Byrne, Reynolds states that Sayers was working on chapter 17, and the letter that follows is to Haddon about the incompetence of Phoenix Films. See *Letters* 1:346n3.

[39]Sayers, *Gaudy Night*, 365. While many film scholars include the "von" with "Stroheim," I follow others who do not, not only because Sayers left it out but also because Stroheim artificially added the "von" to his name. I discuss Sayers's Stroheim allusion in my essay "Through the Screen: Dorothy L. Sayers's Journey into New Worlds," *VII: Journal of the Marion E. Wade Center* 36 (2019): 12-14.

[40]It should be noted that Stroheim was replaced as director during filming of *Merry-Go-Round*, but he wrote the initial scenario.

[41]David A. Cook, *A History of Narrative Film*, 2nd ed. (New York: Norton, 1990), 249.

For years Stroheim had wanted to adapt Frank Norris's novel *McTeague* (1899), and when Goldwyn Pictures gave him the opportunity, he presented them with a film that was over nine hours long—and exceedingly over budget. Asked but not paid to edit the film down to a manageable length, Stroheim mortgaged both his house and his car in order to supervise the editing and thus guarantee the artistic integrity of the film. "Breathing for the love of the job and nothing else" (a phrase from *Gaudy Night*), Stroheim and a friend got the film down to four hours, only to have the merger of Goldwyn with Metro and Mayer undermine the project.[42] For the sake of box-office returns, the new head of MGM had the four-hour film cut almost in half, renaming it *Greed*. To make up for the destroyed footage, MGM inserted what David Cook calls "lengthy and often ludicrous titles," further destroying the artistry of Stroheim's work.[43]

In *Gaudy Night*, then, when Harriett alludes to Stroheim lovers who "sit on the sewer," she refers to one of *Greed*'s famously ludicrous intertitles, "Let's go over and sit on the sewer." An avid reader of newspapers and periodicals, Sayers may have known that Stroheim not only "disowned the film" but also "refused to see it after it was released."[44] Sayers, of course, responded to *The Silent Passenger* similarly, refusing to see the film after Phoenix ignored her offer to get the film "into water-tight condition," language she also employed while constructing *Busman's Honeymoon* around the same time, "making it water-tight."[45]

Nevertheless, Sayers has the honeymooning Wimseys go to the cinema, where they see "a Mickey Mouse and an educational film about the iron and steel industry." Because Harriet and Peter represent different aspects of Sayers's own personality and passions, it seems highly unlikely that she would have them enjoy an activity she currently repudiated. She even has a character in *Busman's Honeymoon* compare the newlyweds to "film-stars," noting Lord Peter wears a monocle like movie celebrity Ralph Lynn (1882–1962), famous at the time for maintaining the "majesty of King's English . . . in all its glory and dignity."[46]

---

[42]Sayers, *Gaudy Night*, 307.

[43]Cook, *History of Narrative Film*, 245.

[44]Cook, *History of Narrative Film*, 246.

[45]Dorothy L. Sayers to David Higham, March 25, 1935, included as carbon copy enclosure with a letter to Muriel St. Clare Byrne with the same date (Wade 185/236); *Letters* 1:348.

[46]Dorothy L. Sayers, *Busman's Honeymoon* (New York: HarperCollins, 1992), 339, 229. See my discussion of how Sayers uses autobiographical elements for the characters of both Peter and Harriet in Crystal Downing, *Writing Performances: The Stages of Dorothy L. Sayers* (New York: Palgrave, 2004), 35-36. The

In March 1935, the month Sayers told Haddon about the "extremely bad" script for *Silent Passenger*, Sayers praised Muriel St Clare Byrne for a screenplay she wrote, complimenting Muriel's ability to focus on what "*only* the camera can tell." And in another letter she mentions a soon-to-be-published Wimsey short story, saying, "It really ought to have been a film in the first place—though not at all the Phoenix's idea of a film."[47] Called "Striding Folly," the story appeared in London's *Strand* magazine the very same month that *Silent Passenger* premiered at London's Plaza cinema, July 1935. Sayers wrote Byrne that she would not be attending the Phoenix premiere, partly due to an appointment in Oxford, but she offered to send Byrne tickets for the opening.[48] Clearly, Sayers was neither renouncing film in general nor even banning friends from *Silent Passenger.*

## THE WAGES OF QUOTA QUICKIES

Rather than rejecting cinema, as biographers repeatedly suggest, Sayers was merely questioning the integrity of the studio that made *The Silent Passenger*. Indeed, producing seven unremarkable films in six years (1932–1938), Phoenix Films seems to have been established in response to Britain's 1927 Cinematograph Act. Passed by Parliament to countermand the cultural and financial dominance of Hollywood talkies, the act stipulated that a certain percentage of movies screened in the UK had to be based on works written by British citizens, produced by and filmed in British-controlled companies, and have 75 percent of production salaries go to British subjects. Ostensibly seeking to inculcate high-quality British films, the act instead resulted in what are derisively called "quota quickies": poorly made low-budget movies.

Hollywood production companies provided financing for quota quickies as a means to exhibit their own films in the UK.[49] Reginald Denham, the director of *Silent Passenger*, explains the complicity of Hollywood with the quota

---

comment about Ralph Lynn was published by *Picture Show* magazine in 1932, quoted in Steve Chibnall, *Quota Quickies: The Birth of the British "B" Film* (London: BFI, 2007), 11.

47Dorothy L. Sayers to Muriel St Clare Byrne, March 15, 1935 (Wade 185/217); Sayers to Byrne, April 2, 1935 (Wade 186/16). Byrne's film, called *Doubles and Quits*, does not seem to have been produced. Reynolds tended not to publish letters in which Sayers speaks positively about cinema.

48Dorothy L. Sayers to Muriel St Clare Byrne, June 2, 1935 (Wade 186/52).

49See Powell, *Life in Movies*, 215-16.

system: "A whole new bunch of incompetent people were churning out these pictures, and the worse they were the more delighted the Americans seemed. The one thing Hollywood didn't want was strong competition from the English film-maker. Contracts were being handed out like religious tracts on street-corners."[50] As a result, quota quickies functioned as "B pictures," a term coined in the early 1930s to describe second-rate, low-budget films shown in conjunction with more expensive Hollywood features.

When the Cinematograph Act was modified in 1938, Phoenix Films went out of business. As Steve Chibnall notes in *Quota Quickies*, "An astonishing 233 new production companies were registered in the first five years of the Act, although few survived to see the next five years." With *Silent Passenger*, then, Sayers experienced what Donald Spoto calls "the lowest ebb" in British film-making.[51] Even the movie's director, Reginald Denham, admits in his autobiography, "Between 1933 and 1939, I directed no less than twenty-four pictures. And weren't they awful!" He actually got exasperated with Sayers's desire to improve *The Silent Passenger*, saying she "blue-pencilled the script with patronizing marginal notes," becoming "rather more than tiresome." Attributing Sayers's interference to her passionate infatuation with Lord Peter, Denham did not realize that Sayers's passion was instead for artistic integrity.[52] She wanted sound film to be soundly crafted.

Significantly, a review of *The Silent Passenger* published soon after its release mentioned the problem with talkies, describing "Sound" as "an alarming upheaval which shook the peaks of film achievement and dislodged the great European directors who, like so many Balboas, stood silent upon them. . . . Articulate emotion somehow paralysed the film's freedom of movement—robbed it of articulation—and reduced it to theatre." Even Peter Hadden commented to Sayers that *The Silent Passenger* "ought to have been 'shot' silent."[53]

---

[50]Reginald Denham, *Stars in My Hair: Being Certain Indiscreet Memoirs* (New York: Crown, 1958), 175.

[51]Chibnall, *Quota Quickies*, 18; Donald Spoto, *The Dark Side of Genius: The Life of Alfred Hitchcock* (Boston: Da Capo, 1999), 168.

[52]Denham, *Stars in My Hair*, 177, 180. Sayers describes Denham years later in Dorothy L. Sayers to Muriel St Clare Byrne, March 28, 1955 (Wade 186/2).

[53]John Marks, "Penny Plain, Twopence Coloured," *The New Statesman and Nation*, July 20, 1935, 95. The article also reviews three other movies, noting that *Silent Passenger* was "at the Plaza." The Hadden comment occurs in Peter Hadden to Dorothy L. Sayers, June 5, 1935 (Wade 186/50).

## THE INTEGRITY OF "BLOOD SACRIFICE"

Feeling she had sacrificed her reputation over *Silent Passenger,* Sayers told her agent that she would not consider film rights to any of her books without "full control" over the shooting script, with "final veto upon every foot of film before it leaves the studio." Six months later her attitude had mellowed, and she informed the agency to consider requests for film adaptations from "any American company" that might "work along the right lines," even offering "to help any such company to get the thing right."[54] Quite clearly, Sayers's contempt was not for cinema in general but for mediocre work, a mediocrity associated with Britain's quota quickies, as her specification "any *American* company" implies. More importantly, due to disgust over *Silent Passenger,* Sayers began to reflect more intensely about the integrity of her own work. That, in fact, may be the lasting value of Phoenix Films.

Almost a year to the day after expressing despair over the script for *Silent Passenger,* Sayers was protesting changes a publisher proposed for one of her new stories. Called "Blood Sacrifice," the story recounts the anguish a playwright experiences when a theater director changes the script for better box-office appeal. As though allegorizing her experience with Phoenix Films, Sayers has Scales, the playwright, groan, "Like a fool I signed the contract without a controlling clause," and she includes multiple references to film adaptations of Scales's script. Sayers certainly identified with Scales when she includes his disagreements with "the film people": disagreements that got Scales, like Sayers, "agreeing to a number of things he did not approve of but could see no way to prevent." Describing "Blood Sacrifice" to her agent as one of the "best" things she had written, Sayers refused any changes, seeking to protect assaults on her "spiritual integrity"—a phrase she gave Scales, who has to give a blood transfusion to the theater director he despises.[55]

While resisting changes to "Blood Sacrifice," Sayers happened to see an "American gangster film" that included a blood transfusion scene. Describing relevant shots in a letter to Helen Simpson, she notes how a policeman must give his blood to save the life of a criminal he has been chasing, just as Scales

[54]*Letters* 1:365, 399.

[55]Dorothy L. Sayers, "Blood Sacrifice," in *In the Teeth of the Evidence* (New York: HarperCollins, 1993), 156, 161. For additional allusions to film in the story, including a reference to *Steamboat Willie,* one of the first animated sound films, see also 152, 155, 160, 165; *Letters* 1:378.

is forced to give his blood to someone destroying his work.[56] Then, a little over six months later, Sayers was the recipient of a radically different kind of transfusion—one that brought fresh blood not only to her career but also to her faith.

## Rising from Flames: *The Zeal of Thy House*

In October 1936, Sayers was asked to write a play to be performed as part of a yearly festival celebrating the history of Canterbury and its famous cathedral. Having recently been tutored in stagecraft during her collaboration with Muriel St Clare Byrne on the *Busman's Honeymoon* play, she eventually accepted the commission. Nevertheless, she was a bit daunted. After all, a year earlier the Canterbury Festival staged a play about the assassination of Thomas Beckett, *Murder in the Cathedral,* written by adulated poet T. S. Eliot. Sayers therefore chose to write about something closer to her own experience: the integrity of one's craft, an issue that had been ignored by Phoenix Films. Her resulting play, *The Zeal of Thy House,* focuses on William of Sens, the architect who designed and helped rebuild the choir of Canterbury Cathedral after its destruction by fire in 1174. In Sayers's script, the reconstruction rises majestically, because William "thinks of nothing, lives for nothing, but the integrity of his work," which gives him the ability to experience God's "joy of making."[57]

Needing to establish that the architecture of Canterbury Cathedral was constructed to the glory of God, Sayers was forced to contemplate how her construction of a play about the cathedral related to the glory of God as well. Moving beyond her identification with mystery writer Harriet Vane, who regards truth "to one's calling" as the only "way to spiritual peace," Sayers began to consider how Christian doctrine explained one's vocation *as well as* spiritual peace.[58] She therefore repeatedly alludes to God as "the Master architect" and Jesus as "the carpenter's Son, the Master-builder, / Architect, poet, maker" in order to suggest that the architect William of Sens was created in God's image, as pronounced in Genesis 1:27. In fact, at the end of the published

---

[56]Sayers screened the gangster film on March 24, 1936, as made clear in her letter to Helen Simpson, written the next day. See *Letters* 1:376.

[57]Dorothy L. Sayers, *The Zeal of Thy House*, in *Four Sacred Plays* (London: Victor Gollancz, 1948), 27, 41, 46, 68.

[58]Quoted from *Gaudy Night* in Francesca Wade, *Square Haunting: Five Writers in London Between the Wars* (New York: Crown, 2021), 139.

version of the play, Sayers has the archangel Michael explicitly state that God "hath made man in His own image, a maker and craftsman like Himself."[59] By deciding to argue in *Zeal* that human creativity fulfills the *imago Dei* (the image of Creator God), Sayers was able to reconcile her secular commitment to creative work with her withered Christian faith.

## THE ARCHITECTURAL INTEGRITY OF FILM

Sayers was composing *The Zeal of Thy House* just as reviews were being published about Hitchcock's *Sabotage* (1936): the film for which her friend Helen Simpson wrote dialogue. And it is not far-fetched to surmise that published reviews of Hitchcock as a "superb craftsman" influenced Sayers's characterization of William, whom she describes as a "great craftsman."[60] Indeed, Sayers's contemporaries often made analogies between architecture and cinema. Famous Soviet filmmaker Dziga Vertov (1896–1954) once pronounced that he was a "builder," reporting that he placed viewers "in an extraordinary room which did not exist until just now when I also created it." Elia Kazan (1909–2003), director of *A Streetcar Named Desire* (1951) and *On the Waterfront* (1954), commented, "A screenplay's worth has to be measured less by its language than by its architecture." And the work of Fritz Lang (1890–1976) was called "animated architecture" by a French film critic. Even into the twenty-first century, film theorists analyze "the architecture" of movies: their visual "construction," as Kazan puts it, rather than mere plotlines and acting.[61]

Sayers constructed *Zeal* with the same "sweat and passion" she gives William of Sens, who desires to "raise up beauty from ashes."[62] One cannot help wondering whether Sayers's sly allusion here to the phoenix, the mythical bird that rises from the ashes of its predecessor, was intentional. Indeed, *The Zeal of Thy House* seems to be her answer to Phoenix Films, explaining why, around the time *Zeal* was finishing its hundredth London performance in

---

59Sayers, *Zeal of Thy House*, 98-99. For other references to God as architect, see 26, 38, 67, 91.

60Spoto, *Dark Side of Genius*, 187; Sayers, *Zeal of Thy House*, 30.

61All but Kazan are quoted in David Bordwell, Kristin Thompson, and Jeff Smith, *Film Art: An Introduction*, 11th ed. (New York: McGraw Hill, 2017), 225, 464. Contemporary references to film architecture appear on 69, 102. For the Kazan quotation, see Paul Kuritz, *Theater and Film: A Christian Perspective* (Enumclaw, WA: Redemption, 2007), 31.

62Sayers, *Zeal of Thy House*, 51.

"a *blaze* of glory," as she put it, Sayers was composing an essay for *Sight and Sound,* "widely acknowledged as the leading cinema publication in the English language."[63] Called "Detective Stories for the Screen" and clearly inspired by the Phoenix Films fiasco, Sayers's article discusses film adaptations of print stories, arguing that "good craftsmen" in each medium must respect the skills of the other. Hence, Sayers argues, when filmmakers adapt detective fiction to for the screen, they "must trust" the original writer "to know his own job," employing the same words she gave the "great craftsman" in *Zeal,* who proclaims, "Allow me to know my own job."[64]

## A Trinitarian *Imago Dei*

When *The Zeal of Thy House* was first performed in 1937, it did not include archangel Michael's closing speech about the *imago Dei,* most likely due to the complexity of his assertion that human creativity is triune. Through St. Michael, Sayers establishes that creativity in a single human has three personas, thus fulfilling a specifically *Christian* vision of the *imago Dei.* As the archangel explains, human creativity begins with a creative Idea, by which a maker conceptualizes a work in its entirety, outside time, paralleling God the Father. Consubstantial with the Idea is its incarnational activity, as when artists talk about *fleshing out* their ideas—even before they put them on paper, canvas, or screen. Michael parallels this activity with the Son of God, the "Energy" of creation "working in time." The third persona of the *imago Dei* is creative Power, which, like the Holy Spirit, generates response in individuals, opening their hearts and minds to Idea and Energy. As with our trinitarian God, these three—idea, energy, and power—"are one" in the mind of each human creator.[65]

Though dropped from the staged performances, St. Michael's speech was included in a 1937 publication of the script. One reader, Father Herbert Kelly, founder of the Society of the Sacred Mission in Nottinghamshire, praised Sayers's ability to "state the vital force of a Christian faith in God and His Christ, not in the abstract fashion which is all we theologians can teach, but in a living,

---

[63]*Letters* 2:84, emphasis added; Ephraim Katz, *The Film Encyclopedia,* 4th ed. (New York: HarperCollins, 2001), 1258.

[64]Dorothy L. Sayers, "Detective Stories for the Screen: Some Advice to Producers," *Sight and Sound* 7, no. 26 (Summer 1938): 50; Sayers, *Zeal of Thy House,* 30, 40.

[65]Sayers, *Zeal of Thy House,* 103.

pictorial fashion which common people can follow."[66] Over the course of many letters, Kelly encouraged Sayers to elaborate her theory about a trinitarian *imago Dei*. The result was a 1941 book called *The Mind of the Maker*, which directly quotes from *The Zeal of Thy House*. In addition to arguing that a "creative artist does, somehow or other, specialize in construction"—reminding us of William of Sens—Sayers also provides a clue that her book was written in defiance of shoddy work such as *The Silent Passenger*. In the ninth chapter, Sayers despairs over people who identify mystery authors not by the integrity of their work but according to popular topics, such as "the latest Trunk Murder" and sleuthing on "wearisome railway journeys."[67] In the Phoenix film, Lord Peter is on a railroad journey unaware the train contains a murdered man stuffed in a trunk.

## The Mind of the Analogy Maker

When it was first published in July of 1941, *The Mind of the Maker* was met with great, if sometimes qualified, acclaim. As late as 1996, theologian John Thurmer argued that the book "provided the most developed and usable analogy of God the Holy Trinity in the English language."[68] The key term here is *analogy*. When Sayers argues that a "characteristic" shared by humans and their Creator is "the desire and the ability to make things," she makes very clear that she speaks metaphorically. As she explains in *The Mind of the Maker*, "All language about God must, as St. Thomas Aquinas pointed out, necessarily be analogical. . . . It may be perilous, as it must be inadequate, to interpret God by analogy with ourselves, but we are compelled to do so; we have no other means of interpreting anything."[69]

Indeed, how can we explain, let alone understand, the Trinity apart from human constructions of language? Even the words *explain* and *understand* are metaphors based on human experience: *ex-plain* means to "flatten out" (flat like the Serengeti plains), and *under-stand* merely means to stand under something (to better see its construction). As Sayers puts it with her typical humor,

---

66Quoted in *Letters* 2:42.

67Sayers, *Mind of the Maker*, 181, 144. She quotes from *Zeal of Thy House* on 37-38.

68John Thurmer, "Sayers on the Trinity," in *Reluctant Evangelist: Papers on the Christian Thought of Dorothy L Sayers* (West Sussex, UK: Dorothy L. Sayers Society, 1996), 38. I will address problems with Sayers's analogy in the next chapter.

69Sayers, *Mind of the Maker*, 22-23.

"If the tendency to anthropomorphism is a good reason for refusing to think about God, it is an equally good reason for refusing to think about light, or oysters, or battleships." We need metaphors, based on experience, to understand and explain most things, including "a mystery as inscrutable as the mystery of the Trinity."[70] Jesus himself recognized the need for human analogies to explain the mystery God's love, as when he asked his disciples, "Which of you, if your son asks for bread, will give him a stone? . . . If you, then, though you are evil, know how to give good gifts to your children, how much more will your Father in heaven give good gifts to those who ask him!" (Mt 7:9-11). Sayers's analogy is similar: if we, though evil, recognize the triadic nature of creativity as a good gift from God, how much more will we value the good gift of creation from our triune God.

Sayers, of course, was not the first to see an analogy between the Trinity and human experience. More than fifteen hundred years before her, Augustine grappled with the inscrutable mystery by paralleling the consubstantiality of Father, Son, and Holy Ghost with the interdependence of human memory, intelligence, and will. However, as Claude Welch notes in *The Trinity in Contemporary Theology*, the argument in *The Mind of the Maker* "goes significantly beyond an (Augustinian) attempt to find an analogy for the divine Triunity and becomes an argument from the trinitarianism of finite creativity to a Divine Trinity."[71]

In Sayers's paradigm, the fleshed-out work is trinitarian as much as the work of creating it. For example, an artistically sound novel can be perceived in terms of "Book-as-Thought" (idea), "Book-as-Written" (energy), "Book-as-Read" (power).[72] However, all three are simultaneously involved in the mind of the maker before the book appears on paper, just as Father, Son, and Holy Ghost were constantly interacting before Christ appeared on earth. In both cases, the three are one during the process of creation.

Confirming Sayers's analogy almost sixty years later, Philip Yancey celebrates *The Mind of the Maker* by describing his own experience: "Every writer begins with an Idea, or an Essence. For instance, I have been thinking about

---

[70]Sayers, *Mind of the Maker*, 23.

[71]Claude Welch, *The Trinity in Contemporary Theology* (London: SCM Press, 1953), 86, parentheses original.

[72]Sayers, *Mind of the Maker*, 122.

this column [in *Christianity Today*] for several days, pondering what to say. Finally the time comes to begin writing, and for that I must choose a medium of Expression." When the medium is a book, Yancey explains,

> I realize that some pages distract from the original Idea; they make the book bog down, or go in conflicting directions at once. The Idea has a life of its own, and I have learned to follow instincts alerting me when my Expression misrepresents the Idea. . . . The act of creation does not end, though, until another person receives the communication. My "trinity of creation" finds fulfillment only at this very instant, as you read this sentence.[73]

As any writer committed to the integrity of work will affirm, the very act of reading one's incarnated idea on the page is part of the creative process. Idea and energy only have power when contemplated by the author, who then rethinks the idea while giving energy to the revision process. As Claude Welch summarizes, "All this may be complete in the author's imagination, i.e. without any material creation, though there may be an urgent desire for material manifestation."[74]

Sayers, of course, intended her trinitarian aesthetic to apply to all the arts, including cinema. Creative film has the power to energize receptive viewers to relish the beauty of creation as well as cause them to perceive truths of existence in new ways. The initial viewers of film, of course, are the writers, producers, director, and actors who assess the unedited product shot each day in order to make changes in their creation—idea, energy, and power simultaneously contributing to the creative work.

### MAKING SOUND METAPHORS

Significantly, Sayers uses a metaphor from cinema to explain the "unending labor of creation" in the mind of a true maker. Each new work "is a 'still' cut out and thrown off from the endless living picture which [the] creative mind reels out. It is a picture in itself, but it leads only from the picture behind it to the picture in front of it, as part of a connected process." Earlier in *The Mind of the Maker*, she employs an analogy from cinema to illustrate God's plan for our lives:

[73]Philip Yancey, "Writing the Trinity," *Christianity Today*, July 12, 1999, 72.

[74]Welch, *Trinity in Contemporary Theology*, 87.

> Thousands of film actors turn up daily at the studios, play through the shots in which they figure (sometimes in the right order, more often in the wrong order) and depart again, ignorant whether they are figuring in a tragedy, a comedy, or a melodrama; or what was the nature of the injury which caused them to shoot the stockbroker in the fifth reel or cut their own throats in the seventh. The actor on the stage of the universe cannot even go to the nearest cinema and see the result of his work when the sequences have been fitted together, for the film is still in the making.[75]

Sayers's understanding of the energy behind filming a movie, most likely learned from Helen Simpson's collaboration with Alfred Hitchcock, provides a superb analogy for individualized instantiations of the *imago Dei*. Because humans cannot see in advance the completion of God's screenplay, we must commit to the integrity of our work in the small film sequence in which we live and move and have our being. Indeed, we are all actors in God's work of creation, many fulfilling the *imago Dei* by exercising God's gift of creativity—whether as artists, parents, employees, and/or friends. And we are all part of a God-guided production that includes Christians from earlier reels, such as Thomas Aquinas (ca. 1225–1274), who argued, "God's knowledge stands to all created things as the artist's to his products."[76]

God's film of creation, as Sayers puts it, is still in the making. This explains why Christian artist Makoto Fujimura cited Sayers more than six decades after her death to argue, "The Bible makes clear that God commissions all people to create for the New."[77] Note the phrase *all people*. The *imago Dei* is not limited to Christians, which may explain why Sayers, despite her Phoenix Films fiasco, met with British director Michael Powell in 1947 to discuss film adaptations of her detective fiction.[78] Sayers must have recognized in Powell a commitment to the integrity of his work. As he proclaims in his autobiography, "I am a craftsman, and a craftsman I shall remain until I die. In know only one

---

[75]Sayers, *Mind of the Maker*, 207, 128-29.

[76]Quoted in Nancy Tischler, "Artist, Artifact, and Audience: The Aesthetics and Practice of Dorothy L. Sayers," in *As Her Whimsey Took Her: Critical Essays on the Work of Dorothy L. Sayers*, ed. Margaret P. Hannay (Kent, OH: Kent State University Press, 1979), 166.

[77]Makoto Fujimura, *Art and Faith: A Theology of Making* (New Haven, CT: Yale University Press, 2020), 7-8.

[78]Powell acknowledges Sayers's willingness to collaborate on a film project, mentioning her novels *The Nine Tailors* (1935) and *Murder Must Advertise*. Michael Powell to Dorothy L. Sayers, February 10, 1947 (Wade 524/5-6).

craft, the craft of making films."[79] By substituting "architecture" for "making films," Powell's statement could have been lifted directly from *The Zeal of Thy House*. Both cognizant of how talkies undermined the creativity of cinematic art, Powell and Sayers recognized in each other a commitment to sound work.

## A SOUND SUMMARY

Creating a sound work—whether cathedral, book, or movie—fulfills the *imago Dei* as proclaimed in Genesis 1:27. As Sayers summarizes in a lecture delivered seven months after the publication of *The Mind of the Maker*, the "creative mind" works "by building up new images, new intellectual concepts, new worlds, if you like, to form new consistent wholes."[80] C. S. Lewis, who valued *The Mind of the Maker* highly, pointed out a year after Sayers died that the Old Testament word translated "true" often means, "in the Hebrew sense," "sound": "what doesn't 'give way' or collapse," like well-built architecture.[81]

This does not mean that creativity can save our souls. Indeed, in *The Zeal of Thy House* Sayers has William eventually acknowledge his need for salvation through Christ. After he confesses his sins, however, William pleads,

> But let my work, all that was good in me,
> All that was God, stand up and live and grow.
> The work is *sound*, Lord God, no rottenness there—
> Only in me.

Sayers felt the exact same way. In fact, a decade later she wrote Lewis about the "proper truth" found in sound "workmanship," saying, "Thousands . . . have spewed at the *sight and sound*" of "shoddy" Christian art.[82] Perhaps she was thinking, if even subconsciously, of the shoddy Phoenix film that ignited her essay for *Sight and Sound*.

---

79Powell, *Life in Movies*, 143.

80Dorothy L. Sayers, "Creative Mind," in *Unpopular Opinions* (London: Gollancz, 1946), 48.

81C. S. Lewis, *Reflections on the Psalms* (New York: Harcourt, 1958), 60.

82Sayers, *Zeal of Thy House*, 99, emphasis added; *Letters* 3:252-54, emphasis added.

5

# The Mind of the Filmmaker

## *Endorsing a Christian Aesthetic*

The same year Horkheimer and Adorno were distributing drafts of *Dialectic of Enlightenment* criticizing the "culture industry," Sayers was spreading her theory about a distinctly Christian response to culture. In 1944, the canon chancellor of St. Paul's Cathedral in London invited her to speak about her understanding of trinitarian creativity. Part of a lecture series that began within weeks of the Normandy invasion, Sayers's talk, "Towards a Christian Aesthetic," outlined the history of aesthetics while foregrounding the contribution of Christianity to the arts.

This chapter begins with that history to demonstrate not only how a trinitarian aesthetic applies to cinema but also how Sayers's Christian vocabulary challenges the Marxist ideology of Horkheimer, in which "critical theory," as he called it, seeks "to liberate human beings from the circumstances that enslave them." As far as Sayers was concerned, only Christ can liberate human beings from slavery to the culture industry.

Nevertheless, like Horkheimer, she despaired over people "doping themselves into complete irresponsibility over the conduct of life," whether through movies, theater, or newspapers.[1]

### Plato Versus the Bible

Sayers begins her 1944 lecture reminding listeners of Plato's famous argument that an *ideal* republic would "banish" all representational art, including theater. By merely "imitating" the Real, asserted Plato, such work distracts viewers from "eternal realities."[2]

[1]Max Horkheimer, *Critical Theory: Selected Essays* (New York: Continuum, 1982), 244; Dorothy L. Sayers, "Towards a Christian Aesthetic," in *Unpopular Opinions* (London: Gollancz, 1946), 35.

[2]Sayers mentions book 10 of Plato's *Republic*, borrowing his word *banish*. For details about the lecture series, see the preface to V. A. Demant, ed., *Our Culture, Its Christian Roots and Present Crisis: Edward Alleyn Lectures 1944* (London: Society for Promoting Christian Knowledge, 1947).

She then works to distinguish Plato's position from a Christian view of the arts, and allusions to film aid her argument.[3] While discussing emotions dramatized on stage and screen, she mentions "cinema organs" and "documentary film." She references concerns about young people who "wallow in day-dreaming at the cinema" to illustrate Plato's reasoning about drama: "He says that even where the action represented is in itself good and noble, the effect on the audience is bad, because it leads them to dissipate the emotions and energies that ought to be used for tackling the problems of life."[4] Rather than mimicking Plato by banning stage and screen, however, Sayers encourages greater engagement with and critical thinking about the arts.

Ironically, all too many Christians mimic what Sayers calls "Plato's heathen philosophy" when it comes to film, considering as mindless entertainment any movie that fails to either ignite "virtuous action" or offer "a moral."[5] Sayers would rather have Christians celebrate a theory of art that reflects the distinctiveness of Christian faith. Noting that the Greeks had no word for creation, she asserts that the "idea of Art as *creation* is, I believe, the one important contribution that Christianity has made to aesthetics." She then proceeds to restate, in more complex terms, her argument in *The Mind of the Maker*, while quoting from Hebrews: "God . . . hath spoken to us by His Son, the brightness of this glory and *express image* of His person."[6] She explains her italicized term "*express image*" by saying Christ "is not the copy, or imitation, or representation of the Father, nor yet inferior or subsequent to the Father in any way." Instead, "the Unimaginable and the Image are *one and the same*."[7]

Similarly, an artist's idea and the energy of fleshing it out are one and the same, as suggested in *The Mind of the Maker* three years earlier. Though Sayers uses different terms from *idea, energy*, and *power* in "Towards a Christian Aesthetic," substituting instead "experience, expression and recognition," her point is the same: a writer "cannot even be conscious of his Idea," generated

---

[3]Alejandro García-Rivera makes a similar distinction fifty-five years after Sayers. See García-Rivera, *The Community of the Beautiful: A Theological Aesthetics* (Collegeville, MN: Liturgical Press, 1999), 27.

[4]Sayers, "Towards a Christian Aesthetic," 32-33.

[5]Sayers, "Towards a Christian Aesthetic," 36, 40.

[6]Sayers collapses together phrases from Heb 1:1-3 (KJV). See "Towards a Christian Aesthetic," 37, emphasis original.

[7]Sayers, "Towards a Christian Aesthetic," 38.

by his *experience*, "except by the working of the Energy," or *expression*, "which formulates it to himself" so he can *recognize* its power. Once the mind of the maker has "imaged forth his experience he can incarnate it . . . in a material body," like that of a film, painting, or poem.[8] After all, the Son, who was with the Father at the moment of creation, was not always incarnate. As the Gospel of John puts it, quoting from the start of Genesis, "In the beginning was the Word, and the Word was with God, and the Word was God. . . . Through him all things were made; without him nothing was made that has been made. . . . The Word became flesh and made his dwelling among us" (Jn 1:1, 3, 14). The relevance of these verses to Sayers's Christian aesthetic is affirmed by Richard L. Harp in an essay about *The Mind of the Maker*: "This is the clearest statement the Bible makes concerning the union of God's creative Idea and the Energy which brings that Idea into being." And, as Harp points out, the Gospel writer follows up with a reference to power: "As many as received Him, to them gave He power to become the sons of God."[9]

## From Failed Power to Future Art

Unfortunately, many people fail to communicate power through their work. Theologian Laura Simmons, in fact, illustrates Sayers's trinitarian aesthetic with the example of a twenty-first-century film critic who "defines a bad movie by how weak it is in concept (which parallels the Idea in Sayers's model), execution (similar to the Energy), or what she calls a 'whammo combination of both' (which would affect the Power)."[10] Bad movies, what Sayers calls "debased and debasing cinema films," are usually made for the love of wages more than for the love of creation.[11] In contrast, as Sayers reiterates in *The Mind of the Maker*, genuine creators, whether Christian or not, recognize a hypostatic union between a creative idea and the energy that gives it shape. Only then can it have power. Furthermore, power can generate new acts of creativity, artists learning from the creativity of predecessors. As Sayers puts it, "Each

[8]Dorothy L. Sayers, *The Mind of the Maker* (San Francisco: HarperSanFrancisco, 1979), 39; Sayers, "Christian Aesthetic," 39.

[9]Richard L. Harp, "The Mind of the Maker: The Theological Aesthetic of Dorothy Sayers and Its Application to Poetry," in *As Her Whimsey Took Her: Critical Essays on the Work of Dorothy L. Sayers*, ed. Margaret P. Hannay (Kent, OH: Kent State University Press, 1979), 181.

[10]Laura K. Simmons, *Creed Without Chaos: Exploring Theology in the Writings of Dorothy L. Sayers* (Grand Rapids, MI: Baker Academic, 2005), 92-93.

[11]Sayers, *Mind of the Maker*, 204.

new work should be a fresh focus of power through which former streams of beauty, emotion, and reflection are directed."[12] Her word *directed* applies to film directors committed to the integrity of their work—as when the makers of *Railway Man*, discussed in chapter three, explicitly allude to works of filmic art that preceded them.

Film scholars identify "former streams of beauty" in the work of D. W. Griffith, calling his tendency to surround lit-up faces with darkness on the screen "Rembrandt lighting," in honor of seventeenth-century Dutch realist painter Rembrandt van Rijn. And many have borrowed a term art historians use to describe a similar effect in other Renaissance painters, such as Leonardo da Vinci, Caravaggio, Johannes Vermeer, and Francisco Goya: *chiaroscuro*. In cinema, chiaroscuro depends on what is known as *low-key lighting*, wherein "illumination . . . *creates* strong contrast between light and dark areas of the shot, with deep shadows and little fill light."[13]

Griffith tapped into "former streams of beauty" in other ways as well. According to an article published in the London *Times* on April 26, 1922, Griffith testified to the influence of Charles Dickens on his filmmaking. Sayers, an avid reader of the *Times*, surely read the article. Not only did she own one of G. K. Chesterton's biographies of Dickens, but she still retained hopes of writing for cinema, not yet having found a publisher for her first detective novel.[14] In fact, the very day the article about Griffith and Dickens appeared in the *Times*, Sayers wrote her parents that she felt her gift was for writing, and one cannot help wondering whether the newspaper essay planted a seed that blossomed when she wrote about idea, energy, and power in *The Zeal of Thy House*.[15] For, as the author of the *Times* article summarizes, "Dickens inspired Mr. Griffith with an *idea*, and his employer (mere 'business' men) were horrified at it; but, says Mr. Griffith, 'I went home, re-read one of Dickens's novels, and came back next day to tell them they could either make use of my *idea* or dismiss me.'" So what was it in Dickens' work that so inspired Griffith? It was "the *idea* . . . of a

[12]Sayers, *Mind of the Maker*, 121.

[13]David Bordwell, Kristin Thompson, and Jeff Smith, *Film Art: An Introduction*, 11th ed. (New York: McGraw Hill Education, 2013), glossary, emphasis added.

[14]The Marion E. Wade Center owns Sayers's personal copy of G. K. Chesterton, *Appreciations and Criticisms of the Works of Charles Dickens* (London: J. M. Dent & Sons, 1911). Sayers wrote her name on the font-free endpaper and made multiple annotations in the margins.

[15]*Letters* 1:190.

'break' in the narrative, a shifting of the story from one group of characters to another group."[16] Griffith's cutting from one group or action to another, then, incarnated Dickens's idea in a new medium—the energy of cinema—generating power for filmmakers to follow. In other words, just as "streams of beauty" in Renaissance paintings inspired a "fresh focus of power" through Griffith's lighting techniques, Dickens's narrative breaks inspired Griffith's splicing together of discontinuous shots.

## Streams of Beauty: From Griffith to Eisenstein

Griffith's editing style was given a "fresh focus of power" by Soviet filmmaker Sergei Eisenstein, as discussed in chapter two. Eisenstein, in fact, quotes from the 1926 London *Times* article about Dickens and Griffith in his book *Film Form: Essays in Film Theory*. Furthermore, Eisenstein acknowledges, the very same year that Sayers wrote "Towards a Christian Aesthetic," how former streams of beauty, emotion, and reflection irrigate works of cinematic creativity:

> Let Dickens and the whole ancestral array, going back as far as the Greeks and Shakespeare, be superfluous reminders that both Griffith and our cinema prove our origins to be not solely as of Edison and his fellow inventors, but as based on an enormous cultural past: each part of this past in its own moment of world history has moved forward the great art of cinematography. Let this past be a reproach to those thoughtless people who have displayed arrogance in reference to literature, which has contributed so much to this apparently unprecedented art.[17]

Celebrating the possibilities of cinematic art, Eisenstein proceeds to quote American cultural critic Gilbert Seldes. Born the same year as Sayers, Seldes addressed American "movie magnates" in 1924, imploring them to encourage creative filmmakers: "*With fresh ideas* (among which the idea of making a lot of money may be absent) these artists will give back to the screen the thing you have debauched—imagination. *They will create* with the . . . *medium* of the camera."[18] As though anticipating *The Mind of the Maker*, Seldes suggests that

---

[16]Quoted in Sergei Eisenstein, "Dickens, Griffith, and the Film Today," in *Film Form: Essays in Film Theory*, ed. and trans. Jay Leyda (New York: Harcourt Brace Jovanovich, 1949), 205, emphasis added.

[17]Eisenstein, "Dickens, Griffith, and the Film Today," 232-33. See also Ana Laura Zambrano, "Charles Dickens and Sergei Eisenstein: The Emergence of Cinema," *Style* 9, no. 4 (Fall 1975): 469-87.

[18]Quoted in Eisenstein, "Dickens, Griffith, and the Film Today," 239, emphasis added.

creative filmmakers generate power for viewing audiences by energizing, with the camera, their fresh ideas.

## STREAMS OF BEAUTY: FELLINI AND BERGMAN

Seldes saw his dreams come true in 1957, when two European directors rocked the moviegoing world with creative films that defied the commercialism of Hollywood. Ingmar Bergman (1918–2007) premiered *The Seventh Seal* and *Wild Strawberries,* both of which repeatedly appear in *Sight & Sound*'s polls of the greatest films ever made. That same year, Frederico Fellini (1920–1993) released *Nights of Cabiria,* a title that alludes to the oft-lauded silent film that captured Sayers's attention in 1916, *Cabiria.* As though endorsing Sayers's perception that "each new work should be a fresh focus of power through which former streams of beauty, emotion, and reflection are directed," *The Nights of Cabiria* earned the Academy Award for Best Foreign Language Film in that year's competition.

It is Bergman, however, who most closely echoes Sayers's trinitarian theory of art. The child of a clergyman, like Sayers, Bergman emphasized the "dynamic interplay" of three components of creativity. Called his "magic triangle," his triadic theory was developed through his work for the stage—much as Sayers's trinitarian aesthetic was developed through work for a Canterbury stage.[19] Bergman starts with a "conceptual design," which we might see paralleling Sayers's emphasis on creative idea. Inseparable from Bergman's "conceptual design" is his "strong conviction that it is the actor and the actor alone who must bring the text to life," what Sayers would call the energy of the performance. Indeed, like Bergman, Sayers illustrates the relationship between idea and energy with "the individual creativeness which the actor brings" to a script, which is why "writing for the stage is so much more interesting" for her than publishing detective novels.[20] Finally, Bergman's commitment to creative power is manifest in "deliberate strategies he has used to realign the audience's imaginative response" to create "an ever stronger bond between the performer and the spectator."[21] Bergman exemplifies that genuinely creative people, even

[19]See Lise-Lone Marker, "The Magic Triangle: Ingmar Bergman's Implied Philosophy of Theatrical Communication," *Modern Drama* 26, no. 3 (Fall 1983): 251-61.

[20]Sayers, *Mind of the Maker,* 65, 64.

[21]Quotations about Bergman's creative process are from Lise-Lone Marker and Frederick J. Marker, *Ingmar Berman: A Life in the Theatre* (Cambridge: Cambridge University Press, 1992), 3.

if they renounce trinitarian Christianity (as did Bergman), nevertheless understand the triadic nature of creativity due to their "direct experience" of how their own acts of creation work.[22] Their creativity endorses a trinitarian Creator even when they do not.

## Cinematic Heresies

Sayers's Christian aesthetic also explains why so many movies fail to rise above conventional, if not mindless, entertainment. Titling a chapter in *The Mind of the Maker* "Scalene Trinities," she proceeds to identify various ways one of the three components, idea, energy, or power, is either overemphasized or overlooked.[23] Distressed by such disregard for the triune *imago Dei*, she aligns such imbalances with heresies that developed during the early centuries of Christianity.

Sayers found especially annoying "propaganda novelists and dramatists," who are so obsessed with communicating an idea that they disregard the energy of artistic excellence.[24] In an essay written while *The Mind of the Maker* was going to press, she gives the example of movies made by Christians who clearly assume that an evangelistic message put together by pious people is all that matters. Arguing that "God is not served by technical incompetence," Sayers states, "The worst religious films I ever saw were produced by a company which chose its staff exclusively for their piety. Bad photography, bad acting, and bad dialogue produced a result so grotesquely irreverent that the pictures could not have been shown in churches without bringing Christianity into contempt."[25] In addition to being embarrassingly incompetent, Christian art intended "to manipulate the minds of others," as Sayers told one correspondent, was "as corrupt as 'Fascist Mathematics' or 'Marxist Music', or any other art or science that is harnessed to the service of an ideology."[26] As far as she was

---

[22]Sayers, preface to *Mind of the Maker*, xiii.

[23]Sayers, *Mind of the Maker*, chap. 10. I discuss "Scalene Trinities" and other aspects of Sayers's Christian aesthetic in two recent essays: "The Wonder of Cinema in Dorothy L. Sayers and Spike Lee," in *God and Wonder: Theology, Imagination, and the Arts*, ed. Jeffrey W. Barbeau and Emily Hunter McGowin (Eugene, OR: Cascade, 2022), 133-48; and "Power of the Spirit: Sayers and Cinema," in *The Spirit and the Screen: Pneumatological Reflections on Contemporary Cinema*, ed. Chris E. W. Green and Steven Felix-Jaeger (New York: Lexington/Fortress, 2023), 55-68.

[24]Sayers, *Mind of the Maker*, 173.

[25]Dorothy L. Sayers, "Why Work?," in *Creed or Chaos?* (Manchester, NH: Sophia Institute, 1974), 80.

[26]*Letters* 4:171.

concerned, "edifying art," as she puts it in "Towards a Christian Aesthetic," is merely the product of a "pseudo-artist corruptly saying, 'This is what you are supposed to believe and feel and do—and I propose to work you into a state of mind in which you will believe and feel and do as you are told.'" She proceeds to distinguish such "propaganda" from authentic creative power: "This pseudo-art does not really communicate power to us; it merely exerts power over us."[27]

Sayers therefore aligns Christians who elevate message over medium with Manichaeism, a heresy that attracted Augustine for many years. Inspired by a third-century Persian prophet named Mani, Manichees believed in a cosmic battle between spirit and matter, aligning the former with goodness and light, the latter with darkness and evil. Hence, the very idea that a good God would enter the world through the medium of flesh was, to them, nonsensical, if not downright appalling. In contrast, and consonant with Christian orthodoxy, Sayers emphatically argued that matter matters for Christians. As she explained in a radio broadcast that aired several weeks after *The Mind of the Maker* was published, "The Church does *not* say that matter is evil, nor that the body is evil. For her very life, she dare not. For her whole life is bound up in the doctrine that God Himself took human nature upon Him and went about this material world as a living man, with a human body and a human brain."[28] Orthodox doctrine establishes that Jesus is a material medium of salvation—a medium that died in the flesh but, as God incarnate, rose again and ascended into heaven. Christ's incarnation leads, therefore, to a "freeing of the images"—images that followers of Jesus often overlook.[29] As a result, many who write about film are more Manichaean than Christian, failing to use vocabulary identified with how images are incarnated on screen: mise-en-scène, montage, tracking shot, rack focus, tilt, pan, dissolve, graphic match, and so on. Focusing only on the spiritual uplift and/or edification of a film's idea, they ignore the energy of the material *medium*.

Eighty years after the publication of *The Mind of the Maker*, Angela Dalle Vacche similarly employed the term *Manichean*, this time to describe filmmakers wanting to make money rather than art. "The causal and linear editing of

---

[27]Sayers, "Towards a Christian Aesthetic," 41.

[28]Dorothy L. Sayers, "The Sacrament of Matter," in *The Christ of the Creeds and Other Broadcast Messages to the British People During World War II*, ed. Suzanne Bray (West Sussex, UK: Dorothy L. Sayers Society, 2008), 40, emphasis original.

[29]Dorothy L. Sayers to the bishop of Coventry, June 26, 1944 (*Letters* 3:28).

Manichean Hollywood," she notes, is "preprocessed into an industrial formula adjustable to what we think we already know and what we are sure of." Furthermore, to provide a contrast to Manichean Hollywood, Dalle Vacche employs language that echoes Sayers's Christian aesthetic. Discussing Chaplin's *The Kid*, Dalle Vacche says, "The *medium* begins to breathe through human *energy*, until it learns to think and create anew."[30]

## Gnostic Cinema

Similar to Manichean repudiation of matter is another heresy Sayers identifies in "Scalene Trinities," Gnosticism, which developed toward the end of the first century after Christ's birth.[31] Gnostics not only endorsed, like Manichees, a "dualistic world in which good and evil contested," but also "the existence of a secret code of knowledge" that must be promulgated from one generation to the next.[32] In both instances, knowledge supersedes the material medium, idea suppressing energy.

Sayers applies this heresy to playwrights and, by extension, screenwriters, whose commitment to communicating their own personal vision leads them to write scripts that do not match how embodied people really talked in a certain place or during a certain era. Take, for example, movies that place contemporary concepts and/or jargon—especially vulgar language—into the mouths of characters living in earlier centuries that did not advance such ideas or use such diction. After all, embodiment implies one's position in a certain context, which affects how one dresses one's language as well as one's body. Even God incarnate reflected the context of first-century Palestine to communicate the truth. After all, Jesus said, "I am the good shepherd; I know my sheep and my sheep know me" (Jn 10:14), not, "I am the good businessman; I know my clients and they know me."

Sayers's repudiation of message-based art doesn't mean she thought Christianity was irrelevant to creativity. Just the opposite. As she explained to a correspondent several years before her death, "If a writer is himself excited about the Faith, and is moved to write about it, his own excitement will

---

30 Angela Dalle Vacche, *André Bazin's Film Theory: Art, Science, Religion* (New York: Oxford University Press, 2020), 11, 121.

31 Sayers, *Mind of the Maker*, 169-72.

32 David L. Jeffrey and Martin E. Marty, "Heresy," in *A Dictionary of Biblical Tradition in English Literature*, ed. David Lyle Jeffrey (Grand Rapids, MI: Eerdmans, 1992), 347.

communicate itself to what he writes; but if he sets out deliberately to manufacture excitement in other people, he will produce nothing but a fourth-rate thriller which will thrill nobody."[33] Fourth-rate thrillers, in fact, reflect a totally different heresy Sayers discusses in *The Mind of the Maker*.

## ARIAN WORK: FROM SUPERHERO TO OUTLAW HERO

Whereas Christian filmmakers and viewers often elevate idea over energy, secular film producers often do the opposite, financing work that, in Sayers's words, is "all technique and no vision."[34] For this imbalance, Sayers coined the term "artistic Arianism," referring to the Arian heresy that came to a head during the First Ecumenical Council at Nicaea in 325 CE. In her play about the council, *The Emperor Constantine* (1951), Sayers includes a debate between two historical Christians: Athanasius, who argued for the coeternal nature of God the Father and God the Son, and Arius, who argued from Scripture that Jesus Christ was not one with God the Father, as when the apostle Paul told the Colossians that Jesus was "the *firstborn* over all creation" (Col 1:15). To counter Arius and his followers, the Nicene Creed established that Jesus Christ was *both* fully God *and* fully human: the two are one. Arian art, then, separates the energy of technique (the Son) from any unifying idea (the Father).

Examples of cinematic Arianism are legion, apparent in movies that offer little more than spectacularly impressive computer-generated imagery (CGI), jaw-dropping chase scenes, graphic sex and violence, stunning costuming, and so on, while providing nary a single insight about human nature. Movies based on comic book heroes provide obvious examples. More insidious, however, are movies about regular people that ignore a fundamental truth of existence, that in the world God has created, actions have consequences. As Sayers explained in a radio talk broadcast the same month that *The Mind of the Maker* appeared, "God's judgments are always the consequences, direct or indirect, of an offence against the universal law: if you hold your hand in the fire, you will be burned; if you swallow prussic acid you will die."[35] This principle exposes the lack of realism in so-called realistic movies, where protagonists get in brutal fights without breaking their fists or smearing their makeup, enjoy multiple sex

[33] *Letters* 4:171.

[34] Sayers, *Mind of the Maker*, 173.

[35] Dorothy L. Sayers, "Touchstone of History," in *Christ of the Creeds*, 69.

partners without getting STDs or causing emotional havoc, consume excessive amounts of alcohol without getting drunk, crash their cars in outrageously violent chase scenes while walking away in one piece, and so on.

In such Arian movies, truths about existence are limited to artificial notions of right versus wrong, *right* usually aligned with protagonists' choices, *wrong* with those who get in their way. A good example is *Greenland* (Ric Roman Waugh, 2020). As a comet heads toward earth, with the potential to destroy all living things, a man in Atlanta, John Garrity (Gerard Butler), seeks to save his family by journeying to Greenland, where protective bunkers have been built underground. Encountering panicking crowds on the way, he not only steals medical supplies for his diabetic son but also a car to help get him to safety. Demanding room on a plane for his family, he attacks anyone standing in his way, which causes the destruction of the plane as well as injuries, if not death, to other people on board. But the movie presents his actions as noble, done in the name of "family," which has become the ethical cliché du jour of cinema. And, of course, by destroying everyone who gets in his way, Garrity succeeds, saving not only his wife and son but also, quite conveniently, himself.

Garrity exemplifies what film scholar Robert B. Ray calls "the outlaw hero" of Hollywood cinema, often borrowing words from Alexis de Tocqueville, the Frenchman who assessed US distinctives in his famous 1835 publication *Democracy in America*. For example, de Tocqueville discusses the mythology of individualism guiding American thought, saying that it "disposes each citizen to isolate himself from the mass of his fellows and withdraw into the circle of family and friends; with this little society formed to his taste, he gladly leaves the greater society to look after itself." Though Ray quotes these words in 1985 to illustrate "a certain tendency of the Hollywood Cinema," he could have been talking about *Greenland* thirty-five years later.[36]

Visually stimulating and well-acted, *Greenland* is all energy with a banal idea of the outlaw hero. Exemplifying Arian work, it merely reproduces the nineteenth-century idolization of family, which becomes, for many, a substitute for confidence in a trinitarian God.[37] In contrast, the Jesus whom

36Robert B. Ray, *A Certain Tendency of the Hollywood Cinema, 1930–1980* (Princeton, NJ: Princeton University Press, 1985), 61.

37For a fuller explanation of this Victorian idol, see Crystal Downing, *Changing Signs of Truth: A Christian Introduction to the Semiotics of Communication* (Downers Grove, IL: IVP Academic, 2012), 133-34.

Arians refused to consider one with God shockingly said, "If anyone comes to me and does not hate father and mother, wife and children, brothers and sisters—yes, even their own life—such a person cannot be my disciple" (Lk 14:26). Jesus illustrated what he meant, of course, by laying down his life so that all humans—not just friends and family—might live.

### RECOGNIZING CONSEQUENCES: *THE INFILTRATOR*

*The Infiltrator* (Brad Furman, 2016) better exemplifies Sayers's point about God's judgment tied to consequences. In the film, Bryan Cranston plays an historical US customs agent, Robert Mazur, who infiltrated and helped destroy the money-laundering cartel of Pablo Escobar in the 1980s. Going undercover as a wealthy businessman, Mazur befriends members of the cartel, along with another undercover agent who plays his beautiful fiancé (Diane Kruger). Several times we see Cranston and Kruger look like they want to kiss when they are alone, but the married Mazur always draws back, wanting to remain faithful to his wife. Viewers used to conventional close-ups of actors moving toward each other while looking at each other's lips may feel disappointment at not seeing a steamy movie cliché fulfilled. But that is nothing compared to the way the filmmakers overturn habitual conventions of spy films.

The undercover couple invites cartel members to their fake "wedding," where the criminals will be rounded up by law enforcement. Having seen the human side to cartel members, many attending the wedding out of affection for the couple, Mazur starts to worry about betraying people he has befriended. He is experiencing the consequences of acting like a friend: genuine affection. Hence, rather than close-ups on a steamy kiss, we get close-ups on Mazur's face in agony, followed by point-of-view shots as he sees military police raid the wedding and arrest people who have treated with him with joyous solicitude. Attentive viewers feel his agony, for the camera has shown us a different side to several of the money launderers. It is as though the filmmakers had internalized Sayers's statement, "The solidarity of mankind is a solidarity in guilt, / and all our virtues stand in need of forgiveness / being deadly."[38]

Viewers responded poorly to *The Infiltrator*, which, despite its star-studded cast, lost money. Habituated by Hollywood to feel elation at the close of crime

---

[38]Dorothy L. Sayers, "Target Area," in *Poetry of Dorothy L. Sayers*, ed. Ralph E. Hone (Cambridge: Dorothy L. Sayers Society, 1996), 144.

movies, which make clear distinctions between the guilt of "bad guys" and the innocence of "good guys," people prefer Arian cinema. Indeed, *Greenland* netted over $70 million, with viewers addicted to artificially happy endings, whereby heroes experience minimal suffering while villains get their just deserts: "poetic justice," as it is often called. As far as Sayers is concerned, poetic justice reflects unsophisticated views of creation, both that of God and of human makers, whereby "rewards and punishments" depend on whether one has been naughty or nice. Reducing movies to Santa Claus treats, artificially "happy" endings, as Sayers puts it in *The Mind of the Maker*, may be "comforting," but they are "very bad art."[39]

## Augustine, Pelagius, and Barth

Though Sayers received great praise for *The Mind of the Maker*, not all theologians embraced the book. Some worried that Sayers's Christian aesthetic could destabilize Augustine's argument that original sin corrupts even human creativity. In fact, famous Swiss Calvinist Karl Barth (1886–1968), an avid reader of Peter Wimsey novels, identified an anti-Augustinian element in Sayers's theological efforts. In September 1939, he wrote Sayers about wanting to translate essays she had originally published in the *Sunday Times*: "The Greatest Drama Ever Staged" and "The Triumph of Easter."[40] Obviously valuing her Christ-centered insights enough to make them available to German readers, Barth nevertheless takes Sayers to task, telling her, "You have not yet entirely rid yourself of . . . Pelagianism," a heresy denounced by Augustine.[41]

Inspired by the writings of a British monk named Pelagius (ca. 355–ca. 420 CE), Pelagianism suggests that, due to God's grace, humans have the ability to choose the good. In fact, something Pelagius said sounds like it could have come straight out of *The Mind of the Maker*: "That we are able to see with our eyes is no power of ours; but it is in our power that we make a good or a bad

---

39 Sayers, *Mind of the Maker*, 79.

40 Sayers evidently wrote the essays to advertise the London opening of *The Zeal of Thy House*. "The Greatest Drama Ever Staged is the Official Creed of Christendom" (*Sunday Times*, April 3, 1938) and "The Triumph of Easter" (*Sunday Times*, April 17, 1938) were later published together as a pamphlet by Hodder & Stoughton (June 1938), which shorted the first essay's title to "The Greatest Drama Ever Staged." It was this booklet that Barth wanted to translate into German.

41 Quoted in David McNutt, "A Surprising Correspondence: How an Exchange of Letters Between Karl Barth and Dorothy L. Sayers Models Gracious Theological Discourse," *VII: Journal of the Marion E. Wade Center* 38 (2021): 18.

use of our eyes. . . . The fact that we have the power of accomplishing every good thing by action, speech and thought comes from him who has endowed us with this possibility, and also assists it."[42] Sayers would certainly agree, believing all goodness originates in God but that humans have power to accept or reject God's pattern for goodness, a power that comes from God in the first place. No wonder, as Diarmaid MacCullough puts it, "Pelagius's views have often been presented as rather amiable, in contrast to the fierce pessimism in Augustine's view of our fallen state." This, MacCullough implies, arises from Augustine's emphasis on original sin, which "seemed to leave humankind helpless puppets who could easily abandon all responsibility for their conduct."[43]

Significantly, Sayers uses the exact same metaphor in the essay Barth found most troubling, "The Triumph of Easter." There she argues that when people question why God failed to stop Nazi evil, they are ultimately asking, "Why did He not make us mere puppets, incapable of executing anything but His own pattern of perfection?"[44] Indeed, Calvinists reinforced Augustine's view by teaching that "total depravity" corrupts even the human will. Humans, then, do not freely choose to accept Jesus into their hearts; God "elects" particular individuals to receive the unmerited favor of "irresistible grace," which predestines them to become followers of Jesus.[45]

Sayers did indeed have trouble with the Calvinist idea of predestination, that God selects some people to go to heaven, others for eternal damnation. Confident that salvation depends on "the direction of the will,"[46] she overtly dismissed Christian "schools of thought" that assume "everything we do (including Jew baiting in Germany and our own disgusting rudeness to Aunt Eliza) is rigidly determined for us, and that, however much we may dislike the pattern, we can do nothing about it." Not coincidentally, these words appear in "The Triumph of Easter."[47] Why, then, did Barth value the essay enough to translate it?

In a revelatory essay on letters between Barth and Sayers, theologian David McNutt provides an answer: Sayers's "Christ-focused attention was sweet

---

[42]Quoted in Diarmaid MacCullough, *Christianity: The First Three Thousand Years* (New York: Viking, 2010), 306.

[43]MacCulloch, *Christianity*, 307, 306.

[44]Dorothy L. Sayers, "The Triumph of Easter," in *Creed or Chaos?*, 12-13.

[45]I quote language made famous by the Calvinist acronym TULIP: Total depravity, Unconditional election, Limited atonement, Irresistible grace, Perseverance of the Saints.

[46]*Letters* 4:353.

[47]Sayers, "Triumph of Easter," 14.

music to Barth's ears."[48] Perhaps less sweet was Sayers's emphasis on the *imago Dei*, that people who value creativity get a glimpse, if even in a glass darkly, of the love of creation for its own sake, as demonstrated by the God who created us all. In contrast, Barth assumes "the total annihilation of the *imago Dei* through sin," as Christian theologian and screenwriter Craig Detweiler puts it.[49] Barth certainly would have questioned Sayers's suggestions in *The Mind of the Maker* that even the craft of despicable sinners might image forth transcendent truth and goodness.

## A Delicate Balance

Ultimately, Sayers sought to walk "a razor-edge of delicate balance" between opposite theological "exaggerations."[50] Indeed, Pelagians and Calvinists are far more extreme in their views than their namesakes, Pelagius and Calvin. By marginalizing God's grace, Pelagians placed "a terrifying responsibility on the shoulders of every human being to act according to the highest standards demanded by God," as MacCulloch explains.[51] Sayers, in fact, admits that she often did not follow Christ's teachings as well as she preached them.[52]

Sayers demonstrates her attempt at balance in a 1955 letter to the *Church of England Newspaper*. Identifying as Anglo-Catholic, she states that she agrees with Augustine, Calvin, *and* Barth, who, among many others, believe that "our nature is in some sense 'depraved' and 'very far gone from original righteousness.'" Assenting that "the whole of nature (body, mind, and spirit) is maimed" by original sin, she nevertheless hesitates to endorse a "total" depravity in which "natural goodness is wholly extinguished." Such a doctrine, she suggests, "tends in effect to exclude God from the nature He created."[53]

Kutter Callaway echoes Sayers's sentiments in a 2013 book on Christianity and film, explaining, "For Barth, the Spirit of God is so completely and wholly Other that there is an utter discontinuity between the Creator and the

---

48McNutt, "Surprising Correspondence," 15.

49Craig Detweiler, *Into the Dark: Seeing the Sacred in the Top Films of the Twenty-First Century* (Grand Rapids, MI: Baker Academic, 2008), 265. See also Richard Vance Goodwin's discussion of Barth in *Seeing Is Believing: The Revelation of God Through Film* (Downers Grove, IL: IVP Academic, 2022), 60-61.

50*Letters* 4:10.

51MacCulloch, *Christianity*, 307.

52See Dorothy L. Sayers to V. A. Demant, June 21, 1938 (Wade 44/76).

53Dorothy L. Sayers, letter to the editor of the *Church of England Newspaper*, May 2, 1955, quoted in Simmons, *Creed Without Chaos*, 100-101.

creation."[54] In contrast, Callaway quotes from Barth's "decidedly Trinitiarian" student Jürgen Moltmann, who, like Sayers, aligns the Holy Spirit with power: "The grounds for the possibility of perceiving God in all things and all things in God originate from an 'understanding of the Spirit of God as *the power of creation* and the wellspring of life.'"[55]

Drinking deeply from this wellspring, the decidedly trinitarian Sayers believed that, despite original sin, humans could generate beauty, whether in action, word, or artistic deed, thanks to God's gift of creativity. As one Christian book on film puts it, "All beauty reflects God's beauty, whether it is understood to be from the Creator or not."[56] Nevertheless, maintaining that "razor-edge of delicate balance" between artistic beauty and human depravity is not easy, as famously exemplified by D. W. Griffith.

## THE SIN IN GRIFFITH'S CINEMA

As we have seen, Griffith generated power through the creative energy of cinematic techniques still used by filmmakers today. In fact, it was Griffith who premiered the first blockbuster feature-length movie made in America. A little over three hours long, his *Birth of a Nation* (1915) was a first in many ways:

- It was composed of more than 1,544 distinct shots when most multireel spectacles at the time employed one hundred shots or fewer.
- It was the longest film yet produced in America (thirteen reels).
- It was the most expensive film yet produced in America.
- It was the first film to charge two dollars for admission.
- It was the first film to be shown in the White House (to Woodrow Wilson).

Though considered a leap forward in the evolution of cinema, Griffith's film presents demeaning images of African Americans while glorifying the rise of the Ku Klux Klan after the Civil War. Many credit Griffith's film, in fact, with intensifying despicable Klan activities after its premiere. *Birth of a Nation* is therefore known as the "first film ever to be widely acclaimed as a great work

---

[54]Kutter Callaway, *Scoring Transcendence: Contemporary Film Music as Religious Experience* (Waco, TX: Baylor University Press, 2013), 158.

[55]Callaway quotes from Moltmann's *The Spirit of Life* (see Callaway, *Scoring Transcendence*, 162, emphasis added). Callaway's phrase "decidedly Trinitarian" is from 233n24.

[56]Peter Fraser and Vernon Edwin Neal, *ReViewing the Movies: A Christian Response to Contemporary Film* (Wheaton, IL: Crossway, 2000), 32.

of art and simultaneously reviled as a pernicious distortion of the truth."[57] African American filmmaker Spike Lee explores the double nature of *Birth of a Nation* in his film *BlacKkKlansman,* which won the Grand Prix at Cannes in 2018. Periodically inserting clips from Griffith's film into his movie about Klan activities in 1970s Colorado Springs, Lee suggests that the artistic camerawork and editing in *Birth of a Nation* should be valued despite the racist subject matter. He would agree with Sayers that art is much more than the idea presented.

Griffith, however, was not as generous as Spike Lee. Angered by protests over *Birth of a Nation,* Griffith made *Intolerance* (1916), which portrayed intolerance during four eras: the fall of Babylon, the crucifixion of Christ, the St. Bartholomew's Day Massacre of French Huguenots, and the American attacks on *Birth of a Nation.* A book published the same year, *The Art of the Moving Pictures* (1916), celebrated Griffith's film, describing it as a "superb example of architecture-in-motion."[58] Like the tower of Canterbury Cathedral, *Intolerance* was beautifully constructed, taking "editing to new heights," as film scholars still recognize.[59] One can only wonder whether the architect of the problematic *Birth of a Nation* ever humbled himself as did Sayers's architect in *The Zeal of Thy House*: "But let my work, all that was good in me, / All that was God, stand up and live and grow."[60]

As though exploring the complexity of these words, a 2014 film titled *Ex Machina* focuses on created works that literally stand up and live and grow. Directed by Alex Garland, the movie alludes to a question that quite legitimately disturbed Barth and should disturb us as well: What if the mind of the maker is not just sinful but downright evil in intent?

## Creativity Ex Machina

The maker portrayed in *Ex Machina* is a computer genius, Nathan Bateman (Oscar Isaac), who retreated to a gorgeous mountain wilderness after developing a search-engine company. Removed from all civilization in a high-tech home, he creates robots so lifelike that they seem fully human, like images of

---

[57]David A. Cook, *A History of Narrative Film* (New York: Norton, 1990), 93.

[58]Vachel Lindsay, quoted in Janet Staiger, "The Politics of Film Canons," *Cinema Journal* 24, no. 3 (Spring 1985): 6. Other scholars identify 1915 as the year Lindsay published his book on film.

[59]David Bordwell, *On the History of Film Style* (Cambridge, MA: Harvard University Press, 1997), 15.

[60]Sayers, *Zeal of Thy House,* 99.

their creator. To test the lifelikeness of Ava, his newest robot, Nathan arranges to have one of his employees, programmer Caleb Smith (Domhnall Gleeson), spend a week at his isolated home. In Sayers's terms, Nathan represents idea incarnated in the energy of Ava, the power of which will be tested on Caleb. Problematically, Nathan creates not for the love of the work itself, but to serve his own selfish interests. Clearly alluding to the Dionysian origins of Greek theater, from which we get the term *ex machina*, the film shows Bateman going on alcoholic binges and using the robots he has created to quench his sexual appetites. In the apt words of Christina Bieber Lake, Bateman has become "a womanizing male god like Zeus."[61] And the medium encourages viewers to wonder whether the robot Ava reflects the image of her Zeus-like creator.

*Ex Machina* emphasizes the idea of reflection with a glass motif, bodies repeatedly reflected in windows and mirrors and on computer screens. Proving that this was its intent, the film begins and ends with a shot of multiple bodies reflected on glass. In the opening shot, glass office walls reflect workers as they walk left to right. After a montage of shots capturing different parts of the office space, a close-up on one worker's face signals that this is our protagonist, Caleb. Staring at his computer, he almost seems to look into our eyes—as though we were on the other side of his computer screen just as he is on the other side of our movie screen. Subliminally, we thus become aware of two sides of a partition—one side having human bodies, the other reflecting programmed images—preparing us for a fundamental theme in the film: the difference between human consciousness and its reflection in artificial intelligence.

Before such thoughts can even register, a point-of-view shot reveals what Caleb sees on his screen: the words "first prize." Sparkling lights reflect off his face, as though to externalize his delight at the announcement that he has been selected to spend a week with the brilliant founder of the software company. Using no spoken words, the medium thus concretizes the concept of de-light, Caleb's face lit up not only figuratively by the written words on his screen but also literally by lights refracted from multiple computer screens and windows around him. Furthermore, the unnatural sparks on his face also make him look like a robot with an electrical short. In only several minutes,

---

[61]Christina Bieber Lake, "Children of a Lesser (but Incredibly Tech-Savvy) God," *The Cresset* 78, no. 5 (June 2015): 34.

Garland has provided a synecdoche for the entire film, encouraging viewers to consider how much Caleb reflects the technological environment created by a computer genius.

The glass/window motif intensifies when Caleb, after a long helicopter ride, enters the home of Nathan, whom he first sees through a window. The shot cuts from Caleb's point of view—Nathan on a deck outside—to that of Nathan looking back at Caleb. As though seeing with Nathan's eyes, the shot reveals two images of Caleb, standing side by side, one his actual body, the other a lifelike reflection on a pane of glass. Which is the real Caleb, and which is only the reflection? Similar shots are repeated throughout the film, reflections off glass not only creating multiple side-by-side images of Caleb but also establishing a parallel between Caleb and the robot Ava (Alicia Vikander). Numerous reflections of Ava appear on the glass walls that surround and limit her living space, the mise-en-scène sometimes including reflections of Caleb watching her, encouraging viewers to wonder how much Caleb's mindset as a computer nerd has been programmed by Nathan as well.

Significantly, the camera never shows Nathan reflected in the many glass walls throughout his house. Only once do we see the top of Nathan's face reflected, on a table. The horizontal line of the table distinguishes Nathan's reflection from the numerous side-by-side reflections of Caleb and Ava, where glass seams and frames emphasize their verticality. Nathan, it would seem, is the only autonomous human in the house, locking Caleb in and out of certain rooms the same way he confines his robots to glass boxes and closed closets. They all seem to be controlled by Nathan's brain, contained in the part of his head reflected on the table, explaining why Nathan asserts, "I'm not a man; I'm a god."

In Sayers's terms, Nathan is "like an autocratic deity," a creator who wants to "compel the characters to do his will," whereas "the perfect work of love demands the co-operation of the creature, responding according to the law of its nature." As she expands this point in *The Mind of the Maker*, Sayers sounds as though she could be discussing the creation of a robot from inanimate matter:

> For the artist who handles inanimate matter, this co-operation is secured without the creature's self-consciousness or will, so long as the creator has rightly conceived the work in relation to the nature of his material. . . . The structure of sand does not, for example, adapt itself to the making of ropes. . . .

> Certain kinds of sand will, however, readily adapt themselves to the making of glass.[62]

The transformation of sand into glass, of course, parallels the transformation of digital codes into artificial intelligence, signaled in the film by Ava's glass limbs, which reveal her robotic mechanisms inside.

To reinforce this issue of godlike control, Garland adds a hand motif to the glass motif in order to get viewers thinking about who has the upper hand in the mountain retreat. We become aware of this motif primarily through repeated focus on Ava's hand. As Caleb watches Ava in her glass box through a live feed on his computer screen, film viewers watch Ava in her glass box on their film screen. All watchers are therefore shocked when, pressing her hand against the wall of her prison, Ava causes the lights of the whole facility to shut down. Having originally seen her as a superbly crafted machine, viewers now see her exercising free will, manipulating the programmed environment that contains her. Garland next draws attention to Caleb's hand by placing the camera on the other side of a frosted glass door, such that Caleb's hand, and only his hand, appears pressing against the glass from the other side.

The image of a hand pressing on glass is repeated several more times, usually by robots, thus reinforcing the parallel between handcrafted machines and Caleb, who wonders how much Nathan is manipulating his behavior as well. (The words *manage, maneuver,* and *manipulate* all come from a Latin root meaning "hand.") The film powerfully symbolizes Caleb's fears in a scene where he sits facing Nathan, who lies in a drunken stupor on a couch. The camera films from behind the couch toward Caleb, such that all we can see are Nathan's hands waving above the back of the couch, Caleb's upper body appearing immediately beyond them. At one point Nathan's fingers wiggle directly in front of Caleb's stationary form, as though to indicate the latter is a mere puppet manipulated by the former.

## The Mind of the Puppet Maker

Sayers mentions puppets repeatedly in her work, usually to discuss the relationship of makers to their creations, including her own. In 1937, the year

---

[62]Sayers, *Mind of the Maker*, 137-38.

her life was changed by *The Zeal of Thy House*, Sayers published "Gaudy Night," an essay explaining how she came to create the character of Lord Peter Wimsey: "I plugged confidently on, putting my puppet through all his tricks and exhibiting him in a number of elegant attitudes. But I had not properly realized . . . that any character that remains static except for a repertory of tricks and attitudes is bound to become a monstrous weariness to his maker."[63] This certainly seems to be the case in *Ex Machina*, where Nathan's "monstrous weariness" of things he has made is manifest through drunken lassitude.

Whereas Nathan keeps his creatures locked up in glass cells so he can selfishly manipulate them to serve his appetites, genuinely creative makers encourage "the complete independence" of their creations.[64] In her chapter of *The Mind of the Maker* titled "The Love of the Creature," Sayers illustrates her point by expressing annoyance with readers who suggest she should turn Lord Peter Wimsey into a Christian—much as Nathan turns his robots into sex slaves: "No; you shall not impose either your will or mine upon my creature. He is what he is, I will work no irrelevant miracles upon him, either for propaganda, or to curry favour, or to establish the consistency of my own principles. He exists in his own right and not to please you. Hands off."[65]

Sayers's "hands off" serves as an apt commentary on the hand motif in *Ex Machina*. Indeed, Caleb's fear of being manipulated like a puppet intensifies when Nathan's Japanese servant reveals to Caleb that she is a robot by pulling sheets of skin off her hardwired body. Rather than employing voiceovers or soliloquies, Garner captures Caleb's subsequent despair visually, having him cut open his arm to make sure that his skin does not hide a mass of wires and microchips as well. As he makes incisions in his body, bright lights sparkle off his face, reminiscent of the sparkles highlighting his amazement in the film's opening scene. Rather than relief from seeing his flesh bleed, Caleb displays anger as he punches his hand against the mirror, spreading his blood on the glass. Does he have any hand in his own creation? Must blood be shed to save others from selfish impulses?

---

[63]Dorothy L. Sayers, "Gaudy Night," in *The Art of the Mystery Story: A Collection of Critical Essays*, ed. Howard Haycraft (New York: Simon & Schuster, 1946), 210.

[64]Sayers, *Mind of the Maker*, 138.

[65]Sayers, *Mind of the Maker*, 131.

Unlike the selfish Nathan, Caleb desires not only "the complete independence" of Ava but also what Sayers calls the creature's "willing co-operation."[66] Hence, in response to Ava's words, "Help me," as she presses both hands against the glass walls of her prison, Caleb sets her free. However, when Nathan encounters the liberated Ava in a hallway, he holds up *his* hand, fingers spread like someone seeking to manipulate a puppet. Instead, Ava's hand succeeds in killing her maker, even as she leaves Caleb locked behind a frosted glass door, his hands ineffectually banging on the glass. Ava's mind quite clearly reflects the mind of her evil maker, manipulating others to achieve self-serving ends.

The film closes with a symmetrical framing device that once again creates a parallel between Ava and Caleb. At the start of the movie, after capturing multiple reflections in Caleb's workplace, the camera shows Caleb flying to Nathan's isolated retreat via helicopter—the same kind of machine employed for deus ex machina effects in other films. Indeed, Caleb exits the machine only to find himself in the role of savior several days later: deus ex machina. Then, toward the end of the film, we see Ava climb into a helicopter waiting for Caleb outside Nathan's retreat. We never see her get out of the helicopter, however. Instead, a low-angle shot of the helicopter flying away from Nathan's retreat cuts to a high-angle shot focusing on city pavement, reflecting shadows of scurrying walkers. Soon we discover that the shot has been inverted, such that people walking on the pavement are upside down, while their shadows are right-side up, as though to symbolize how Ava has inverted the relationship between creator and creature.

The film ends as it begins, showing reflections on glass of human bodies walking left to right. But this time, overlaid on top of the storefront reflections, is the stationary image of Ava, much as we saw Caleb's reflection in his computer glass. Whom, then, does Ava most reflect: Caleb, her sacrificial savior, or Nathan, her devilish maker? *Ex Machina*, like many artistic films, refuses a clear-cut happy ending. As one reviewer aptly puts it, "Like both Caleb and Ava, we [viewers] are being tested, to see how far we will extend the boundary of humanity."[67]

---

[66]Sayers, *Mind of the Maker*, 138.

[67]Sayers, *Mind of the Maker*, 79; Jennifer L. Miller, "Of Tortoises and Turing: Creating a Test for Humanity," *The Cresset* 53, no. 1 (Michaelmas 2016): 50. I have borrowed phrasing for this discussion from Crystal L. Downing, "Out of the Machine: Cinema and Science Fiction," in *The Robot Will See You Now: Artificial Intelligence and the Christian Faith*, ed. John Wyatt and Stephen N. Williams (London: SPCK, 2021), 28-42.

## The Problem of Evil Makers

Like the inverted shadows in the final sequence, *Ex Machina* turns the mind of the maker upside down, presenting an indulgent inventor who is more like Satan than God. Nathan's evil is subsequently reflected in his invention, which becomes its own god as well. The film thus captures how Sayers might respond to Barth's accusation of Pelagianism. As she puts it in *The Mind of the Maker*, "Any Idea whose Energy manifests itself in a Pentecost of Power is good from its own point of view. It shows itself to be a true act of creation, although, if it is an evil Idea, it will create . . . by destruction."[68]

As though illustrating these words, Nathan destroys each robotic woman he creates, building a more advanced robot out of its body parts. For him, creation is not a good in itself; instead, it merely serves his own interests. Ava, his creation, seems to follow his selfish example, leaving Caleb to rot in a locked cell. Nevertheless, as Sayers argues, "no creative Idea can be wholly destructive: some creation will be produced together with the destruction; and it is the work of the creative mind to see that the destruction is redeemed by its creative elements."[69] Indeed, *Ex Machina* leaves us wondering whether Ava, a robot as creative as its maker, may positively influence people in the city she enters.

Though this speculation may disturb many, we need to consider it in light of Sayers's emphasis on the freedom of the art object, which reflects, as though in a glass darkly, the free will God gave to every human being. Sayers would respond to complaints about the problem of evil with the counterintuitive suggestion that evil results from the goodness of Creator God, who lovingly gifted humans with freedom. As free creatures, humans can choose either submission to their Creator or becoming their own gods, as do Adam and Eve in the creation story and Ava in *Ex Machina*. Unlike Nathan, our Maker glories in the free will of his human creations, allowing each to choose either reconciliation with or rejection of their Creator. As Sayers summarizes in *The Mind of the Maker*, the *imago Dei* reflects "the perfect relation of Creator and creature, and the perfect reconciliation of divine predestination with free created will."[70]

---

[68]Sayers, *Mind of the Maker*, 112.
[69]Sayers, *Mind of the Maker*, 112.
[70]Sayers, *Mind of the Maker*, 138.

## A Power-Full End

Though Sayers believed in the wages of sin, from which Christ alone provides the gift of salvation, she clearly affirmed creation as a good in and of itself. As a godly prior puts it in *The Zeal of Thy House*, "All the truth of the craftsman is in his craft. / Where there is truth, there is God; and where there is glory, / There is God's glory too."[71] Similar to *Zeal*, *Ex Machina* is a well-crafted exploration of the mind of a maker, a maker whose self-centered pride leads to his fall. The primary difference, of course, is that the architect in *Zeal* confesses his sins and thus dies into life after realizing that God transcends all human constructions. Indeed, we humans are merely two-dimensional reflections in glass compared to the substantive multidimensionality of our Creator. For now, we see in that glass darkly; but someday we will meet face to face.

[71]Sayers, *Zeal of Thy House*, 59.

# 6

# Film Theory

## *Making Meaning of Cinematic Form*

Sayers's trinitarian aesthetic illuminates not only the creativity of filmmakers but also complex theories about the essential artistry of film form. The word *theory* comes from a Greek root that means "spectator," the same root from which we get *theater*. Theories, like theaters, help us see in new ways, and this chapter combines the two by exploring divergent theories based on different ways of seeing. The multiple ways Christians responded to Sayers's theory of creativity in *The Mind of the Maker* can help illuminate various viewpoints among film theorists.

### Theories About *The Mind of the Maker*

The most scathing responses to Sayers's trinitarian theory, as might be expected, were from people who questioned doctrine about the Trinity in the first place. In 1953, Kathleen Nott, who trusted hypotheses based only on empirically verifiable evidence, derided *The Mind of the Maker* for basing its aesthetic on dogma that cannot be scientifically proven. As Nott puts it in her book *The Emperor's Clothes*,

> Unless we can start with the doctrine of the Trinity and show that it is a true and essential description of the structure of the whole universe without which human creativity, with all other processes, is unintelligible, the two subjects, theology and aesthetics, remain in departmental obscurity, until we can illuminate them by some more scientific examination.

Not surprisingly, she takes Sayers to task for suggesting that scientists inevitably rely on the metaphoric nature of language, as do theologians. Disturbed that Sayers questioned belief in "the open-minded inquiry" of science, Nott mounts ad hominem attacks against Sayers and her friend C. S. Lewis: "I know that they are braver and stupider than many of their orthodox literary fellows, but it is interesting to consider why an orthodoxy which is not only less muscular but less pinheaded than theirs should be relatively cautious in its minimal claims."[1] Nott's book was so popular that a second edition appeared five years later.

Ironically, Lewis had reservations about *The Mind of the Maker* as well, but for very different reasons. In a review published for the journal *Theology* (October 1941), Lewis describes the book as "full of illumination," and hence recommends it "heartily to theologians and critics." Nevertheless, he expresses concern over the parallel Sayers draws between Creator God and creative humans, wishing she had spent more than four pages emphasizing that it is "merely an analogy." He especially dislikes Sayers's statement "that 'between the mind of the maker and the Mind of his Maker' there is 'a difference, not of category, but only of quality and degree.'" As far as Lewis was concerned, "There is a greater, far greater, difference between the two than between playing with a doll and suckling a child."[2] For him, it would seem, Sayers's theory about the *imago Dei* sullies the mystical nature of the Trinity.

Someone who profoundly influenced Lewis's interest in mysticism critiqued *The Mind of the Maker* several months later. British philosopher Edwyn Bevan, whose book *Symbolism and Belief* (1938) Lewis valued greatly, focuses his review on the problem with "anthropomorphic" analogies: "It may be a bit of the truth when Miss Sayers thinks of God as the Supreme Creative Artist and another bit of the truth when someone else thinks of God as the Supreme Mathematician. Falsehood only arises when we take any of these conceptions of God as more than partial adumbration of the incomprehensible Reality."[3] And though Sayers explicitly states in *The Mind of the Maker* that "it may be perilous" and is indeed "inadequate" to develop analogies for God, especially concerning "a mystery as inscrutable as the mystery of the Trinity," Bevan evidently thought she should not have made the attempt at all.[4] Never once

---

[1]Kathleen Nott, *The Emperor's Clothes* (Bloomington: Indiana University Press, 1954), 286, 298, 68.

[2]C. S. Lewis, untitled review, *Theology* 43 (October 1941): 248-49.

[3]Edwyn Bevan, "Mind of the Maker," *Hibbert Journal* 40 (January 1942): 202-3. For the influence of Bevan on Lewis, see David C. Downing, *Into the Region of Awe: Mysticism in C. S. Lewis* (Downers Grove, IL: InterVarsity Press, 2005). See especially 114-15, which discuss the problem with metaphors about God.

[4]Dorothy L. Sayers, *The Mind of the Maker* (San Francisco: HarperSanFrancisco, 1979), 23.

praising Sayers's book, he compares its author to Job's comforters. Ironically, when C. S. Lewis was asked near the end of his life to list people who had influenced his spiritual life, he named both Bevan and Sayers.[5]

Agreeing with Bevan (and Sayers!) about the "incomprehensible" and "inscrutable" mystery of the Trinity, Lewis had a far more practical reason to question *The Mind of the Maker*. In his review he states, "I think that in an age when idolatry of human genius is one of our most insidious dangers Miss Sayers would have been prudent to stress more continuously than she does the fact that the analogy *is* merely an analogy. I am afraid that some vain glorious writers may be encouraged to forget that they are called 'creative' only by metaphor."[6] In other words, modernist artists of their day, most of whom shared Kathleen Nott's disdain for Christianity, might be reinforced by Sayers's book to think of themselves as gods, producing work that can save human souls from mundane existence. Indeed, one contemporary of Lewis and Sayers asserted that literary art was "one of the chief temples of the human spirit, in which all should worship," another arguing that a "poem is absolute; it is eternal and indestructible."[7] Famous literary critic I. A. Richards, whom both Sayers and Lewis mention in their writings, argued that poetic art "is capable of saving us; it is a perfectly possible means of overcoming chaos."[8] No wonder Lewis was concerned.

When postmodernism started exposing the problematic assumptions of high modernism (hence *post*modernism), cultural critics felt free to critique the modernist "religion of art," as Jacques Barzun called it.[9] Wendy Steiner, for example, parodied modernism with these words: "The public is meant to receive art as manna from the demigod artist and to accept the insult that goes along with it: that they are, by virtue of their status as nonartists and capitalists, incapable of truly understanding high culture. They should consume art,

---

5C. S. Lewis, "Cross-Examination," in *God in the Dock: Essays on Theology and Ethics*, ed. Walter Hooper (Grand Rapids, MI: Eerdmans, 1970), 260.

6Lewis, "Cross-Examination," 248.

7Quoted in Crystal Downing, *How Postmodernism Serves (My) Faith: Questioning Truth in Language, Philosophy and Art* (Downers Grove, IL: IVP Academic, 2006), 71, 82.

8I. A. Richards, *Science and Poetry* (New York: Norton, 1926), 95.

9Jacques Barzun, *From Dawn to Decadence: Five Hundred Years of Western Cultural Life, 1500 to the Present* (New York: HarperCollins, 2000), 663. Significantly, Barzun coined the phrase "aesthetic theology" in his review of *The Mind of the Maker*. See Barzun, "Aesthetic Theology," *Nation* 154 (February 21, 1942): 238. On the same page, Barzun critiques Sayers's "needless technicalities, Latin derivatives, and awkward circumlocutions."

because that is all they know how to do with anything, but leave the judgment of art to its priests."[10] Steiner's parody helps explain why the stigma of cinema lasted so long. Movies, especially after the development of synchronized sound, were constructed for mass audiences as money-making commodities, the box office more important than artistic integrity. Seeking to protect the temple of eternal art, modernist priests disdained such consumerism, considering popular movies as contemptible as bestselling novels, both of which appealed to what they considered lowbrow tastes. As Sayers recounts, someone once told her that, as far as modernist critics were concerned, she and Lewis "have committed the two unforgivable sins: you believe in God and your books sell."[11]

It is no wonder that cinephile contemporaries of Sayers sought to distinguish a blockbuster movie made for profit from a prophetic film that manifest the integrity of the work. By developing theories about distinctive artistry in the medium itself, they echoed modernists who elevated art above the mass appeal of rhymed poetry and representational paintings. Such film theorists, as Malcolm Turvey summarizes, reflected "conceptions of art prevalent in modernism—anti-imitation, medium-specificity."[12] What they *specified* as essential for the medium, however, differed from critic to critic. Sayers's trinitarian aesthetic can therefore help clarify their attempts to distinguish wages-driven movie entertainment from cinematic art. Indeed, throughout the history of film theory, some theorists primarily consider creative idea, others focus on creative energy, whereas many emphasize creative power.

## EARLY FILM THEORY

In 1916, German psychologist Hugo Münsterberg published *The Photoplay: A Psychological Study*, often considered one of the earliest attempts at film theory. Exploring how movies influence human perception and imagination, Münsterberg suggests that some day film will encourage "the free and joyful play of the mind" better than any other art form.[13] His "play of the mind," of course,

[10]Wendy Steiner, *Venus in Exile: The Rejection of Beauty in Twentieth-Century Art* (New York: Free Press, 2001), 20.

[11]*Letters* 4:318.

[12]Malcolm Turvey, "Belázs: Realist or Modernist?," in *The Film Theory Reader: Debates and Arguments*, ed. Marc Furstenau (New York: Routledge, 2010), 86.

[13]Quoted in Janet Staiger, "The Politics of Film Canons," *Cinema Journal* 24, no. 3 (Spring 1985): 6. For Munsterberg's interest in close-ups, see Noël Carroll, *Theorizing the Moving Image* (Cambridge: Cambridge University Press, 1996), 295.

reminds us of power in Sayers's triadic paradigm. Due to his emphasis on viewer psychology, however, Münsterberg attends to the power of film much more than the energy by which filmmakers generate power. As Sayers reminds us, a "creator must still adapt the work to the *material*."[14] Imperative to the success of a creative work is the energy of the material medium. Not surprisingly, then, the actual *makers* of movies, the ones working with the medium itself, were the first to explore this issue, perhaps because they understood that the free play of the mind, Sayers's power, was inseparable from the energy of filming and editing an idea.

In the 1920s, when German Expressionist cinema was generating international acclaim, filmmakers in France were developing theories about film form. Known as French Impressionists, these postwar cineastes were publishing essays "proclaiming cinema to be an art comparable to poetry, painting, and music." As the authors of *Film Art* continue to explain, these "young theorists compared Chaplin to a ballet dancer and the films of [American William S.] Hart to the *Song of Roland*," analogies that would have delighted Sayers, who refers to Chaplin in her sixth detective novel and who translated *The Song of Roland*, an eleventh-century French poem, for Penguin books.[15]

In 1924, one of the French Impressionists, Jean Epstein, suggested that truly artistic films do not need any verbal language, including the explainers or intertitles discussed in chapter four, because "cinema is made to narrate with images and not with words," a view also held by Münsterberg.[16] That same year, Hungarian film critic and screenwriter Béla Balázs published *Visible Man, or the Culture of Film*, which endorses Epstein and Münsterberg by emphasizing how the close-up distinguishes the language of cinema from spoken words performed on theatrical stages. Like modernists of his day, he implies such language has religious power: "The art of film seems to hold out the promise of redemption from the curse of Babel."[17] In other words, people from all nations can understand the visual language of cinema, thus

---

[14] Sayers, *Mind of the Maker*, 138, emphasis added.

[15] David Bordwell, Kristin Thompson, and Jeff Smith, *Film Art: An Introduction*, 11th ed. (New York: McGraw Hill, 2017), 467; Dorothy L. Sayers, trans., *The Song of Roland* (Middlesex, UK: Penguin, 1957). Sayers began to translate the book-length poem during her student days at Oxford, returning to the project in 1954.

[16] Jean Epstein, "For a New Avant Garde," trans. Stuart Liebman, in *The Avante-Garde Film*, ed. P. Adams Sitney (New York: New York University Press, 19780), 27.

[17] Béla Belázs, "Visible Man, or the Culture of Film," in Furstenau, *Film Theory Reader*, 71.

surmounting the incoherence of Babel's multiple tongues. As we have seen, awareness that film images generate a universal language powerfully influenced Soviet cineastes such as Sergei Eisenstein.

Only two years after Eisenstein's industry-changing *Battleship Potemkin*, however, sound came to American cinema, which, as discussed in chapter four, destabilized attentiveness to the integrity of film form. With the spread of talkie technology to other countries, no longer could Balázs promise redemption from the curse of Babel. Instead, Babel was overpowering cinema, forcing cineastes to develop new theories about the distinctive artistry of cinema.

## OVERCOMING BABEL

The Christian answer to Babel, of course, occurs in Acts 2, when the Holy Spirit falls on Christ's disciples during Pentecost, causing them to speak in multiple tongues. As Christian philosopher James K. A. Smith explains, "At Pentecost Yahweh's *pneuma* affirms the multiplicity of creation and the post-Babelian era, in direct contrast to the quest for unity that initiated the construction of the tower." God thus celebrates "diversity and the multiplicity of others. And that is why creation is a pluralist idea and why a creational hermeneutic attempts to honor this diversity not as the original sin but rather as primordially good."[18] Sayers, of course, was implying something very similar almost sixty years earlier. Her "creational hermeneutic," or the principle on which she bases her interpretation of Genesis 1, arose from her belief that Creator God is multiple, a Trinity of Father, Son, and Holy Ghost who creates humans in its own image, endorsing not only the goodness of creation but also the "diversity and multiplicity" of human creativity. Not coincidentally, Sayers titles a chapter in *The Mind of the Maker* "Pentecost."

Exploring when and how a creative work generates "a Pentecost of Power," Sayers alludes to the moment when the power of the Holy Spirit became manifest in "tongues of fire that separated and came to rest" on diverse believers (Acts 2:3). As she puts it, "From some quarter or other, the Power will descend, to flame or to smolder until it is ready to issue in a new revelation,"

[18]James K. A. Smith, *The Fall of Interpretation: Philosophical Foundations for a Creational Hermeneutic* (Downers Grove, IL: IVP Academic, 2000), 59-60.

even, she suggests, from "Hollywood."[19] Perhaps Sayers was remembering a review of *The Silent Passenger* that stated, "When the gift of tongues descended on Hollywood . . . it was merely a splutter that slowed down the tempo of films."[20] Only six years after the disastrous Phoenix film that ignited her Christian aesthetic, Sayers was admitting that, if creatively constructed, even Hollywood talkies had the power to energize receptive viewers to relish the beauty of creation, as well as cause them to perceive truths of existence in new ways.

Many of Sayers's contemporaries, however, still only heard babel. The same year Sayers wrote "Towards a Christian Aesthetic," Eisenstein published *Film Form,* endorsing a nonverbal "special film language, by way of a special form of film *speech.*" A year later, French film theorist André Bazin argued in his famous 1945 essay, "The Ontology of the Photographic Image," that cinema spoke a new "language."[21] For both, the language was primarily visual, like the tongues of fire that *visually* appeared over disciples before they began babbling in different languages. Nevertheless, Eisenstein and Bazin spoke in very different tongues when it came to the power of cinema, developing radically diverse theories about *how* the visual language of cinema speaks.

## The Power of André Bazin

Whereas Eisenstein argued that montage, especially the collision of discontinuous shots, provided the essential language of cinema, Bazin emphasized mise-en-scène, encouraging contemplation of screen images that appear in any *one* shot, whether through deep focus, long shot (the camera far from the subject matter), or long take (a lengthy run of the camera). As far as Bazin was concerned, montage sequences usually "impose an interpretation" on viewers. Far preferable, for him, was the work of Erich von Stroheim, the filmmaker mentioned in Sayers's *Gaudy Night,* who "rejects . . . the tricks of montage." By using long takes, depth-in-field, and astute camera movements, Stroheim encourages viewers to contemplate—and interpret for themselves—what

---

[19]Sayers, *Mind of the Maker,* 112-13.

[20]John Marks, "Penny Plain, Twopence Coloured," *The New Statesman and Nation,* July 20, 1935, 95.

[21]Sergei Eisenstein, "Dickens, Griffith, and the Film Today," in *Film Form: Essays in Film Theory,* ed. and trans. Jay Leyda (New York: Harcourt Brace Jovanovich, 1977), 245, emphasis original; André Bazin, "The Ontology of the Photographic Image," in *What Is Cinema?,* trans. Hugh Gray (Berkeley: University of California Press, 1967), 1:16.

appears in the mise-en-scène. "One could easily imagine," Bazin writes, "a film by Stroheim composed of a single shot as long-lasting and as close-up as you like."[22] As James Monaco explains, Stroheim was "among the first to recognize that the observer of a film had to be given freedom to operate *in concert with the creator*."[23] Many filmmakers follow his lead, as when Steven Spielberg pronounced, "I'd love to see directors start trusting the audience to be the film editor with their eyes," selecting "who they would choose to look at while a scene is being played."[24]

To explain the difference in Sayers's terms, Bazin emphasized the medium of the camera, believing that the energy of cinematography created thought-inducing mise-en-scène; Eisenstein, in contrast, thought power arose from the energy of cutting the cinematic medium to splice together discontinuous shots. Their differing theories could be compared to the divergent ways Christians tend to visualize the medium of salvation in their churches. Whereas Protestants seem to prefer the symbolism of an empty cross, Roman Catholics tend to depict Jesus still nailed to the crucifix, the blood of our salvation apparent in cuts on his flesh. Analogically, then, Bazin would want us to spend time looking at an empty cross while reflecting on the fact that Christ conquered death, whereas Eisenstein would rather have us be shocked by each cut we see, remembering how much our Savior suffered for our sins. Nevertheless, just as Catholics and Protestants similarly believe in Christ as the resurrected medium of salvation, both Eisenstein and Bazin similarly believed that the energy of the medium communicated power to audiences—even if in radically different ways.

## The Power of Film Noir

The same decade that Eisenstein and Bazin were theorizing about the essence of cinematic art, a new style of film developed in the United States, ignited by the 1941 release of John Huston's *The Maltese Falcon*, in which Humphrey Bogart plays detective Sam Spade. The famous film was an adaptation of a novel Dashiell Hammett published in 1930, the same year Sayers and G. K.

---

[22]André Bazin, "The Evolution of the Language of Cinema," in *What Is Cinema?*, 1:26-27.

[23]James Monaco, *How to Read a Film: The Art, Technology, Language, History, and Theory of Film and Media*, rev. ed. (New York: Oxford University Press, 1981), 240.

[24]Quoted in Bordwell, Thompson, and Smith, *Film Art*, 213.

Chesterton helped form the London Detection Club. Hammett, however, was reacting "against traditional British detective stories, which often involved staid country-house settings and upper-class characters"—like Lord Peter Wimsey. Film adaptations followed suit, employing low-key lighting and other chiaroscuro effects influenced by German Expressionism to destabilize clear-cut distinctions between noble-minded sleuths and evil criminals.

By 1946, French critics had coined the term *film noir* to describe such films in which protagonists have a pessimistic view of the world, with thoughts as dark as the mise-en-scène in which they appear. Indeed, shadows crossing over characters' bodies and faces, often caused by venetian blinds, are common to film noir, as though signaling the divided nature within both protagonists and criminals, including the femme fatale. In fact, as Kristin Thompson and David Bordwell note, "Film noir was the one type of Hollywood film that permitted an unhappy ending."[25] Sayers would have been intrigued, having published *The Mind of the Maker* the same year Warner Brothers released *The Maltese Falcon*. In a chapter titled "Problem Picture," she questions, like Dashiell Hammett a decade before, the legitimacy of traditional detective fiction, wherein the story always provides a "solution" at the end, thus perpetuating the artificial "miracle-mongering" of happy endings.[26]

Impressed with the distinctive style of film noir, the French began grappling with another kind of problem picture: Who is responsible for the stylistic distinctions of a moving picture? As Thompson and Bordwell summarize, "Since the mid-1940's French directors and screenwriters quarreled over who could properly be considered the *auteur*, or author, of a film."[27] Was it the screenwriter or the director?

## The Camera Pen

The quarrel intensified in 1948 when a French film critic named Alexandre Astruc published an essay that some consider "the most important critical theory the cinema has yet produced."[28] Translated into English as "Birth of a

---

[25]Thompson and Bordwell, *Film History*, 215-16.

[26]Sayers, *Mind of the Maker*, 188, 79.

[27]Kristin Thompson and David Bordwell, *Film History: An Introduction*, 3rd ed. (New York: McGraw-Hill, 2010), 381.

[28]Quoted in "Alexandre Astruc," New Wave Film Encyclopedia, www.newwavefilm.com/french-new-wave-encyclopedia/alexandre-astruc.shtml.

New Avant-Garde: The Camera Pen," Astruc's essay argues that directors are most clearly the auteurs of film, the camera serving as their writing implement. With their *caméra-stylo,* or camera pen, directors can "write *ideas* directly on film without even having to resort to those heavy associations of *images* that were the delight of silent cinema."[29] For Astruc, in other words, autonomous directorial idea is far more important than visual images given energy either by montage or mise-en-scène—quite a radical departure from early film theorists who regarded the image as the primary language of cinema.

In terms of the crucifix analogy, Astruc draws attention away from the image of the cross to the person who stands in front of it, the preacher who develops profound ideas that direct our thoughts about Christ's sacrifice in new ways. In fact, Astruc argued that cinema would "gradually break free from the tyranny of what is visual, from the image for its own sake, from the immediate and concrete demands of the narrative, to become a means of writing just as flexible and subtle as written language."[30] He seems reminiscent of radical Protestants who renounce images altogether. As art historian Christopher W. Wood explains, "John Calvin as well as some radical followers of Martin Luther had argued that sculpted and painted representation of the human figure distracted worshippers from Christian teaching, if not from God himself. Reformed congregations removed the offending depictions from their places of worship."[31] In Sayers's terms, ideas based on the Bible and preached from the pulpit were the "one thing . . . needful" (Lk 20:42 KJV).

Sayers's 1938 essay in *Sight and Sound,* in fact, anticipates debates over the authorship, and hence authority, of film. Whereas she argued for the need to honor the initial story on which a screenplay was based, the first issue (1951) of *Cahiers du cinéma,* France's counterpart to *Sight and Sound,* identified films entirely by their directors, reviewing "*Sunset Boulevard* as a Billy Wilder film, *Diary of a Country Priest* as a Robert Bresson film, *The Little Flowers of Saint Francis* as a Roberto Rossellini film, and so on."[32] This changed the way people have discussed film ever since. Unlike theater, which continues to identify stage plays by the writer—a Shakespeare production or Lorraine Hansberry

---

[29]Quoted in Monaco, *How to Read a Film,* 331, emphasis added.

[30]Quoted in Monaco, *How to Read a Film,* 331.

[31]Christopher S. Wood, *A History of Art History* (Princeton, NJ: Princeton University Press, 2019), 218.

[32]Thompson and Bordwell, *Film History,* 381-82.

play—today we identify a film by its director, an Alfred Hitchcock movie or a Spike Lee film. Film scholars reinforce this initiative, almost always listing the director's name along with the premiere date anytime they mention a film.

### Truffaut and the French New Wave

In January 1954, a twenty-one-year-old disciple of André Bazin, François Truffaut, published an essay in *Cahiers du cinema* that influenced theories about cinema as much as Dante influenced theories about purgatory. Titling his piece "Une Certaine Tendance du Cinéma Française" ("A Certain Tendency of the French Cinema"), Truffaut denounces what he calls the "tradition of quality": self-consciously literary movies, often based on famous novels or plays. The directors of such "quality" fare, claims Truffaut, merely follow directions that screenwriters write into their scripts. Rather than exercise genuine creativity, such directors parallel people who paint landscapes by using paint-by-numbers kits. Auteur directors, in contrast, *create* films themselves, wherein, to use Sayers's terms, idea, energy, and power are simultaneously operative in the mind of the auteur maker.

Indeed, Truffaut often reinforces *The Mind of the Maker*. When he argues, "The artist cannot always dominate his work. He must be sometimes God, and sometimes his creature," he echoes Sayers's statement in a chapter called "The Love of the Creature": "The creator's love for his work is not a greedy possessiveness; he never desires to subdue his work to himself but always to subdue himself to his work."[33] Of course, Truffaut's metaphor "He must sometimes be God" might also reinforce C. S. Lewis's concern over the modernist deification of artists. Nevertheless, Lewis would highly value something else in "A Certain Tendency of the French Cinema," that is, the essay's indictment of cineastes who justify gratuitous blasphemy, vulgarity, and adultery by calling it "psychological realism." As Truffaut puts it, "Under the cover of literature—and, of course, of quality—they give the public its habitual dose of smut, non-conformity and facile audacity." Truffaut follows up with a simple question: "Is this realism?"[34]

[33] François Truffaut, "A Certain Tendency in French Cinema," in *Film Manifestos and Global Cinema Cultures: A Critical Anthology*, ed. Scott MacKenzie (Berkeley: University of California Press, 2014), 218; Sayers, *Mind of the Maker*, 130.

[34] Truffaut, "Certain Tendency," 216-17.

Truffaut powerfully influenced filmmakers to follow, helping generate *la Nouvelle Vague* in cinema, or the "French New Wave."[35] Defying the traditional language of cinema, New Wave directors employed handheld cameras, unknown actors, digressive scenes, unmotivated tracking shots, natural lighting, unusual jump-cuts, and random plots. While filmmakers in the "tradition of quality" wanted audiences to fantasize that the screen was a window to reality, these directors drew attention to the energy of the medium as they incarnated their ideas on film, thus creating a new wave of power.

New Wave directors also placed into their films references to and sometimes clips from movies and directors of the past. In the words of Sayers, they honored "former streams of beauty" while employing a new language that changed the future. Celebrating the mind of the maker, they practiced what Sayers preached: "All the truth of the craftsman is in his craft."[36] Indeed, though Truffaut helped to ignite the French New Wave through his writings, he didn't fully experience "the enormous privilege of the act of creation," as he puts it, until he made his first feature-length film, *Les Quatre Cents Coups* (*The Four Hundred Blows*).[37]

Earning him the Cannes Award for Best Director in 1959, Truffaut's black-and-white movie echoes film noir by refusing to deliver a happy ending. After the film's adolescent protagonist escapes from a detention center, tracking shots follow the boy as he runs to a beach and into the water, at which point the camera zooms in to a close-up, the boy's eyes breaking the fourth wall with a neutral expression. The final freeze-frame leaves viewers baffled: is the boy feeling liberated or regretful? What will he do now? Truffaut's famous finish confirms Sayers's sense that "life is no candidate for the Detection Club."[38]

*The Four Hundred Blows* was like nothing produced in the "tradition of quality" that Truffaut had critiqued five years earlier. Even though Truffaut

---

[35]The term originally described a new art form appearing in France and later was applied to tradition-breaking filmmakers. See Genette Vincendeau, "Fifty Years of the French New Wave: From Hysteria to Nostalgia," in *The French New Wave: Critical Landmarks*, ed. Peter Graham (London: Palgrave Macmillan, 2009), 6.

[36]Sayers, *Mind of the Maker*, 121; Dorothy L. Sayers, *The Zeal of Thy House*, in *Four Sacred Plays* (London: Victor Gollancz, 1948), 59.

[37]François Truffaut, *The Films in My Life*, trans. Leonard Mayhew (Boston: Da Capo, 1994), 13.

[38]Sayers, *Mind of the Maker*, 202. For more in-depth discussion about Truffaut's famous film, see Crystal Downing, *Salvation from Cinema: The Medium Is the Message* (New York: Routledge, 2016), 100-102.

oversaw what his cinematographer filmed, he gave up mastery over the film by allowing unanticipated events and images captured during location shooting to guide his creativity, willing to change his original vision—idea, energy, and power participating together in the act of creation. Sayers could be talking about Truffaut when she writes, "The only way of 'mastering' one's material is to abandon the whole conception of mastery and to co-operate with it in love."[39]

Truffaut sounds even more like Sayers after having created fifteen films. In 1975 he suggested a relationship among idea (intentions), energy, and power:

> A perfectly ordinary movie with *energy* can turn out to be better cinema than a film with "intelligent" *intentions* listlessly executed. . . . Cinematic success is not necessarily the result of good brain work, but of a harmony of existing elements in ourselves that we may no have even been conscious of. . . . The public's desire to see a film—its *power* to attract—is a stronger motivation than the power of any criticism.[40]

Sayers, of course, would add that when the three elements of trinitarian creativity fail to harmonize, we are left with "Scalene Trinities" in various kinds of movies, as discussed in the preceding chapter. The same might be said about film theories, some so scalene that many cinephiles started denouncing film theory altogether. Ironically, an early example of scalene theory was influenced by Truffaut.

## Father-Ridden Auteur Theory

Like many new wave directors, Truffaut had internalized Astruc's theory that film directors wrote movies with the "camera-pen." He therefore celebrated French filmmakers Robert Bresson (1907–1999) and Jacques Tati (1908–1982) by stating, "A film by Bresson or Tati is necessarily a work of genius *a priori*, simply because a single, absolute authority has been imposed from the opening to 'The End.'"[41] The word *authority*, of course, is based on the word *author*, or *auteur* in French. Truffaut's sense of cinematic authority, in other words, depends on the unique vision of the auteur director, the father of the film, whose idea reigns above all. Auteur cinema thus exemplifies what Sayers

---

[39]Sayers, *Mind of the Maker*, 107, 186.

[40]Truffaut, *Films in My Life*, 15, emphasis added.

[41]Truffaut, *Films in My Life*, 235.

called "father-centered" art, insofar as "all the writer's work and every part of it can be referred to a coherent and controlling unity of Idea."[42]

By the 1960s, American critic Andrew Sarris was using the term "auteur theory" to describe the elevation of "any director with a personal style or a distinct worldview."[43] For auteur theorists, then, a creative film projects an overarching idea, whether of style or message, that shapes all the work of a filmmaker, an idea that distinguishes a given auteur's films from those of all other directors. For instance, Alfred Hitchcock, considered an auteur by Truffaut, has a highly recognizable style and/or subject matter, a "controlling unity of Idea" symbolized when Hitchcock briefly appears on screen in most of his movies, as though to say that he, the father of the film, controls what we see. The viewer, therefore, has little power other than to recognize the distinctive auteur idea manifest in the energy of a film.

## Power and the Viewer: Psychology and Politics

By the late 1960s, attitudes had changed. Echoing rebellions of the radical sixties, discussions about the power of cinema started dominating film theory. Jean-Luc Godard, who contributed to the French New Wave with his 1960 film *Breathless*, became more and more interested in the psychology of film viewers. Whereas his early film criticism published in *Cahiers du cinéma* focused on how the energy of montage and mise-en-scène express auteur idea, Godard later focused on the political relationship between makers and consumers. James Monaco summarizes the change with language relevant to Sayers's triadic aesthetic, saying Godard's "emphasis" was no longer on "how cinema relates to an ideal system (aesthetics) but rather on how it directly affects us as viewers. Film's ethics and politics therefore determine its nature."[44]

After being identified as part of the French New Wave, Godard started making movies that explore how film manipulates viewers to see reality in a certain way. In other words, rather than use film stories to preach political propaganda, Godard made films that encouraged people to think about how cinematic techniques *themselves* are inherently propagandistic, perpetuating inaccurate views of reality. Horkheimer and Adorno, of course, had addressed

---

[42]Sayers, *Mind of the Maker*, 156.

[43]Thompson and Bordwell, *Film History*, 382.

[44]Monaco, *How to Read a Film*, 338.

the problematic politics of cinema decades earlier, but their answer was to banish cinema, saying, "This bloated pleasure apparatus adds no dignity to man's lives."[45] Godard, in contrast, wanted to transform lives by transforming the power of cinema. He was not alone.

## The Power of Third Cinema

A decade after the French new wave revolutionized theories about cinema, a different kind of revolution affected filmmaking in Latin America. Like Sayers, who encouraged a threefold approach to creativity in "Towards a Christian Aesthetic," two Argentine filmmakers took a threefold approach toward film in a manifesto titled "Towards a Third Cinema" (1969). However, rather than celebrating triadic creativity, the authors, Fernando Solanas and Octavio Getino, outlined three kinds of cinema in order to banish all but the third. Calling big-budget Hollywood fare "first cinema," they argued that such entertainment fills the screen with titillating images that anesthetize audiences to political realities, thus reinforcing the status quo. Solanas and Getino also repudiated "second cinema," which they aligned with the French New Wave and auteur theory. Though second cinema eschewed the Hollywood commercialism of first cinema, it failed, in their minds, to adequately address social inequities due to its obsession with the brilliant uniqueness of each auteur director.

In Sayers's terms, first cinema idolizes entertaining energy, while second cinema idolizes director idea. Third cinema, in contrast, brings power to the people, film viewers considered more important than the originality of auteur idea or the energy of images on screen. Solanas and Getino therefore encouraged people to discuss what they were screening, suggesting that films be shown outside established cinema spaces so that impoverished people didn't have to pay to join the conversation. Their award-winning 1968 documentary, *The Hour of the Furnaces*, halted midreel with a directive to viewers: "Now it is up to you to draw conclusions, to continue the film. You have the floor."[46] Their words echo something Sayers wrote a member of Parliament in 1940. Celebrating that "cinemas are open again," she states, "there are plenty of

[45]Max Horkheimer and Theodor W. Adorno, "Dialectic of Enlightenment," trans. John Cumming, in *The Norton Anthology of Theory and Criticism*, 2nd ed., ed. Vincent B. Leitch (New York: Norton, 2010), 1117.

[46]Thompson and Bordwell, *Film History*, 504.

people eager and anxious to do things—but what they chiefly needs is to learn to think, and to be made to understand their own *power*."[47]

Solanas and Getino would emphatically agree. Their third cinema, as Thompson and Bordwell summarize, regards "the viewer a 'participant-comrade,' ready to think and debate." Unlike Sayers, however, Solanas and Getino wanted each participant-comrade to primarily think and debate in order to incite "populist rebellion."[48] The power of cinema was reduced to a political agenda, exemplifying what Sayers dismissively calls "spell-binding art," which channels "energy into a sort of mill-stream to turn the wheel of action."[49]

Not surprisingly, other film theorists dismissed the very idea that cinema might turn the wheels of action. Some argued, in fact, the exact opposite, that film generates passivity through the manipulation of viewer psychology. Rather than focusing on the positive effects of power, these theorists obsessed about the negative effects of energy, eliminating the possibility of viewer power altogether. Their theory dominated the 1970s, the era in which more and more universities were developing majors in film studies.

## ENERGY OF THE APPARATUS

The turning point came with the publication of two extremely influential essays in 1970, "Ideology and Ideological State Apparatuses," by Louis Althusser, and "Ideological Effects of the Basic Cinematographic Apparatus," by Jean-Louis Baudry. The origins of what became known as apparatus theory, however, go back to the decade in which Sayers was developing her Christian aesthetic.

In 1946 a Freudian psychoanalyst named Bertram D. Lewin coined the term "dream screen" to describe "a surface on which a dream seems to be projected."[50] The very next year Marxist theorists Horkheimer and Adorno were denouncing the "bloated pleasure apparatus" of cinema, and their indictment affected the way film theorists started talking about the dream screen of cinema. Echoing Godard, who asserted in 1966 that "cinema is capitalism

[47]*Letters* 2:161, emphasis added.

[48]Thompson and Bordwell, *Film History*, 504.

[49]Dorothy L. Sayers, "Towards a Christian Aesthetic," in *Unpopular Opinions* (London: Gollancz, 1946), 35.

[50]Quoted in Jean-Louis Baudry, "The Apparatus: Metapsychological Approaches to the Impression of Reality in Cinema," in *Film Theory and Criticism*, 4th ed., ed. Gerald Mast et al. (New York: Oxford University Press, 1992), 691.

in its purest form," these theorists argued that the apparatus of movie techniques blinds viewers to social injustices.[51] By making fantastical stories appear realistic, the cinematic dream screen, though seeming like a window to reality, instead offers artificial images that reinforce capitalist ideology.

Apparatus theorists went one step further to suggest that not only viewers but also filmmakers themselves have been psychologically manipulated to endorse assumptions and practices of the culture in which they are embedded. By creating protagonists who successfully defy cultural expectations to fulfill their desires, Hollywood filmmakers imply that systemic problems—racism, sexism, poverty, and so on—do not affect authentic individualists. This becomes obvious when producers market a movie by celebrating the protagonist as a cop, surgeon, detective, pilot, soldier, and so on "who doesn't play by the rules," thus fulfilling the American paradigm of outlaw heroes, as discussed in the previous chapter.

For apparatus theorists, then, power does not reside in the viewer, or even in the mind of the maker, whose idea is itself manipulated by capitalist ideology. Both filmmakers and viewers, they assert, are controlled by the energy of the apparatus itself—cinematic techniques that disguise the artifice of their view of reality. They would agree with Sayers's sense that sole emphasis on energy, what she calls "son-ridden" art, is manifest by "thrilling and moving the senses but producing no genuine rebirth of the spirit."[52] Furthermore, they argue that the ideological manipulation operates on multiple levels. First is the need to fund multimillion-dollar projects, investors wanting to please audiences in order to make money. Producers therefore hire big-name directors, having extrapolated from auteur theory the importance of branding. Those directors then engage the apparatus of camera and editing—close-ups, over the shoulder and point-of-view shots, and so on—which influence viewers to identify with the protagonist's point of view. Hence, when protagonists escape limitations and consequences, viewers who identify with them assume they can escape as well, thus giving them no incentive to change inequities in culture.

Sayers would endorse various aspects of apparatus theory, especially its emphasis on distribution and exhibition, wherein theater owners show psychologically manipulative blockbusters in order to make money,

---

[51]Quoted in David A. Cook, *A History of Narrative Film*, 2nd ed. (New York: Norton, 1990), 567.
[52]Sayers, *Mind of the Maker*, 151-52.

entertainment-art that "dissipates the energies of the audience and pours them down the drain."[53] While many Christians reduce cinematic sins to curse words and sex scenes, she would rather have us question whether movies encourage us to be uncritical endorsers of capitalist individualism more than to become a people called to love our neighbors as ourselves, sacrificing self-interest in order to serve those in need. As she puts it in an essay on the seven deadly sins, "Do the vigilance committees who complain of 'suggestive' books and plays make any attempt to suppress the literature which 'suggests' that getting on in the world is the chief object in life?" Confirming that she was thinking of suggestive movies as well, she soon follows her question with an allusion to the manipulative apparatus of film: "When we go to the cinema and see a picture about empty-headed people in luxurious surroundings, do we say: 'What drivel!' or do we sit in a misty dream, wishing we could give up our daily work and marry into surroundings like that?"[54] She too worries about the dream screen.

Unlike Sayers, however, apparatus theorists tended to assume the misty dream was inescapable. For them, Truffaut's call for realism on screen, along with his celebration of auteur freedom, reflect his naivete. Apparatus theory is thus the most extreme reaction to the modernist deification of artists and their so-called original art, suggesting that no one can escape the manipulation of cultural practices—except, evidently, apparatus theorists themselves. Even one of the most brilliant of film scholars, Christian Metz, fell under the spell of apparatus theory. Though his early work provides a rigorously nuanced understanding of how film functions as a "language" his later work focuses on the psychological manipulation generated by the way images are placed on screen.[55]

## THE POWER OF SIGNS: SEMIOLOGY

Much of apparatus theory drew on Freudian and Marxist appropriation of semiology, or the science of signs, made famous by Ferdinand de Saussure (1857–1913), who focused on the relationship between a signifier/image and

[53]Sayers, "Towards a Christian Aesthetic," 35.

[54]Dorothy L. Sayers, "The Other Six Deadly Sins," in *Creed or Chaos?* (Manchester, NH: Sophia Institute, 1974), 98-99.

[55]See, e.g., Metz's earlier *Language and Cinema* (1971) versus his later *The Imaginary Signifier: Psychoanalysis and the Cinema* (1977).

its signified meaning.[56] The relevance to the language, or signifiers, of cinema is obvious. Apparatus theorist Louis Althusser argued that the signifiers of capitalist culture, reinforced by cinema, make people believe they are free when they are actually being manipulated by signs of success. In his "Ideology and Ideological State Apparatuses," Althusser argues that every citizen "is interpellated [given an identity] as a (free) subject in order that . . . he shall (freely) accept his subjection." He uses a term made famous by theater and film scholars to expose "the way the 'actors' in this *mise-en-scène* of interpellation, and their respective roles, are reflected in the very structure of all ideology."[57]

In other words, just as actors perform a script in the mise-en-scène of stage or screen, citizens perform an ideological script that subtly makes them think they freely chose the words themselves. The easiest examples are clichéd compliments that change from generation to generation, such as *groovy, neat, hip, phat, hot, cool, lit,* and so on. Hearing these terms applied to cultural practices, then, affects the way people actually *see* things. When a tan was called ugly centuries ago, people actually saw a tanned person as ugly, in radical contrast to the twentieth century, when people showered praise on a tan as cool or awesome. Language therefore changes not only seeing but human behavior, as when women in one era never walked in the sun without a parasol (a word that means "against the sun"), whereas a century later women would lie for hours in the sun to work on their tans. Both groups are manipulated by signifiers of their culture. Cinema, of course, has its own language of signs, leading another disciple of Saussure, Roland Barthes, to use photography and film to argue, in 1967, that "only language acts, 'performs,' and not 'me.'"[58] Like Althusser, Barthes turned Saussure's theory of signs into an inescapable theater, where the scripts of ideological state apparatuses control what all people think, say, and do—from auteur directors to popcorn guzzling spectators.

---

[56]Peter Wollen, "The Semiology of the Cinema," in Furstenau, *Film Theory Reader*, 171.

[57]Louis Althusser, "Ideology and Ideological State Apparatuses (Notes Towards an Investigation)," in *Lenin and Philosophy and Other Essays*, trans. Ben Brewster (New York: Monthly Review Press, 1971), 182, 177. Althusser was heavily influenced by Saussure's semiology through the work of anthropologist Claude Lèvi-Strauss and psychologist Jacques Lacan.

[58]Roland Barthes, "The Death of the Author," trans. Stephen Heath, in Leitch, *Norton Anthology*, 1323. For more about the power of language to change behavior, see Crystal Downing, *Changing Signs of Truth: A Christian Introduction to the Semiotics of Communication* (Downers Grove, IL: IVP Academic, 2011).

In reaction to the determinism of apparatus theory, Peter Wollen published *Signs and Meaning in the Cinema* in 1969, a book so highly regarded that an expanded version was released forty-four years later, in 2013. Wollen offers a different theory of signs, one developed by a contemporary of Saussure, American philosopher Charles Sanders Peirce (1839–1914). After earning Harvard University's first summa cum laude chemistry degree, Peirce became fascinated with the logic of perception, developing a science of signs that he called semiotic rather than semiology. The Greek root word for both words, *sēmeion*, means "sign" and appears repeatedly in the Greek New Testament, as with the birth of Jesus: "This will be a *sēmeion* to you: you will find a baby wrapped in cloths and lying in a manger" (Lk 2:12). That baby, of course, was part of the Trinity. For Peirce, all signs are part of a trinity as well.

## C. S. Peirce and the Mind of the Viewer

Saussure saw every *sēmeion* as dyadic, made up of a signifier and its signified meaning, or, as Wollen summarizes, a preexisting "code" and its culturally determined "meaning."[59] Peirce, in contrast, considered every *sēmeion* triadic, composed of an object, a representamen, and an interpretant. For example, an object such as a piano can represent different things to different people, each interpretant actually seeing (not "interpreting") the representamen differently, a difference resulting not from capitalist manipulations but from life experiences, which are nevertheless influenced by culture. For example, one person may see a piano as a representamen of oppression due to onerous years of parent-enforced piano lessons; another may see a piano as the source of uplifting beauty. It is the same object for both, but each interpretant sees the representamen according to what Peirce calls "habits of perception."

Many well-crafted films focus on habits of perception, often playing with the perceptual habits of their viewers. Take, for example, *Das Leben der Anderen*, or *The Lives of Others* (Florian Henckel von Donnersmarck, 2006), which rightly won many awards, including the Oscar for Best Foreign Language Film. The protagonist, Gerd, a member of the secret police in 1984 East Germany, has been molded by habits of Marxist perception that justify spying on citizens, especially artists suspected of challenging communist ideology. Numerous

---

[59]Wollen, "Semiology of the Cinema," 171.

shots of Gerd wearing earphones in a dreary attic space are intercut with the bright, art-filled apartment of the playwright whose apartment he has bugged. Soon comes the *sēmeion* of a piano. Crosscutting allows us to see the playwright playing a piece called "Sonata for a Good Man," with Gerd listening in the attic. Then, after a medium shot from Gerd's left side, his earphones central to the screen, the shot pans clockwise from the viewers' perspective to show a faint appreciative smile on Gerd's formerly dour face. The diegetic music not only changes Gerd's habits of perception but also challenges us to contemplate the *sēmeion* "Sonata for a Good Man." Who is the good man here? It depends on habits of perception that shape the interpretant.

Peirce became so fascinated with the dependence of perception on the triadic nature of signs that he developed an exhausting "ten trichotomies by which signs can be classified . . . yielding a possible 59,049 classes of sign."[60] Woolen, along with film theorists to follow, focused attention on the most understandable of Peirce's numerous triads, wherein the interpretant sees the representamen as either an icon, an index, or a symbol. Wollen uses the cross for illustration: "There is no doubt that the cross can serve as a phatic signal [icon] and as a degenerate index, but this should be radically distinguished from the conceptual content articulated by the symbolic sign."[61]

Here's how Christians might understand what Wollen means. Most believers see the cross as an index, something that points to that which caused it. Just as smoke is an index of fire, a cross points to the fact that God loved the world so much that he took on flesh to die for our sins. By calling it a "degenerate index," Wollen probably means that the cross has become a magic token for many, worn around the neck because it points to the "magic" of Christ's resurrection, as when someone holds up a cross in horror movies to keep a demon at bay: degenerate indeed!

In contrast, many see the cross as a culturally constructed symbol, representing multiple aspects of Christian faith, much as a crescent and star symbolizes Islam. Indeed, we know the cross was culturally constructed because it was rarely used as a sign for Christianity until Emperor Constantine outlawed the persecution of believers and convened the first Ecumenical Council in

---

[60]Jonathan Culler, *The Pursuit of Signs: Semiotics, Literature, Deconstruction: An Augmented Edition with a New Preface by the Author* (Ithaca, NY: Cornell University Press, 2002), 23.

[61]Wollen, "Semiology of the Cinema," 183.

325 CE. In Peirce's terms, Christians before Constantine saw the cross not as symbol of their faith but as an icon, "a sign which represents its object mainly by its similarity to it."[62] For these early Christians, then, the image of a cross sustained its similarity to torture devices still being used by Roman soldiers, explaining why, instead of crosses, they drew images of Noah's ark in the catacombs where they worshiped.[63] The cross, for them, was an icon of persecution, whereas Noah's ark provided a symbol of God's salvation for the faithful.[64]

How one sees signs, then, depends on perceptions shared by a community. As Peirce puts it, "The very origin of the conception of reality shows that this conception essentially involves the notion of a COMMUNITY, without definite limits, and capable of a definite increase of knowledge."[65] Rather than the psychoanalytic emphasis of apparatus theory, then, Peirce's semiotic is incarnational, for it emphasizes the *bodies* of those seeing a sign—bodies made up of different races, ethnicities, sexualities, and so on, all of which are situated in particular times and places that affect their beliefs. Peirce's notion of community, of course, has powerful implications for Christians, who are called to worship our trinitarian God in community, where our interpretants might be infused with Christlike habits of perception.

The implications for screening movies should also be clear, as any English speaker who has viewed a Hollywood film in another country can testify: audiences that do not speak English often laugh and groan at different places, for they see signs differently.

### SEEING WITH PEIRCED EYES

Art historian Kaja Silverman endorsed Wollen's focus on Peirce in a 1983 book titled *The Subject of Semiotics*. Saussure's semiology, she argues, "provides no way of distinguishing between linguistic signifiers, photographic signifiers, or

---

62Wollen, "Semiology of the Cinema," 173-74. As Wollen goes on to explain, Peirce also considered diagrams to be indexical, for they visualize what they communicate, like a diagram of the number of deaths each month from a virus.

63Jack P. Lewis, *A Study of the Interpretation of Noah and the Flood in Jewish and Christian Literature* (Leiden: Brill, 1968), 11.

64For more details about early Christian icons, in Peirce's sense, see Downing, *Changing Signs of Truth*, 211-13.

65Quoted in Kaja Silverman, *The Subject of Semiotics* (New York: Oxford University Press, 1983), 17. See also Roger A. Ward, *Peirce and Religion: Knowledge, Transformation, and the Reality of God* (Lanham, MD: Lexington Books, 2018), 3.41, 3.60.

signifiers generated by the codes of editing, camera movement, lighting, and sound. Peirce's scheme, on the other hand, enables us to make a number of valuable distinctions."[66] On the most obvious level, images on screen are icons in Peirce's sense, looking like what they represent, whether a refrigerator, a dragon, or a kiss. But, as Silverman adds, an image on screen can also be seen as indexical, pointing to what caused it, whether "exposing film stock to light which organizes objects in space" or editing the exposed stock to create crosscutting, dissolves, match cuts, and so on.[67] Unfortunately, many Christians value images on screen only by turning them into symbols, thus ignoring the multiple signs of indexical artistry in a film. Such viewers become one-dimensional seers, much like apparatus theorists who see film only as an index of ideological state apparatuses.

The same decade Silverman published *The Subject of Semiotics*, French philosopher Gilles Deleuze explained that he "borrowed from Peirce a certain number of terms whilst changing their meaning" in order to offer another way to view cinema, by seeing the passage of time itself through the creation of disorienting signs on screen.[68] Then, almost twenty-five years after Wollen applied Peirce's semiotic to film theory, Johannes Ehrat published *Cinema and Semiotic: Peirce and Film Aesthetics, Narration, and Representation*.[69] Admirably seeking to explain the complexity of Peirce's work, which Peirce himself calls "a very snarl of twine," Ehrat employs vocabulary based on Peirce's 59,049 classes of sign, leading to sentences such as, "'Once upon a time' functions semiosically as an 'uncoupling' de-Dicent, 'de-Indexizer'; it quite literally disorients spatiotemporally and constructs a new universe with a Symbolic, Legisign Interpretant: the plot."[70]

Between the cynicism of apparatus theory and the snarled complexity of Peirce's semiotic, it is no wonder that many film scholars called for the end of film theory altogether.

---

[66]Silverman, *Subject of Semiotics*, 222-23. Some might indict Silverman for still supporting apparatus theory in this, her first book, but her accessible prose draws subtle distinctions helpful for understanding the nuances of film theory.

[67]Silverman, *Subject of Semiotics*, 23.

[68]Gilles Deleuze, "Recapitulation of Images and Signs," in Furstenau, *Film Theory Reader*, 190.

[69]Johannes Ehrat, *Cinema and Semiotic: Peirce and Film Aesthetics, Narration, and Representation* (Toronto: University of Toronto Press, 2005), 11. For more on Peirce and film, see Warren Buckland, *The Cognitive Semiotics of Film* (Cambridge: Cambridge University Press, 2000).

[70]Charles Lock, "Peirce Unbound," *The Semiotic Review of Books* 4, no. 3 (1993): 2-3; Ehrat, *Cinema and Semiotic*, 134.

## Peering Past Peirce: Cognitivism and Reception Theory

Even though, or perhaps because, Peirce is impenetrably complex at times, many film scholars indiscriminately lumped his semiotic theory together with the semiology of apparatus theory, repudiating both together as "grand theory."

The most famous challengers of grand theory are David Bordwell and Noël Carroll, who published a book in 1996 called *Post-theory: Reconstructing Film Studies.* They sought to turn attention back to the importance of cinema history, which includes the history of a movie's reception, as well as to the historical development of film form. The latter, often called neoformalism, celebrates cinematic techniques as artistic developments instead of psychological manipulators. Bordwell and Carroll thus encourage a more scientific approach known as cognitivism, which assesses how "perceptions, thoughts, beliefs, desires, intention, plans, skills, and feelings" affect each viewer's understanding of and response to a movie.[71] Ironically, Peirce, a Harvard-trained chemist, would readily agree.

The cognitive approach of Bordwell and Carroll parallels the development of reception theory, which relies on empirical evidence from viewer surveys. As Henry Jenkins summarizes, "Reception theory and audience research asks basic questions about how we make sense of the movies and what they mean in our lives. Within this paradigm, audiences are understood to be active rather than passive, to be engaged in a *process of making,* rather than simply absorbing, meanings."[72] Sayers would be delighted by the suggestion that viewers participate in the process of creative making by exercising receptive power.

## New Technologies, New Analogies

Harmonizing with reception theory, some film scholars have contemplated whether the development of digital technology affects cognition and hence the way viewers see cinema. While many scholars considered digital projection revolutionary, theorist John Belton calls it a "false revolution," noting, "Audiences viewing digital projection will not experience the cinema differently, as those who heard sound, saw color, or experienced widescreen and

---

[71]David Bordwell and Noël Carroll, eds., *Post-theory: Reconstructing Film Studies* (Madison: University of Wisconsin Press, 1996). The quotation is from David Bordwell, "A Case for Cognitivism," *Iris: A Journal of Theory on Image and Sound* 9 (Spring 1989): 13.

[72]Henry Jenkins, "Reception Theory and Audience Research: The Mystery of the Vampire's Kiss," emphasis added, https://web.mit.edu/~21fms/People/henry3/vampkiss.html.

stereo sound for the first time did." In Sayers's terms, the power over viewer response differs little from the power of "traditional 35mm film."[73]

The real revolution therefore lies in the energy of the making, an energy that affects the idea in the mind of the filmmaker. As Noel Carroll recognizes, "We tend to understand our own tools and inventions more readily than that which we have not created. . . . We know a great deal about what we create in virtue of making them to perform the tasks that they successfully perform."[74] In fact, as Belton notes, computer-generated imaging and editing has created better opportunities for independent filmmakers, including Christian filmmakers, due to "the relative cheapness of the technology."[75] Rather than being subservient to money-minded producers, independent filmmakers have greater freedom to exercise the mind of the maker while maintaining the integrity of the work.

Along with this revolution of digitized energy comes a new analogy for creativity in filmmaking: the art of painting rather than that of architecture. After all, in film-based cinema, directors use actual buildings for establishing shots; the set dresser places props into the mise-en-scène for architectonic effect; film editors cut and reassemble film shots like the builders in Sayers's *Zeal of Thy House*, who cut and reassemble materials to construct the tower of a cathedral. In contrast, as William J. Mitchell argues, "computational tools for transforming, combing, altering, and analyzing images are as essential to the digital artist as brushes and pigments to a painter."[76] Film theorist Lev Manovich appropriates this analogy to the digital making of movies, wherein computer programs enable the creation of outrageous special effects or naturalistic background scenes on the canvas of a green screen: "Given that an artist is easily able to manipulate digitized footage either as a whole or frame by frame, a film in a general sense becomes a series of paintings." Furthermore, "Digital hand-painting is also the most obvious example of the return of cinema to its nineteenth-century origins—in this case, the hand-crafted images of magic-lantern slides . . . and Zoetrope."[77] According to this analogy, digital

---

[73]John Belton, "Digital Cinema: A False Revolution," in Furstenau, *Film Theory Reader*, 286.

[74]Noël Carroll, "Film/Mind Analogies," in Furstenau, *Film Theory Reader*, 67.

[75]Belton, "Digital Cinema," 287.

[76]William J. Mitchell, *The Reconfigured Eye: Visual Truth in the Post-photographic Era* (Cambridge, MA: MIT Press, 1992), 7.

[77]Lev Manovich, "Digital Cinema and the Moving Image," in Furstenau, *Film Theory Reader*, 250.

technology generates the kind of power Sayers exercised in childhood, having seen both magic-lantern and zoetrope displays (see the coda of this book).

## FOR THE LOVE OF CREATION: THE END(S) OF FILM THEORY

This chapter demonstrates the relevance of Sayers's Christian aesthetic to secular, sometimes downright anti-Christian film theorists. Sayers would have been especially intrigued by Peirce, who inspired film scholars to see beyond the mere manipulation of icons on screen, instead assessing the indexical and symbolic power of the triadic sign.

In fact, Peirce, whom Wollen calls "the most original American thinker there has been," came to believe that every sign functions as "a divine trinity," and, "in many respects, this trinity agrees with the Christian trinity."[78] Quite tellingly, this statement remains unpublished. Though scholars understand that Peirce focused on logical assertions that might reconcile science with Christianity, few know that Peirce believed creativity fulfilled the *imago Dei.*

During a lecture to British logicians in 1869, Peirce invoked St. Augustine to proclaim, "He who does not take refuge in reason has abandoned the honor of his creation, since it was by reason that he was made in the image of God." He also argues, "The power of judging the unseen by the seen—even if it be applied to the most sordid and wicked objects—*affiliates man to the Creator of all things.*"[79] His words should remind us of Sayers's insight, first quoted in the introduction, which is shared by many film theorists: "Art that is the true image of experience is true art, even though the experience is ugly or immoral (as the image of God is still the image of God, even in a wicked man)."[80]

Studied by both film theorists and theologians, Peirce provides an apt culmination to this chapter. Commenting on the apostle John's statement, "Whoever does not love does not know God, because God is love" (1 Jn 4:8), Peirce writes, "Everybody can see that the statement of St. John is the formula of an evolutionary philosophy, which teaches that growth comes only from love. . . . Suppose, for example, that I have an *idea* that interests me. It is *my creation.* It is my creature; . . . it is a little person. *I love it*; and I will sink myself

[78]Wollen, "Semiology of Cinema," 173. Peirce's unpublished statement is quoted in Donna M. Orange, "Peirce's Conception of God: A Developmental Study," *Peirce Studies* 2 (September 1984): 21.

[79]Quoted in Ward, *Peirce and Religion*, 6.37, 2.30, emphasis added.

[80]*Letters* 3:27.

in perfecting it."[81] We are reminded not only of the love for both creative process and product that Truffaut and Sayers shared, but also of their common emphasis on wanting to perfect an idea. C. S. Peirce's phrase "it is a little person" also foreshadows a 1958 statement by C. S. Lewis: "For poetry too is a little incarnation, giving body to what had been before invisible and inaudible."[82] Despite his reservations over *The Mind of the Maker*, C. S. Lewis may have been more influenced by Sayers than he realized.

---

[81]Quoted in Ward, *Peirce and Religion*, 4.52.

[82]Sayers, "Christian Aesthetic," 39; C. S. Lewis, *Reflections on the Psalms* (New York: Harcourt, 1958), 5.

7

# Seeing Women

## *From* King Kong *to* Barbie

In the 1970s another kind of film theory became pronounced—in more ways than one. This chapter explores how Christians might respond to feminist film theory, with Sayers once again serving as our Virgil, guiding us through the purgatory of blazing rhetoric to a vision of the Son of God.

### In Front of or Behind the Camera: Vane or Vain?

After Sayers invented the character of Harriet Vane (in *Strong Poison*), planning to marry off Lord Peter, she found herself writing more novels to make the aristocratic sleuth worthy of a woman committed to professional integrity. Significantly, she aligns that integrity with photography and cinema in her second Harriet Vane novel.

In *Have His Carcase* (1932), Harriet discovers a crumpled dead man splayed on a beach rock and proceeds to take shots from multiple angles and distances from the corpse. Sayers's description of Harriet's camera work, in fact, sounds like a collection of shots photographed for a cinema montage, from an establishing shot to a long shot to a high-angle shot:

> She had now four films left in the camera. On one, she took a general view of the coast with the body in the foreground, stepping a little way back from the rock for the purpose. On the second, she took a closer view of the line of footprints, stretching from the rock across the sand. . . . On the third, she made a close-up of one of the footprints, holding the camera, set to six feet, at arm's length above her head and pointing the lens directly downwards.[1]

[1]Dorothy L. Sayers, *Have His Carcase*, in *Dorothy L. Sayers: On the Case with Lord Peter Wimsey* (New York: Wings Books, 1991), 160.

After the tide comes in, washing the corpse to sea, Harriet's photographs become the only record of an apparent murder.

Harriet's ability to see and record truth through a camera lens stands in stark contrast to one of the conspirators behind the murder. Wandering around London, the suspect walks through places that emphasize the importance of seeing, cinema theaters as well as the British Museum. Tailed by Wimsey's manservant, Mervyn Bunter, the suspect finally takes a seat in a Haymarket "picture-palace," where Bunter watches his head "outlined against the comparative brightness at the foot of the screen." After the "film shuddered to its close," the suspect makes his way to a lavatory behind the screen while Bunter views a comic short. The suspect, however, puts on a disguise in the restroom, escaping from Bunter's viewing eye. Sayers thus contrasts Harriet Vane, whose camera work reveals truth, with a criminal who merely uses cinema for his own best interests, a distinction between critical engagement and movie escapism as relevant today as in the 1930s. Proving that this reference is not merely coincidental, Sayers has Lord Peter find a "cinema-ticket," confirming that the murdered man enjoyed "talkies."[2]

Harriet's professionalism behind the lens puts her in front of lenses, journalists seeming more interested in photos of this woman once accused of murdering her live-in lover (as recounted in *Strong Poison*) than in the corpse she discovered. As with Harriet, so with cinema: in her day and beyond, women have been valued more for their images before the camera than for their professionalism behind it. As though to reinforce this idea, Sayers inserts into the novel a fashion model whose photograph, signed by another woman's name, is discovered on the victim's body. Rather than an image of truth, the photograph had manipulated the man to believe a fiction, turning the model into the victim's object of desire. We should not be surprised, then, that the idea of women as objects of male desire, rather than as subjects committed to professional integrity, became part of Sayers's Canterbury play several years later. It also becomes key to the history of feminist film theory.

---

[2]Sayers, *Have His Carcase*, 373, 382, 376, 388, 258.

### FEMALE ZEAL: IS IT HUMAN?

As we have seen, *The Zeal of Thy House* celebrates William of Sens as a master craftsman so committed to the integrity of his work that he fulfills the *imago Dei*. At the same time, however, William disdains the power and integrity of women. When he hears that an intelligent widow providing funding for the cathedral wants to peruse his blueprints, he snidely comments about the limits of female intelligence, ending with, "I've no use for women—not in working hours." For him, women are meant to meet the physical needs of zealous males who have finished their creative work for the day.

A year after *The Zeal of Thy House* was first performed in Canterbury Cathedral, Sayers delivered a lecture titled "Are Women Human?" Commissioned in 1938 by a women's society that wanted Sayers to talk about the feminist movement and "sex-equality," the lecture begins with Sayers proclaiming that she refuses to call herself a feminist. Avoiding labels, she practices sex equality rather than preaches it, *The Zeal of Thy House* clearly informing her talk when she states, "There is perhaps only one human being in a thousand who is passionately interested in his job for the job's sake," reminding us of William of Sens. But then she goes on to explain that when the "one person in a thousand is a man, we say, simply, that he is passionately keen on his job; if she is a woman, we say she is a freak."[3] Sayers wrote another play to prove her point.

### *LOVE ALL* AND THE VENICE FILM FESTIVAL

After a successful run of *The Zeal of Thy House* in Canterbury during June 1937, Sayers relaxed by traveling to Venice and Yugoslavia with a friend. On August 8, she wrote a cousin from Venice, sending the address of their hotel. Two days later, Venice hosted its annual film festival. Initiated in 1932, the Venice International Film Festival is the oldest in the world, considered by many to be as important as the Cannes Festival, founded seven years later. Though we have yet to discover letters in which Sayers describes the 1937 Venice festival, we have strong clues that she attended. The very next summer, Sayers once again vacationed in Venice, soon after a London revival of *The Zeal of Thy House*. On August 10, 1938, Sayers wrote her son,

[3]Dorothy L. Sayers, "Are Women Human?," in *Are Women Human?* (Grand Rapids, MI: Eerdmans, 1971), 21, 36.

saying she was enjoying Venice.[4] If Sayers had been annoyed by a city overrun with tourists due to a film festival in 1937, she would not have returned to the very same location at the very same time of year the following summer. Later, in a 1946 lecture, Sayers stated that her only visits to Venice were during August, when mosquitos were "triumphant."[5] The film festival must have surmounted her annoyances.

In between her two trips to Venice, Sayers began writing *Love All*, a play about Brits visiting Venice in August. One character complains about the miserable heat and annoying mosquitos. Significantly, that character, Lydia, acts in film as well as theater and talks about moving with Godfrey, her lover, to the Lido, a Venetian island that became the permanent location of the film festival the year that Sayers first visited (1937).[6] We should not be surprised, then, that Sayers also references Hollywood and "film-star" crushes in *Love All*.[7] She has Godfrey describe Venice as "a type of glorified Piccadilly. Piccadilly in its resurrection body," as though alluding to the London Pavilion in Piccadilly Circus, which had been converted from a declining music hall to a successful cinema palace.[8] Nevertheless, Sayers makes no reference to the Venice Film Festival in her play—perhaps because she had a more important issue to address.

## The Zeal of the Woman

Not long after developing a theology for "the integrity of work" in *The Zeal of Thy House*, Sayers seems to have constructed *Love All* to address the integrity of female work in her own era. After all, William's sexism in *Zeal* might easily be attributed to the fact that he lived in the twelfth century, and Sayers wanted to address her 1930s audiences. Hence, like the sexually promiscuous William, who constructs buildings, she created the sexually promiscuous Godfrey, who constructs novels while sneering at any female vocation besides motherhood. Leaving his wife and son in England while running away to Venice with Lydia,

---

4 *Letters* 2:84, 86-87.

5 Quoted in Barbara Reynolds, "'I Wrote It Just for Fun': A Review of Alzina Stone Dale, ed., *Love All together with Busman's Honeymoon*," *VII: An Anglo-American Literary Review* 6 (1989): 86.

6 Dorothy L. Sayers, *Love All together with Busman's Honeymoon*, ed. Alzina Stone Dale (Kent, OH: Kent State University Press, 1984), 131-33.

7 Sayers, *Love All*, 164, 144.

8 Quoted in Reynolds, "'I Wrote it Just for Fun,'" 90.

Godfrey later discovers that his wife has become a successful playwright during his absence. Apparently assuming that *male* adultery is far more acceptable than mothers working outside the home, he also "hates the idea" of his mistress "going back to the stage."[9] As with William of Sens, Godfrey believes women are meant merely to gratify male sexual desires and domestic needs.

Sayers was not able to give *Love All* the attention it needed, not only due to London productions of *The Zeal of Thy House* in 1938 but also because of her commitment to write a second Canterbury play for the 1939 festival. Having no time "to alter and improve" *Love All,* Sayers was nevertheless pleased to hear audiences "roaring with laughter" when it opened in April 1940.[10] Reminiscent of Shakespearean comedy, *Love All* unmasks hidden identities. Godfrey's mistress, Lydia, gets cast in a play created by Godfrey's wife, who writes under the pseudonym Janet Reed. After discovering their common male partner, the women acknowledge that they love their work more than the self-serving, egocentric Godfrey. As Janet tells Godfrey, "A job's a real thing. Something one's *made*. You ought to know—you're a writer. Wouldn't you rather be valued for your work than for yourself?" When he protests that an author's popularity can wane, Janet tells him, "The work remains," thus paralleling Sayers's repentant William at the end of *Zeal*: "Wipe out my name from men / But not my work."[11] *Love All* is thus Sayers's secular addendum to *Zeal,* giving a woman's point of view.

A little over a year after the opening of *Love All,* Sayers wrote an article called "The Human-Not-Quite-Human," largely in response to the deficiencies she saw in a 1941 symposium called "The Emancipated Woman Comes of Age," published in *Christendom: A Journal of Christian Sociology.*[12] In her response, Sayers imaginatively puts a man in the same position as women: "When he had succeeded in capturing a mate, his name would be taken from him and society would present him with a special title to proclaim his achievement. . . . He would be regaled daily with headlines, such as "Gentleman-Doctor's Discovery," [or] 'Men-Artists at the Academy.'"[13]

---

[9]Sayers, *Love All,* 148.

[10]*Letters* 2:126, 159-60. Though Sayers started approaching theater managers about the play in September 1938, *Love All* did not open until April 1940. See Alzina Stone Dale, ed., introduction to *Love All,* xxx.

[11]Sayers, *Love All,* 174, emphasis original; Sayers, *Zeal of Thy House,* 99.

[12]*Letters* 2:275.

[13]Dorothy L. Sayers, "The Human-Not-Quite-Human," in *Are Women Human?,* 56-58.

Using ironic reversals like those employed by Virginia Woolf in *A Room of One's Own* (1929), Sayers exposes how language perpetuates the idea that women are not quite human. Doing so, she anticipates by four decades French filmmaker Agnès Varda (1928–2019), who explained why she didn't want to be known as a *woman* filmmaker, echoing Sayers's commitment to the integrity of work: "Filmmaking is specific work. I do it. I try to do it well. . . . Do you ask a man who doesn't have hair if he considers himself a bald filmmaker? He's a man with no hair, and he's a filmmaker."[14] Ironically, the early years of cinema welcomed female creativity, providing far-reaching opportunities for women committed to the integrity of work. A contemporary of Sayers provides a superb example.

## June Mathis: Screenwriter and Studio Executive

When Sayers joyfully tried her hand at screenwriting, her 1920 adaptation of *Blood and Sand* by Vicente Blasco Ibañez went nowhere. Little did she know that the person in Hollywood who turned *Blood and Sand* into one of the most commercially successful films of 1922 was a woman she would have liked immensely, June Mathis (1887–1927). Though Sayers was born in highbrow Oxford and Mathis in the mining district of Leadville, Colorado, the two demonstrated a similar exuberance over theater during their adolescence. While Sayers was performing in plays at boarding school and during her university days, Mathis was earning money on the Broadway stage. Both, however, decided they wanted to be writers, Sayers starting a women's writing group at Somerville College soon after she matriculated to Oxford in 1912, even as Mathis, by 1913, was "spending most of her spare time writing."[15]

Their careers went different directions because Sayers began her screenwriting efforts in France during the postwar decline of its film industry, whereas Mathis moved to California during the rise of Hollywood. By 1920, when Sayers was constructing cinema scenarios for a little-known British director, Mathis had already become the head of the scenario department at Metro, where she wrote her first adaptation of a Vicente Blasco Ibañez novel,

---

[14]Quoted in Ally Acker, *Reel Women: Pioneers of the Cinema 1896 to the Present* (New York: Continuum, 1991), 305.

[15]Thomas J. Slater, "June Mathis: A Woman Who Spoke Through Silents," in *American Silent Film: Discovering Marginalized Voices*, ed. Gregg Bachman and Thomas J. Slater (Carbondale, IL: Southern Illinois University Press, 2002), 203.

*The Four Horsemen of the Apocalypse*. The 1921 film became one of the highest-grossing silent movies of all time, turning Rudolph Valentino, a Mathis discovery, into an international star. In *The Rise of the American Film*, Lewis Jacobs notes that many consider *The Four Horsemen* "a magnificent work of art," largely due to the visionary leadership of Mathis, one of the first screenwriters to consider how visual settings and actor movements written into the script itself might lead to more coherent visual artistry.[16] Mathis, in other words, had what Sayers would later call the mind of the maker, a commitment to creativity that she passed on to many who worked for her, such as highly regarded Irish film director Rex Ingram (1892–1950), who later mentored Michael Powell, the director who dined with Sayers.

The parallels continue. The year Mathis's acclaimed *Four Horsemen* premiered was the same year Sayers turned from screenwriting to the work that brought her acclaim, detective fiction. In 1921 Sayers began composing *Whose Body?*, which was published by an American company in April 1923, the same month *Photoplay* published the following statement about June Mathis, who was now working for Goldwyn: "Probably the most powerful woman in the motion picture industry today is June Mathis. This well known writer seems to be the head and shoulders of the Goldwyn organization at present, and rumor says her word is law and is final upon every angle of every production being made."[17] As Anthony Slide explains in *Early Women Directors*, "During the silent era, women might be said to have virtually controlled the film industry."[18] Since many scholars believe film reached its apex as an art form during the silent era, why have most people never heard of June Mathis and other female powerhouses of silent film?

## Silent Cinema and the Silencing of Women

In *Reel Women: Pioneers of the Cinema 1896 to the Present*, Ally Acker notes that once filmmaking "began to be a big business," women who had been holding studios together "were promptly shown the door."[19] Alfred Hitchcock summarizes the problem with disturbing irony: "American scriptwriters were all

---

16Quoted in Acker, *Reel Women*, 164.

17*Photoplay*, April 1923, quoted in Slater, "June Mathis," 202.

18Anthony Slide, *Early Women Directors* (New York: A. S. Barnes, 1977), 9.

19Acker, *Reel Women*, xxiv. For another brilliant woman in the industry later lost to history, see Alice McMahan, *Alice Guy-Blache: Lost Visionary of the Cinema* (New York: Continuum, 2003).

women, and I learned screenplay writing from them. There were many opportunities at that time for women to work in films. This kind of sedentary work was considered appropriate for women, like sewing. When films became more important, these positions were no longer readily available to women."[20] Such attitudes were not unique to Hollywood, as Sayers exemplifies. Though doing all the work required of males at Oxford University, outperforming many of them by achieving first-class honors in 1915, she was not granted a bachelor's degree. It was assumed that women did not need degrees since their primary calling—caring for children, as either mothers or teachers—did not require it. Change came with World War I as women heroically kept "the wheels of academic life turning" at Oxford while males were being sent to the front.[21] Hence, not long after the Great War ended, Oxford decided to grant women degrees, many retroactively, in recognition for all they had achieved.

Nevertheless, as in Hollywood, money seemed to have been the university's primary motivation. In a book about Sayers's alma mater, Somerville College, Pauline Adams explains that the Great War depleted Oxford's financial resources, making it economically advantageous to welcome and reward female students. Hence, during the same month Sayers conferred on the director her scenario for a film adaptation of *Blood and Sand*, Oxford University retroactively conferred on Sayers a bachelor's and a master's degree in recognition for her past academic accomplishments. She and the other women honored in the 1920 ceremony, however, were given soft caps rather than the traditional hard mortarboards worn by males at Oxford.[22] Though a problematic symbol, it is not as distressing as the disappearance from film history of June Mathis, hailed soon after her death in 1927 as "one of the two greatest [screenwriters] who have yet lived."[23]

Like Sayers, June Mathis was more committed to the integrity of her work than to preaching an ideological agenda. Sayers, in fact, was suspicious of any art made for the "betterment" of society, believing that authors should never write "for money, or for reputation, or for edification," arguing, "To

---

20Quoted in Charlotte Chandler, *It's Only a Movie: Alfred Hitchcock, A Personal Biography* (London: Simon & Schuster, 2005), 40.

21Pauline Adams, *Somerville for Women: An Oxford College 1879–1993* (Oxford: Oxford University Press, 1996), 150.

22Adams, *Somerville for Women*, 150, 152.

23Slater, "June Mathis," 283n49.

make any work with one eye on the audience does, in fact, tend to damage the integrity of the work."[24] Mathis expressed something similar: "Many look at the monetary success of well-known writers and their whole thought is centered on that; whereas, if they will forget ultimate success and simply write because they cannot help writing, and for the very love of the work, success will come unawares."

Sayers uses the exact same phrase, "love of the work," in *The Mind of the Maker*.[25] Knowing that love can generate more change than "loud slogans or hard-and-fast assertions," Sayers refuses to endorse the feminist rhetoric of her day: "'A woman is as good as a man' is as meaningless as to say, . . . 'a poet is as good as an engineer' or 'an elephant is a good as a racehorse'—it means nothing whatever until you add: 'at doing what?'"[26] Sayers's rhetorical question, "at doing what?" was also asked by feminist film theorists.

## GAZING AT THE HUMAN-NOT-QUITE-HUMAN ON SCREEN

In the 1970s, film theorist Laura Mulvey argued that cinema has tended to present female protagonists as "objects" of the "gaze," valued primarily for how they look, the camera often focusing on certain body parts, with close-ups on lips, legs, breasts. In a landmark essay, reproduced in almost every film theory anthology ever published, Mulvey explains that the "determining male gaze projects its fantasy onto the female figure, which is styled accordingly. In their traditional exhibitionist role women are simultaneously looked at and displayed, with their appearance coded for strong visual and erotic impact so that they can be said to connote *to-be-looked-at-ness*."[27] Few realize that Sayers anticipated the famous Mulvey by forty-five years, having alluded to a male gaze while delivering "Are Women Human?" the same year she was working on *Love All* and her essay for the British Film Institute's *Sight and Sound*. In her 1938 speech she comments to her female audience, "We are asked: 'Why do you want to go about in trousers? They are extremely unbecoming to most of you.'" And then she counters such to-be-looked-at-ness with, "As a human

[24]*Letters* 2:218, 326.

[25]Quoted in Slater, "June Mathis," 281n29; Dorothy L. Sayers, *The Mind of the Maker* (New York: HarperCollins, 1987), 218.

[26]Sayers, "Are Women Human?," 21-22.

[27]Laura Mulvey, "Visual Pleasure and Narrative Cinema," in *Visual and Other Pleasures* (Bloomington: Indiana University Press, 1989), 19.

being, I like comfort and dislike draughts. If the trousers do not attract you, so much the worse; for the moment I do not want to attract you."[28] That clearly was not the message presented by classical Hollywood movies.

Take, for example, *Romancing the Stone* (Robert Zemeckis, 1984), a high-action romantic comedy that won a Golden Globe Award for Best Motion Picture. In the opening scene, Kathleen Turner, the glamorous "it" actress of the early 1980s, looks not just disheveled but downright frumpy. Typing away at a romance novel in overwrought solitude, she plays a mousy writer who finds release by breaking open one of the many tiny alcohol bottles she has spirited away from assorted airplane rides. During a trip to Colombia, however, the wallflower novelist is saved from villains by an exotic bird hunter (played by a dashing Michael Douglas), and together they experience adventures more exciting than any she has ever imagined. Transforming into a gorgeous woman, she sports better hair and makeup in the jungles of South America than in the urban flat where the film begins. All she needed was love of a chivalric man, not love for her work as a novelist. Sayers would be appalled, having criticized such outrageous scenarios over forty years earlier, suggesting that chivalric romance tends to deny women "an opportunity for intelligence in their work."[29]

Though *Romancing the Stone* is now considered entertaining fluff, it earned Kathleen Turner the Golden Globe for best actress in 1985, probably due to her willingness to look so frumpy at the film's start. Attitudes have changed considerably since then, with beautiful female actors now willing to perform without coiffed hair and heavy makeup for the entire film. And specialists in LGTBQ studies note that different sexualities gaze in different ways. Mulvey has therefore been criticized for thinking too much like the apparatus theorists discussed in the preceding chapter, theorists who imply that viewers have no control over their responses to gender and sex on screen. It is a critique Mulvey acknowledges.[30] Nevertheless, honorific ceremonies like the Golden

---

[28]Sayers, "Are Women Human?," 28-29.

[29]*Letters* 2:274. I have borrowed several sentences in this paragraph from my essay "Romancing the Crone," *The Cresset* 70, no. 4 (Easter 2007): 45.

[30]See E. Ann Kaplan, "Is the Gaze Male?," in *The Film Theory Reader: Debates and Arguments*, ed. Marc Furstenau (New York: Routledge, 2010), 210; Kenneth MacKinnon, "After Mulvey: Male Erotic Objectification," in *The Body's Perilous Pleasures: Dangerous Desires and Contemporary Culture*, ed. Michelle Aaron (Edinburgh: Edinburgh University Press, 1999), 13-29. For summaries of feminist theorists who have challenged Mulvey, see Robert Stam, *Film Theory: An Introduction* (Malden, MA: Blackwell, 2000),

Globes and Academy Awards perpetuate women as objects of the gaze, evident as cameras linger on celebrity females posing on the red carpet in revealing apparel, the press highlighting presumed embarrassment when two women wear the same designer dress. In contrast, most male celebrities sport similar black tuxedos, as though to say it is the integrity of their work, not their appearance, that identifies them as distinctively human. Women thus become complicit with their own degradation as sexualized objects of the gaze.

Sayers identifies another complicity in "Are Women Human?" Rather than pursuing a job for which they have both love and talent, women all too often merely decide "to copy the men" to garner respect. Though Sayers identified this problem in 1938, it has become especially evident in the last several decades of cinema, when female protagonists can kick, punch, knock out, or outrun any male—while never smearing their makeup or compromising their form-fitting, sexy outfits. Such movies deliver a counterfeminist message, that women are strong primarily when they copy male actions. Sayers, in contrast, argues, "It is ridiculous to take on a man's job just in order to be able to say that 'a woman has done it—yah!' The only decent reason for tackling any job is that it is your job, and you want to do it."[31] Our gaze should be directed toward the integrity of their work, not the beauty of their bodies.

## APING THE GAZE: KING KONG

The King Kong franchise provides an interesting lesson in beauty on screen. Setting records for film attendance when it was released in 1933, the original *King Kong,* one of the few films screened by Sayers's friend C. S. Lewis, was itself about filmmaking.

Directed and produced by Merian C. Cooper and Ernest B. Schoedsack, *King Kong* begins with a film director named Carl Denham, who takes his crew to the isolated Skull Island for movie footage. Island natives kidnap Denham's fledgling actress, Ann, to offer her as a sacrifice to appease a twenty-five-foot gorilla that has broken through a gated wall they had erected. Film crew and sailors attempt a rescue, battling primeval creatures until Driscoll, Ann's love

174-77; and Julie Kelso, "Gazing at Impotence in Henry King's *David and Bathsheba,*" in *Screening Scripture: Intertextual Connections Between Scripture and Film*, ed. George Aichele and Richard Walsh (Harrisburg, PA: Trinity Press International, 2002), 165.

[31]Sayers, "Are Women Human?," 27, 30.

interest, steals her away from Kong. After subduing the giant ape, Denham and Driscoll ship it to New York to display it as "The Eighth Wonder of the World." Shackled to a Manhattan theater stage, King Kong breaks his chains when flashbulb-popping cameras anger him. The huge creature ravages Manhattan until he finds the female object of his gaze, eventually climbing to the top of the Empire State Building with Ann in tow. On top of the skyscraper, Kong swats at biplanes reminiscent of flying pterodactyls he had battled from the summit of his island lair. When bullets finally bring him down, the film ends with the iconic line, "It wasn't the airplanes; it was beauty killed the beast."

Lewis described his response to *King Kong* sixteen years later, telling a correspondent, "I thought parts of 'King Kong' (especially where the natives make a stand after he's broken the gate) magnificent, but the New York parts contemptible."[32] Peter Jackson, who adapted for the screen J. R. R. Tolkien's *Lord of the Rings* trilogy, seems to have shared some of Lewis's views. When he cowrote, directed, and produced an adaptation of *King Kong* seventy years later, Jackson totally subverted the traditional gaze, most remarkably in the New York scenes. Though he ends the 2005 film with the famous line "It was beauty that killed the beast," he deflects beauty from Ann as the object of Kong's gaze, focusing instead on the beauty of creation, both God's and that produced by the *imago Dei*.[33]

## Darker Aspects of Creative Love

A sequel to Jackson's *King Kong* entered development in 2013, with Jackson in the role of producer. When Warner Brothers acquired the rights, however, the project went through multiple directors and alterations in scripting, to the end that Jackson had little to do with the final film. Nevertheless, *Kong: Skull Island* (Jordan Vogt-Roberts, 2017) intensifies Jackson's vision, focusing on the very idea of vision itself. Rather than simply challenging the way people have interpreted the line "It was beauty that killed the beast," the film drops the line while changing the plot, encouraging viewers to think about how *they* see truth, beauty, and goodness, including the truth, beauty, and goodness of cinema.

---

32 Walter Hooper, ed., *The Collected Letters of C. S. Lewis*, vol. 2, *Books, Broadcasts, and the War, 1931–1949* (San Francisco: HarperSanFrancisco, 2004), 910. In a letter to Arthur Greeves on September 1, 1933, Lewis mentions he and Warnie recently screened *King Kong* but says nothing about it (120).

33 For a lengthy analysis of Jackson's film, see Crystal Downing, "The Ape(x) of Beauty," *The Cresset* 69, no. 5 (June 2006): 25-29.

*Skull Island* begins during World War II, with Japanese and American pilots shooting down each other's aircraft, both parachuting onto a fog-covered island where a huge ape disrupts their land combat. The diegesis then jumps to 1973, during the Vietnam War, when a military unit accompanies researchers seeking to explore an island hidden from view until new technologies exposed its existence. Thus begins the film's emphasis on how people see, the researchers hoping to witness primeval creatures unhindered by human civilization. One, in fact, seeks to prove the hollow-earth theory proposed in the seventeenth century by Edmond Halley, of Halley's comet fame. Indeed, the concept of a hollow earth still has endorsers in our own day, especially among conspiracy theorists, even though most scientists discounted Halley's theory in the eighteenth century. Different people see reality differently.

In the film, different visions generate antagonisms among the American and British visitors, especially once Kong appears. Lieutenant Colonel Packard (Samuel Jackson) and some of his Vietnam soldiers seek to destroy Kong, whereas others point out that the giant ape saved them from a dinosaur-like lizard. Film viewers are thus encouraged to reflect on how they see their own enemies, as well as to consider their assumptions about war. Indeed, the professional photographer accompanying the expedition is antiwar, making clear her disdain for military activities in Vietnam. Both sides, of course, can justify the divergent way they see the truth of war—as can Christians, some advocating Augustine's just war theory, others endorsing the Bible-based pacifism of Amish Christians, whose views become clear in the award-winning *Witness* (Peter Weir, 1985).

To symbolize the different ways individuals see reality, the makers of *Skull Island* take advantage of their medium, inserting extreme close-ups on Lieutenant Colonel Packard's eyes, which fill the entire screen, followed by graphic match cuts to extreme close-ups on Kong's eyes. Which eyes see most accurately? Packard, who earned viewer respect at the start of the film, becomes more and more irrational in his violence, aiming his gun at his own men, whereas the ape, whom viewers first see as a threat to life, saves the visitors from a dinosaur-like lizard. Who is the real savage here?

To further emphasize that *Skull Island* is more about vision than about monsters and heroes, the filmmakers include multiple shots of three-foot-high stakes, painted with random lines, bunched together inside the native islanders' fortress. As the camera moves along the stakes, however, viewers suddenly see that, from a certain perspective, the arbitrary lines create pictures of island creatures, including Kong. By thus creating a point-of-view shot for those outside the diegesis, the filmmakers show how seeing depends on one's perspective. This also relates to the way viewers of *Skull Island* see the native islanders who presumably set up the stakes. All natives appear to have been painted with random lines, making it difficult to distinguish male from female, followers from leaders. Point of view changes only as the nobility of the indigenous people's actions becomes apparent—which, of course, is how Christians should see all people: not by external appearances but by the integrity of their character. As with the painted stakes, true seeing comes when we are willing to change our perspective.

Film adaptations often serve as perspective-changing tools, as when Peter Jackson's *King Kong* changed viewer perspective on beauty that killed the beast. Not surprisingly, *Skull Island* alludes to Jackson's film, as well as to *Apocalypse Now* (Francis Ford Coppola, 1979), a film also set during the Vietnam War. Many viewers first recognize the allusion when they hear Richard Wagner's "Ride of the Valkyries" in *Skull Island*'s soundtrack—music used to powerful effect in *Apocalypse Now*, which itself alludes to Joseph Conrad's 1899 novella, *The Heart of Darkness*.

*Apocalypse Now* has its mysterious Kurtz, famously played by Marlon Brando, use the exact same lines as Kurtz in *The Heart of Darkness*: "The horror! The horror!" Almost sixty years earlier, T. S. Eliot, a friend of Sayers, placed Conrad's famous repetition, "The horror! The horror!" in his original epigraph for *The Waste Land* (1922), later mentioning Kurtz at the start of "The Hollow Men" (1925). Not coincidentally, the makers of *Apocalypse Now* placed on Kurtz's desk two books that Eliot said influenced *The Waste Land*. Allusion on top of allusion on top of allusion.

What does this have to do with seeing? Sayers, as we have seen, would answer that great artists recognize how much their own seeing is shaped by art that precedes them: "former streams of beauty, emotion, and reflection."[34] Beauty is not simply about seeing women on screen, as in the 1933 *King Kong*, or even about seeing the beauty of nature and architecture, as in the 2005 *King*

[34]Sayers, *Mind of the Maker*, 121. For implications of Sayers's phrase, see chapter five.

*Kong*. For Sayers and most cinephiles, works of genuine creativity often direct our eyes (and/or ears) to the emotion and reflection elicited by earlier works of art. Hence, upon hearing Wagner's piece from *Der Ring des Nibelungen,* cinephiles suddenly see why most of *Skull Island* is set during the Vietnam War, for that era echoes the diegesis of *Apocalypse Now,* a former stream of beauty that itself echoes Joseph Conrad's 1899 novella, *Heart of Darkness.*

As John Gatins, one of the screenwriters for *Skull Island,* explains, "I liked the idea [from *Heart of Darkness,* echoed in *Apocalypse Now*] of people moving upriver to face a misunderstood force that they think of as a villain, but ultimately they come to realize is much more complicated."[35] People, in other words, change their points of view when they gain new information and/or insight, which also happens with the viewing of film. The more one pays attention to the cinematic medium and becomes acquainted with earlier works of art, the more one can see truth, beauty, and goodness within creatively made film. Rather than simplistically reducing cinema to interesting stories starring gorgeous guys and lovely ladies, viewers can participate in the integrity of the work. This, then, returns the chapter to where it started, cinema's historic emphasis on the to-be-looked-at-ness of females.

Desiring to challenge how people see reality, especially on screen, the makers of *Skull Island* include a challenge to the *viewing* of women, in both senses of the term. They do so by turning the character that most closely resembles the blond Ann of earlier Kong movies into the expedition's professional photographer, standing behind her own camera more than in front of their cameras. Rather than becoming the object of Kong's gaze, she controls the gaze by gazing through her own lens. Rarely does she appear without her camera, usually up to her eyes as she photographs realities of the island. *Skull Island* thus emphasizes what Sayers commended—the integrity of work for both males and females. Perhaps this explains why the filmmakers make it difficult to distinguish males from females among the native islanders as well.

Released in 2017, *Skull Island* thus addresses an issue that females in the industry were still encountering, that is, dismissal of the integrity of their work.

---

[35]Mike Fleming, "King Kong Tale 'Skull Island' Gets Rewrite from 'Flight' Scribe John Gatins," Deadline Hollywood, October 30, 2014, archived https://web.archive.org/web/20200701072911/https://deadline.com/2014/10/skull-island-flight-scribe-john-gatins-rewrite-1201268217/.

For example, Jessica Chastain, after winning an Oscar for her performance in *The Eyes of Tammy Faye* (Michael Showalter, 2021), bemoaned "what everyone has been trained to love in actresses: bubbly, sweet, not super intelligent, naïve, blond and boobs." Oscar winner Lupita Nyong'o, who stars in *Black Panther: Wakanda Forever* (Ryan Coogler, 2022), makes a similar point, if even far more subtly: "the undervaluing of women because of their gender doesn't exist in Wakanda."[36] Both would most likely endorse a comment made by Sayers over eighty years earlier: "A woman is just as much an ordinary human being as a man, with the same individual preferences, and with just as much right to the tastes and preferences of an individual."

Later in the same paragraph, however, Sayers comments that denial of this truth is also an "error into which feminist women are, perhaps, a little inclined to fall about themselves."[37] No movie encapsulates this "fall" better than the movie phenomenon of 2023, *Barbie.*

## The Fall of Barbie

Cowritten and directed by Greta Gerwig, *Barbie* was the highest-grossing movie of 2023, the highest-grossing movie ever produced by Warner Brothers, and the highest-grossing movie ever directed by a female. Of course, financial wages from cinema do not reflect film artistry, and movies that fail to recoup their production costs are sometimes considered classics years later.

The rich returns of *Barbie* resulted in part from a money-making phenomenon that began sixty-four years earlier with Mattel's release of the Barbie doll. Baby boomers as well as their grandchildren enjoyed the film's clever visualizations of what it was like to create a pretend world for their Barbies, carrying their dolls from a Barbie dream house into a pink Barbie car. In the movie, a subplot about tensions between a real-world mother and her rebellious adolescent daughter, Sasha, also ignited real-world memories for many. Ironically, Sasha's denunciation of Barbie dolls differs little from Christian excoriations of the *Barbie* movie, both sides falling into error, as Sayers might put it. She should know, having been excoriated by Christians for her radio plays about Jesus. Like repudiations of *The Man Born to Be King,* Christian

[36]Quoted in "Jessica Chastain," *Parade,* October 23, 2022, 12; quoted in "Walter Scott's Personality," *Parade,* November 6, 2022, 2.

[37]Sayers, "Are Women Human?," 24-25.

denunciations of *Barbie* demonstrate a failure to value the energy of the medium itself.[38]

Director Greta Gerwig and her cowriter, Noah Baumbach, quite intentionally call attention to the cinematic medium from the very opening of *Barbie,* as though honoring Sayers's assertion about the importance of "former streams of beauty, emotion, and reflection." The former stream in this case is the famous opening of *2001: A Space Odyssey* (Stanley Kubrick, 1968), a movie repeatedly appearing in British Film Institute lists of the greatest films of all time.[39] Beginning with apes fighting over a water hole, Kubrick's film suddenly cuts to a low-angle shot of a monolith standing among the losing apes, who had returned to their desert surroundings. Accompanied by nondiegetic music from "Thus Spake Zarathustra," a stream of beauty and emotion composed by Richard Strauss in 1896, some apes shyly touch the monolith. Soon they start using bones at their feet as tools, not only to break rocks but also as weapons against their competitors, as though the monolith energized their evolution. Next, a low-angle lens captures one bone flung into the sky, followed by "one of the boldest graphic matches in narrative cinema," the shot cutting to a spaceship matching the same space on our screens. As the authors of *Film Art* go on to explain, "The cut eliminates millions of years of story time."[40] The language of cinema, in other words, communicates powerfully without any need for words.

Rather than apes by a watering hole, *Barbie* begins with little girls sitting on a rocky coast playing with old-fashioned baby dolls, a voiceover (Helen Mirren) pronouncing, "Since the beginning of time . . ." Suddenly, the shot cuts to a monolith-sized Barbie doll appearing among them, accompanied by "Thus Spake Zarathustra" on the soundtrack. After multiple point-of-view shots, the girls start using their baby dolls to smash their toy paraphernalia,

---

[38]Christian denunciations of the film also tend to overlook the fact that *Barbie* is one of those rare twenty-first-century films that does not signal a woman's power through her explicit erotic advances, sexual overtures that merely have women copy traditional male privilege. Instead, when the newly virile Ken makes sexual overtures toward Barbie, she slaps him. Rather than a sign that "she hates Ken," as one critic intones, it is a sign that women need to exercise their empowerment not by falling into bed with any Tom, Dick, or un-hairy Ken—a very Christian implication, especially considering that Barbie tells Ken she loves him.

[39]Sayers, *Mind of the Maker,* 121. "Revealed: The Results of the 2022 Sight and Sound Greatest Films of All Time poll," BFI, December 1, 2022, www.bfi.org.uk/news/revealed-results-2022-sight-sound-greatest-films-all-time-poll.

[40]David Bordwell, Kristin Thompson, and Jeff Smith, *Film Art: An Introduction,* 11th ed. (New York: McGraw Hill, 2017), 252.

until a doll flung into the air is graphically matched by the pink title *Barbie*. By thus mimicking a profoundly serious film, Gerwig signals the satiric intent of her movie, which proceeds to satirize gender relationships. Unfortunately, one "leading Christian film critic," calling *Barbie* "terrible" due to its "hardcore" feminist "propaganda," seems not to have recognized the energy of the medium, describing the opening scene as girls implying "'We don't have to be mothers anymore.'"[41] Instead, the satiric opening alludes to historical reality that girls in the 1960s switched from baby dolls to Barbies.

The film's script also undermines Christians who reduce *Barbie* to feminist screed. Not only do Gerwig and Baumbach include an affirmation of motherhood toward the end of the film, but they also put the most emphatic feminist statement of the film in the mouth of its least likable character, the sneering Sasha (Ariana Greenblatt), who treats her loving mother (America Ferrera) with scornful disdain—until she learns balance from a chastened Barbie. By the end of the film, Sasha is visually transformed. Dressed in Barbie-like clothes, she affectionately responds to her mother, who articulates, without feminist disdain, the difficulties women still encounter. Rather than "an attack on men," as the critic puts it, Gerwig has created a film that visually illustrates what Sayers verbally argued in 1938: "It is no good saying: 'You are a little girl and therefore you ought to like dolls'; if the answer is, 'But I don't,' there is no more to be said. Few women happen to be natural born mechanics; but if there is one, it is useless to try and argue her into being something different."[42] *Barbie*, then, satirizes this age-old cultural problem by putting males in the position of females, as when Ken dolls function merely as objects of the *female* gaze. Indeed, Beach Ken (Ryan Gosling) remarks that his only good days occur when Stereotypical Barbie (Margot Robbie) looks at him. It is as though Gerwig and Baumbach decided to visualize Sayers's suggestion that a male, if put in the same position as females, would find it quite odd "if everything he wore, said, or did had to be justified by reference to female approval."[43]

The filmmakers clearly know that cultural context, rather than "integrity of work," often defines who has power, implying as much when Beach Ken gets

---

[41]Billy Hallowell, "'Hardcore Propaganda': 'Barbie' Movie Excoriated in Film Critic's Alarming Warning to Parents," Faithwire, www.faithwire.com/2023/07/20/hardcore-propaganda-barbie-movie-excoriated-in-film-critics-alarming-warning-to-parents/.

[42]Sayers, "Are Women Human?," 39-40.

[43]Sayers, "Human-Not-Quite-Human," 56.

treated as a person with value only after he enters the "real world" (a term repeated throughout the film). The opposite happens to Stereotypical Barbie, who notices that "men look at me like an object" after she arrives in the real world of Los Angeles. Suddenly defined by her "to-be-looked-at-ness," she suffers the slings and arrows of outrageous catcalls and inappropriate touching. The film thus visualizes something G. K. Chesterton suggested in 1906: "The real world is not clear or plain. The real world is full of bracing bewilderments and brutal surprises."[44]

*Barbie* also implies that much of the film industry has contributed to the brutal surprises of real-world inequity. For example, an image of Marlon Brando briefly appears on a small screen in the mise-en-scène as a Ken, newly empowered by the real world, explains to a rapt Barbie *The Godfather* (Francis Ford Coppola, 1972)—a famous film in which females have little agency. This follows an earlier "stream of beauty," in which we briefly see Colin Firth on a television watched by "Depression Barbie." Many will recognize the shot as an image of Darcy from the 1995 BBC adaptation of *Pride and Prejudice*. In the 1813 novel by Jane Austen, Elizabeth Bennet defies the cultural constructions of her day by refusing to marry a man of wealth and power until he is humbled. But Austen goes on to show that Elizabeth must be humbled as well so that they can marry as equals, not reversing the hierarchy but practicing both/and truth. It is no wonder that C. S. Lewis loved Jane Austen novels as much as he loved Sayers's *The Man Born to Be King*.

Like Austen and Sayers, then, Gerwig establishes that responding to inequity by reversing the hierarchy merely perpetuates an either-or model, as when individuals are admitted to universities or are hired for jobs not in recognition for the integrity of their work but merely to meet quotas. As Sayers asserts in *Are Women Human?*, women desire to be considered "not as an inferior class and not, I beg and pray all feminists, as a superior class."[45] Gerwig and Baumbach visualize the idiocy of turning females into a superior class through mise-en-scène. The garishly painted sets and obviously false backgrounds in Barbieland, where Barbie dolls have all the power positions in society, are as inhuman as the patriarchy so gleefully appropriated by Ken dolls in the garish mise-en-scène of Los Angeles.

---

[44]G. K. Chesterton, *Charles Dickens, the Last of the Great Men* (New York: Press of the Readers Club, 1942), 110.
[45]Sayers, "Are Women Human?," 45.

## The Mind of the Barbie Maker

The artificial backdrops of Barbieland also lend special significance to sequences in the movie where the mise-en-scène has no backdrops at all, with human figures performing against an empty green screen. The first comes after the Ken dolls stage a revolution by taking over all the houses and jobs in Barbieland, until they start fighting among themselves for dominance. After Barbie-like sparkles appear between some of the fighters, the shot cuts to the Ken dolls all dressed in black against a bare screen divided by pink and blue colors. At first dancing like separate gangs in a musical, one side surrounded by pink, the other by blue, they start performing in unison, including hugs and kisses between both sides. The symbolism is obvious: pink versus blue, like female versus male, must work together, all exercising the integrity of work. This then contrasts with scenes in the real world, where Los Angeles backgrounds contextualize a patriarchy that does not depend on the integrity of work at all—a point the film makes clear when Beach Ken thinks he can apply for prestigious jobs in Los Angeles with no credentials or training whatsoever.

The second contrasting scene eliminates color and backdrop altogether as Barbie talks to her creator. This is the culmination of Barbie's journey to discover what it means to be human, a journey that begins early in the film when she suddenly asks, during a dance party in Barbieland, "Do you guys ever think about dying?" After a brief freeze-frame before the dance goes on, the next sequence shows Barbie experiencing consequences of mortality: her pretend shower is too cold, her pretend toast is burned, her pretend milk is soured, and more. The biblical idea of the fall is soon literalized when, rather than gracefully floating down into her Barbie car as shown earlier, Barbie awkwardly falls from the second floor of her Barbie house onto the ground.

After the fall, Barbie is advised to seek her owner in the real world, a world where woman "is defined and differentiated with reference to man and not he with reference to her; she is the incidental, the inessential as opposed to the essential. He is the Subject, he is the Absolute," as a Sayers contemporary put it in 1949.[46] Sayers, however, offered a different absolute: God incarnate. As she states near the close of "The Human-Not-Quite-Human,"

---

[46] The statement is from *The Second Sex* by Simone de Beauvoir and is quoted in Christina Bieber Lake, "Barbie . . . and Ken," *Current*, August 7, 2023, https://currentpub.com/2023/08/07/barbie-and-ken/.

> Perhaps it is no wonder that the women were first at the Cradle and last at the Cross. They had never known a man like this Man—there never has been such another. A prophet and teacher who never nagged at them, never flattered or coaxed or patronized; . . . who took their questions and arguments seriously; who never mapped out their sphere for them, never urged them to be feminine or jeered at them for being female.[47]

Jesus Christ, *both* fully God *and* fully man, modeled both/and thinking about gender.

*Barbie* also implies that a real absolute transcends culture. Having represented artificial constructions of gender with the gaudy colors of Barbieland, the filmmakers eliminate those colors when Stereotypical Barbie meets with her maker, the inventor of the Barbie doll, named Ruth Handler (Rhea Perlman). Their first meeting seems to be by accident, when Barbie escapes confinement within the garishly painted all-male boardroom at Mattel Headquarters in Los Angeles. Running down colorless corridors, Barbie enters a gray-toned kitchen, where Handler introduces herself. Later, Handler enters Barbieland to take Barbie away, the shot dissolving from the backs of Barbie and Ruth walking toward a small white light to an all-white screen. After Ruth tells Barbie, "Humans make things up like patriarchy and Barbie," the doll replies, "I want to be part of the people that make meaning, not just a thing made." Soon referring to Handler as her "creator," Barbie wants to be an *imago Creator*, a calling that defines both male and female, as Sayers makes clear in *The Mind of the Maker.*

Sayers, in fact, would have valued one of the songs included in *Barbie*, "What Was I Made For?," that begins with these words:

> I used to float, now I just fall down
> I used to know but I'm not sure now . . .
> What was I made for?[48]

Though Sayers clearly knows that only Christ can save us from the fall, she also believes that the well-crafted architecture of creative fiction, whether in plays, novels, or films, can communicate a two-thousand-year-old truth, that in Christ, there is neither male nor female (Gal 3:28), both called by God to discover what they were made for.

---

47Sayers, "Human-Not-Quite-Human," 68.

48Billie Eilish, "What Was I Made For?," *Barbie* soundtrack, 2023.

8

# Love on Screen

## *Finding the Real Thing*

Immediately after establishing that both males and females fulfill the *imago Dei,* the first chapter of the Bible tells us that God encourages *pro*creation: "God blessed them and said to them, 'Be fruitful and increase in number" (Gen 1:28). Sexuality is essential to our humanity. We should not be surprised, then, that a vast number of movies celebrate erotic love. Viewers enjoy losing themselves in romance, if not the titillation of hot sex, as they watch protagonists find their soulmates, that special someone who satisfies all emotional, psychological, and sexual needs. Addicted to the drug of all-conquering romance, many viewers go to the movies for the same reason they go to a pharmacy.

Significantly, the Greek word from which we get *pharmacy, pharmakon,* can refer to either medicine or poison. People watch artificial happy endings, absorbing them like a feel-good cure-all. Medicine, however, becomes poisonous when overdosed. By ignoring the kinds of love that can be pro-creative in Sayers's understanding of creativity, viewers poison their ability to appreciate artistry in the medium itself. Sayers, in fact, once told C. S. Lewis that "the only kind of love" she fully understood was "the love of the artist for the artefact."[1]

Inspired by both Sayers and Lewis, this chapter looks at beautiful films that celebrate other kinds of love than "the carnal or animally sexual element within Eros," as Lewis defined it.[2] In fact, Lewis could be talking about Hollywood when he refers to "people who are in love again every few years, each

[1]*Letters* 3:257.

[2]C. S. Lewis, *The Four Loves* (New York: Harcourt, Brace, Jovanovich, 1960), 131.

time sincerely convinced that 'this time it's the real thing,'" a cliché that appears in many a screenplay.[3] Celebrating other kinds of love instead, this chapter weaves together multiple threads from *The Wages of Cinema,* starting with the influence of theater on cinema.

## DREAMING OF LOVE: THE COMEDY TRADITION

Centuries ago, a comedy was defined not by its inclusion of humor but by a happy ending in which romantic love prevails over social impediments, such that life will go on through procreation. William Shakespeare's *A Midsummer Night's Dream* (ca. 1595), for example, begins with an aristocratic father refusing to allow his daughter, Hermia, to marry the man of her choice. Meanwhile, Hermia's best friend, Helena, is in love with the man the father has chosen for Hermia. To escape these patriarchal demands, the women and Hermia's two suitors run to the woods, the place of nature that might allow a more natural, companionable love to flourish. There, craziness ensues, a natural result of cultural defiance. But, by the end of the play, all four lovers achieve happiness by marrying the person of their dreams.

This was an edgy message in Shakespeare's time. Marriages within the royalty and among the aristocracy were almost entirely arranged for political and socioeconomic advantages. The children from such marriages, as inheritors of privilege and wealth, maintained a family's cultural power and hence the status quo. Furthermore, since marriage had little to do with friendship or even sexual attraction, male aristocrats often fulfilled their urges in adulterous affairs, while punishing any wife who did the same, as portrayed in *The Last Duel* (Ridley Scott, 2021), set in the fourteenth century. Shakespearean comedy, in contrast, was about defying such cultural constructions, characters marrying for love and companionship rather than to sustain cultural expectations. Hence, in the last scene of *A Midsummer Night's Dream,* multiple couples go off to bed, thus fulfilling the traditional message of comedy, "Be fruitful and increase in number!"

In his 1999 film adaptation of *A Midsummer Night's Dream,* Michael Hoffman beautifully captures the biblical roots of this tradition while sustaining Shakespeare's magnificent language. The diegesis begins at a sumptuously baroque

---

[3]Lewis, *Four Loves,* 131, 158.

country estate, nature tamed in elaborately terraced gardens. Escaping this architecture—literal constructions of privilege—the four young lovers experience the realm of freedom in the woods, where no human constructions appear. But, as in Scripture, the realm of Edenic free choice—an inherent good—is corrupted by self-serving and petty behavior. Shakespeare illustrates the point with the king and queen of the fairies, who despite their supernatural powers squabble in the woods over possession of a "changeling," as though to imply that the Eden of free will inevitably changes human relationships. Indeed, the four lovers proceed to squabble as well, Hoffman's adaptation placing their most vicious argument in a dirty sinkhole. A symbol of the fall, lovers fight in the mud, each obsessed with desire and jealousy, behavior that muddies their bodies as well as their minds. Choosing self-interest over love for others, they crawl out of the muck to fall asleep, all isolated by their own vicious desires.

Shakespeare, of course, has the fairies cast a spell that cleanses the lovers from their hateful thoughts, directing their love instead to the most natural soulmate. Following the bard's dialogue, Hoffman takes advantage of the stigmata of cinema, creating a symbolic mise-en-scène. We see the four actors lying at the edge of a lush meadow, all entirely nude except for discretely placed rose petals over their spotless skin. Each couple looks like Adam and Eve awaking after their creation, innocent of lust or self-interest. They are now ready to experience pro-creation, and the film, like the play, ends with a wedding banquet. Honoring Shakespeare, then, Hoffman's film implies that society can be transformed by marriage based on love, because the creation of new life—symbolized by procreation—has the potential to change human hearts. It is no coincidence that God saved humanity from the muddy sinkhole of sin by entering the world in the form of a baby—the divine comedy.

## Less Than Divine: A New Kind of Love

By the mid-twentieth century, romantic comedies explicitly alluded to the necessity of sex for love. A telling example is *A New Kind of Love* (1963), starring two superb actors, Paul Newman and his wife, Joanne Woodward. The film begins cleverly with a voiceover by Newman's character, who describes the "canyon" of Manhattan, where shoppers stampede through the streets. As we watch masses of women waiting for stores to open their doors, we hear the lowing of cattle, as though Fifth Avenue were one big corral.

The film then cuts to a radically contrasting image: a lone woman (Woodward) wanders the streets of Manhattan at night, contemplating mannequins in the windows with the goal of designing less expensive clothes for middle-class women. The independent woman, Samantha (Sam), is so committed to the integrity of her work that she pays no attention to her own appearance, so much so that her cropped hair and determined walk in mannish, comfortable clothes sometimes cause observers to assume she is male. Watched with twenty-first-century eyes, the film seems to offer an intriguing alternative to the conformist females stampeding into stores at the start of the film.

Then, in romantic comedy style, Sam meets someone who views women much as the adulterous womanizer does in Sayers's *Love All.* A reporter named Steve (Newman) is sent on assignment to Paris after an affair with his boss's wife has come to light. Meanwhile, Sam has gone to Paris with her own boss to study haute couture designs. Viewers rightly expect a Shakespearean encounter where witty male and female protagonists clash and despise each other until they eventually fall in love as intellectual equals, like Beatrice and Benedict in *Much Ado About Nothing* (ca. 1599).

But, alas, many filmmakers of the 1950s and '60s were not as enlightened as was Shakespeare. For rather than Steve discovering that the blonde bimbos he beds every night are not as enjoyable as an intelligent, feisty woman like Sam, the film shows Sam deciding to turn herself into a blonde bimbo to catch a man. And it works: Steve falls for "Mimi" (the disguised Sam), believing her to be an expensive call girl that he needs to interview for a newspaper article describing sexual conquest as a sport. Sam sustains the illusion, regaling Steve with false stories of her sexual exploits. Hence, just as she made money by copying expensive clothing designs, she now makes a relationship by copying expensive call-girl designs.

Of course, because the Hays Code was still in effect in 1963, we see no nudity or even passionate encounters.[4] But the message is ultimately more disturbing than any gratuitous sex scene. It establishes that the sexually promiscuous Steve would only marry a woman who is not sexually active—unlike

[4]Named after Will H. Hays, president of the Motion Picture Producers and Distributors of America (MPPDA) from 1922 to 1945, the Hays Code (1934-68) required studios to eliminate sex and violence from their films.

the women he sleeps with. And he gets what he desires, but only when she attracts him with false stories of her sexual exploits. Steve has his cake and gets to eat it too. Viewers in the 1960s thus bought into a fiction as outrageous as the stories "Mimi" tells Steve, that a man accustomed to having a different woman every night (Steve) will settle down with only one woman (Sam) because she can talk about sex without having ever done it.

*A New Kind of Love,* then, is not new at all, perpetuating the problematic mythology that builds on the established autonomy of its protagonists. As a reporter who "doesn't play by the rules" unites with a fashion designer who "doesn't play by the rules," they create a new kind of love that supposedly doesn't play by the rules. Instead, their love plays not only by the rules of 1960s gender constructions but also by the clichés of Hollywood cinema.

Dorothy L. Sayers has taught us a better kind of love, manifest by viewers who creatively distinguish generic conventions from the artistry of films in which idea, energy, and power are consubstantial. For Sayers, a pro-creative film intelligently challenges the clichés of its own era—as did Shakespeare in his own day.

### **Comedy *Lost in Translation***

A good example of creative subversion can be seen in *Lost in Translation* (Sophia Coppola, 2003), an award-winning film that plays off our knowledge of the medium's sexual clichés in order to draw attention to more significant issues. Bill Murray plays an aging actor named Bob who meets a gorgeous woman, Charlotte (Scarlett Johansson), in a Tokyo hotel. Though decades apart in age and married to others, they hit it off and end up in bed together.

Put that way, of course, it sounds like a film cliché . . . which is part of the point. Bob and Charlotte do indeed grow intimate, but not sexually. They instead develop the intellectual and psychological intimacy of friendship through multiple conversations, where they discuss differences not only in Japanese and American cultures but also in cultural values between their two generations. More significantly, they talk about their struggles with insomnia, as they similarly agonize over the ultimate meaning of existence. The image of them in bed together, then, is done with a high-angle crane shot, such that we look down on a bed removed of all coverlets, where we see Bob and Charlotte sleeping fully clothed and not touching each other.

Sophia Coppola, who wrote and directed the film, thus made literal the euphemism "sleeping together" to subvert the common convention that happiness depends on finding a good sexual partner. Instead, the film implies that contentment, as symbolized by the ability to sleep, comes from intellectual and emotional connection. The movie's title, *Lost in Translation,* therefore refers to many different things: the translation of phrases between English and Japanese, the translation of cultural values from one generation to the next, the translation of the phrase "sleeping together," and the translation of movie conventions.

Coppola won the 2003 Oscar for Best Original Screenplay due to her ability to translate film clichés into something new. She, in fact, signals that was her intent through a powerful scene in her film. Bob is on a soundstage in Tokyo, where he has come to act in a whiskey commercial. The director tells Bob's interpreter, "The translation is very important, OK? The translation," and then proceeds to reference one of the most famous films of all time, *Casablanca.* The director states in Japanese, "Mr. Bob. You are sitting quietly in your study. And then there is a bottle of Suntory whisky on top of the table. You understand, right? With wholehearted feeling, slowly, look at the camera, tenderly, and as if you are meeting old friends, say the words. As if you are Bogie in *Casablanca,* saying 'Here's looking at you, kid.'" After this impassioned plea for acting nuance, the interpreter merely says to Bob, "He wants you to turn, look in camera. OK?" This difference in translation parallels the difference between artistic films that draw from what Sayers calls "former streams of beauty" such as *Casablanca* (Michael Curtiz, 1942), and movies that merely offer a new spin on the same old mind-numbing clichés.

### TRANSLATING CONVENTIONS: *SALMON FISHING IN THE YEMEN*

The subversion of romantic clichés enters *Salmon Fishing in the Yemen* (Lasse Hallström, 2011). An oft-overlooked subplot focuses on the translation of unsavory facts into palatable press releases. Patricia Maxwell (Kristin Scott Thomas), the press secretary to Britain's prime minister, regularly finds herself in the position of covering up political embarrassments, such as illicit sexual hookups, by turning them into news feeds that eliminate or change the sordid details. Maniacally manipulative, Patricia's efforts feed the movie's main plot, putting her clout behind a sheikh's plan to transport ten thousand British salmon to the Yemen so she can distract media attention from a recent mosque bombing.[5]

Patricia witnesses the televised bombing from bed while her husband sleeps next to her. Significantly, the scene immediately follows a passionate kiss between one of the film's protagonists, Harriet (Emily Blunt), the sheikh's investment counselor, and Harriet's new boyfriend, Robert. Both scenes are shot in low-key lighting, creating a visual connection between the two women. Indeed, Patricia later uses Harriet as a public-relations ploy by flying Robert into the Yemen to surprise Harriet, who assumes he has been killed in Afghanistan, and then gathering the press to record the artificially arranged romantic moment. Like artificially arranged romantic moments in cinema, the reunion of the two gorgeous lovers is heartwarming and passionate. True to Hollywood convention, the lovers walk toward each other oblivious to everything around them until they finally dash into each other's arms.

Viewer satisfaction in the scene, however, is undermined by sympathy for the film's other protagonist, Fred (Ewan McGregor), a geeky but goodhearted scientist coordinating the fish transport to Yemen. Believing Robert dead, he has recently proclaimed his love to Harriet, and, like most mainstream films, *Salmon Fishing* has manipulated us to root for the protagonist, even to the point of forgiving Fred for declaring his love to Harriet while he's still married to another woman, Mary. After all, we see Mary so caught up in her career that she shows no interest in procreation, dismissing Fred's desire to have a baby together. When his lumbering, pajama-clad body climbs on top of her in bed, Mary responds to his successful fulfillment of conjugal rites with, "That should do you for a while." Of course, another film could have presented the wife sympathetically, as a committed career woman whose husband, failing to satisfy her in bed, wants her to stay home and make babies rather than to take advantage of significant professional advancement, as in Sayers's play *Love All.* The medium directs our allegiances by giving close-ups on Fred's earnest face, which contrast with shots of his wife's stony countenance. Film viewers can be as manipulated as the people Patricia manipulates with her media *pharmakons.*

---

[5]I analyze *Salmon Fishing in the Yemen* in Crystal Downing, *Salvation from Cinema: The Medium Is the Message* (New York: Routledge, 2016), 154-58, but make no mention of the subplot discussed here.

The film would have been more subversive if the awkward Fred had been single, foregrounding instead Harriet's *unconventional* romantic choice between a gorgeous, sensitive boyfriend, with whom she experienced great sex before he left for Afghanistan, and the nerdy Fred, with whom she shares a vision for salmon fishing in Yemen. By choosing nerdy Fred over the dashing Robert, Harriet chooses companionable friendship love over steamy erotic love, a choice that subverts Hollywood convention.

C. S. Lewis writes of friendship love, "Friends are not primarily absorbed in each other. It is when we are doing things together that friendship springs up—painting, sailing ships, praying, philosophizing, fighting shoulder to shoulder. Friends look in the same direction. Lovers look at each other."[6] Add "fishing" after "philosophizing" in Lewis's list, and it could be describing *Salmon Fishing in the Yemen*. Contrasting with the clichéd run toward each other of Harriet and Robert, the camera captures Fred and Harriet multiple times with their backs to the camera, shoulder to shoulder as they look in the same direction at their shared project.

Furthermore, after Harriet chooses to stay with Fred in the Yemen rather than fly off with the handsome Robert (who desires her but mocks the salmon project), we do not see a conventional Hollywood kiss. Instead, the penultimate shot of the film shows their reflection in the water they helped bring to Yemen. Rather than their faces, the water reflects one hand grabbing another as the two stand shoulder to shoulder. The medium thus subverts the convention by which lovers "look at each other."

This, then, might give us more sympathy, if not total forgiveness, for Fred turning his back on his marriage to Mary. The problem, the medium itself implies, is that Mary does not regard him as a friend, made clear when she pays more attention to her cell phone than his conversation, going off on a six-week business trip without consulting him. When Mary snidely comments on the attractiveness of Harriet, Fred yells, "She's just a friend, Mary . . . a *friend*." That indeed captures the subversive love in *Salmon Fishing*: it is about friendship love. We must therefore take note that Fred ends his marriage *after* he discovers Robert has returned to Harriet. Assuming Robert and Harriet will stay together forever, Fred seeks a divorce because he

[6]C. S. Lewis, "Equality," in *Present Concerns: Essays by C. S. Lewis*, ed. Walter Hooper (London: Harcourt, Brace, Jovanovich, 1986), 20.

decides that love should be about the marriage of true minds (to once again invoke Shakespeare).

*Salmon Fishing in the Yemen* ends with instant messaging between Patricia and her boss, who discuss how to manipulate political journalism to satisfy consumers. It is as though the film were commenting on its own status as people-pleasing medium. However, it also forces attentive viewers to think about the Patricia-like spin conventional movies give to romantic love, which is almost always about face-to-face eroticism rather than shoulder-to-shoulder passion. Nevertheless, the film's unconventional happy ending relies on viewers endorsing the breaking of marriage vows, an issue that forces Christians to think about foundations for married love. Indeed, while Jesus never once comments on homosexuality, he argues against divorce (Mt 19; Mk 10), a biblical truth that many Christians choose to ignore.

## Building the Happy Ending: *Brick Lane*

The breaking of marriage vows is a bit more understandable in the British-made *Brick Lane* (Sarah Gavron, 2007), which focuses on a seventeen-year-old sent by her parents from Bangladesh to London for marriage with a Bengali, twice her age, whom she has never met. The film cuts from the young girl, Nazneen, boarding a boat to England, to her life sixteen years later, with two daughters and an oafish, overweight husband who expects Nazneen to wait on him hand and foot—quite literally, we see, when she cuts the corns off his swollen toes.

Nazneen escapes the dreariness of her sequestered life in a tenement on Brick Lane, an actual Muslim ghetto in London, by reading letters in which her sister describes her exciting love life in Bangladesh. Then, true to the romantic genre, Nazneen develops her own satisfying relationship with a virile young clothing worker, Karim, who engages her services as a seamstress. Their relationship develops into erotic desire, and we see them, even if quite discretely, fulfill their sexual longing in the bed she usually shares with her well-meaning but insensitive husband.

The sex scenes are filmed with extreme close-ups on the lovers' faces, communicating adoration as they gaze into each other's eyes. Low-key lighting allows a golden sheen to glint off their youthful skin, as though to express the precious beauty of their relationship, another movie convention. In fact, during their tender enjoyment of each other's bodies, the film interpolates images of Nazneen as a girl playing in golden Bengali sunlight with her beloved sister. We are thus led to believe that the love between Nazneen and Karim is as pure as that of the young sisters and as natural as the grass and flowers through which they run.

The beauty of their tender, "natural" sex is further reinforced by its contrast to a scene earlier in the film. Nazneen's portly husband, Chanu, rolls on top of her with nary a kiss, fulfilling his sexual desire with no concern for her pleasure. Rather than the golden tints of youthful skin, we witness sleeping apparel made gray by the darkness, seeing nothing of Chanu's face as it is buried in Nazneen's pillow, as though symbolizing a dehumanizing sexual encounter. What we do see is the wife's fist raised, as though in agony, next to the husband's humping body.

Like many films before it, *Brick Lane* thus gets viewers to see adultery as more beautiful and natural than married sex. Habits of perception, manipulated by the cinematography, encourage us to cheer on the relationship, especially when Karim tells Nazneen that he wants to rescue her from an old-fashioned husband whose outlandish get-rich-quick schemes have thrown the family into debt. *Brick Lane,* however, refuses to leave us with such an obvious Hollywood scenario. It therefore employs as its turning point an actual historical moment—al-Qaeda's destructive acts on September 11, 2001. As Nazneen watches on television the fall of New York's Twin Towers, she has no idea that the demise of the phallic towers signals the end of her adulterous relationship.

Due to the post-9/11 harassment of Muslims who live on Brick Lane, Nazneen's lover becomes serious about his religious identity. Renouncing the Western clothes in which he seduced Nazneen, Karim starts wearing traditional Muslim garb while participating in rallies defending Islam. As Karim's Western identity falls, Nazneen's idealization of her Eastern identity similarly falls. She discovers that her sister has become little more than a prostitute; what Nazneen thought was beautiful Bangladeshi love was merely self-serving lust. Around the same time, she sees another side of her husband. At a Karim-led rally for Islamic solidarity, Chanu boldly expresses reservations about Islamic violence, leading Nazneen to take his hand as they leave the meeting, the first sign of affection we have seen between the heavyset husband and his long-suffering wife.

Nevertheless, having been trained by Hollywood, viewers suspect that the beautiful love Nazneen experiences with Karim will win out over her perfunctory relationship with the annoying Chanu. Think, for example, of the romantic comedy *Jerry Maguire* (Cameron Crowe, 1996), when viewer fantasies are fulfilled as Jerry, played by Tom Cruise, falls into bed with struggling single mom Dorothy (Renée Zellweger). Like Karim, who is distracted from love as he seeks to establish his Muslim identity, Jerry becomes similarly distracted, emotionally distancing himself from Dorothy as he seeks to become a successful sports agent. In both films, the men, after achieving their personal goals, return to their lovers, now ready for a lifetime of wedded bliss. As Jerry enters Dorothy's home, he says, "Hello," before pronouncing his love for her. Dorothy responds, in one of the most famous cheesy lines of cinema, "You had me at hello." The film thus gives us an artificially happy ending, Jerry getting not only the girl but also several multimillion-dollar sports contracts for his clients. Money and sex, the American dream!

*Brick Lane,* in contrast, subverts the trance of romance. After a period of separation, partially due to Nazneen's trauma over her sister's tawdry lifestyle, Karim, like Jerry Maguire, tells Nazneen he wants to spend the rest of his life with her. Expecting that Karim had her "at hello," we are therefore surprised to hear Nazneen say, "I do not want to marry you." Karim, similarly shocked, asks, "Is it the sin of it?" In response, Nazneen focuses not on their sin ("That we've already done," she explains) but on the trance of romance, telling him, "I am not *the real thing.* I am no longer a girl from the village." When Karim protests, "Yes, you are!" she replies "No. You just wanted me to be. We just made each other up." With these profound words, *Brick Lane* exposes what most Hollywood movies fear to reveal, that the romantic fictions we see on screen are usually as false as George Washington's wooden teeth.

The medium reinforces the message. The conversation between Karim and Nazneen is shot in low-key lighting, with the same blue-grays as in the joyless sex scene between Nazneen and her husband. This contrasts markedly, of course, with the glowing golden tones that sparkle off the skin of Karim and Nazneen during their earlier sex scenes, golden tones intercut with the high-key lighting of Nazneen's childhood memories. But just as her sister's love life is exposed as fraudulent, so is Nazneen's love life with Karim. Both were false gold.

The film ends with Nazneen returning to her dark apartment on Brick Lane, multiple shots portraying her return in the form of black silhouettes against bright backgrounds, including her shadow along a gray wall. The film thus suggests Nazneen's awareness that she lost the substance of her selfhood when she became the romantic girl from the village that both she and Karim desired, only a shadow of "the real thing." Once she enters her flat, however, we see the real Nazneen as she recites a letter to her sister, expressing what she has learned about love. As she crawls into bed, smiling at her sleeping husband, we hear her state these words:

> No one told me there are different kinds of love: the kind that starts big and then slowly wears away, that seems you will never use it up and then one day it is finished. Then there is the kind that you do not notice at first but that adds a little bit to itself every day, as an oyster makes a pearl grain by grain, a jewel from the sand. That is the kind I have come to know.

Nazneen has embraced the kind of love difficult to portray in cinema. After all, it is easy to portray the excitement of sexual passion. But, as numerous celebrity relationships attest, love based solely on erotic attraction rarely lasts. *Brick Lane* gives us instead a slow-growing pearl of great price.

### LOVE OF GREAT PRICE: *LADIES IN LAVENDER*

Diving for pearls is hard work, necessitating focused attention on the oyster in which a pearl lies hidden. In Sayers's terms, viewer power is part of the work, opening the medium in which the energy of pearl creation lies hidden. Many viewers prefer being handed a fake gem at the end of a film, where all problems are resolved, protagonists glorying in the fool's gold of all-conquering romance. Consider *Ladies in Lavender* (Charles Dance, 2004), a film with "an ending that fizzles out disappointingly," according to one reviewer.[7] Indeed, those who desire conventional romance will feel fizzle rather than sizzle at the end of *Ladies*. But those with sizzling minds will find much to contemplate in the ending of the film.

[7]Peter Bradshaw, "Ladies in Lavender," *The Guardian*, November 12, 2004, www.theguardian.com/film/News_Story/Critic_Review/Guardian_review/0,4267,1348661,00.html.

The ladies in lavender are spinster sisters in their sixties who live along the coast of Cornwall in 1936, Ursula and Janet Widdington (the extraordinary Dame Judi Dench and Dame Maggie Smith, respectively). The difference between the sisters is revealed in the opening scene as they walk along the shore. Ursula, gleefully wading into the water while Janet sedately sits on shore, splashes her more reticent sister with ocean water. The very practical Janet lovingly rebukes her sister's childlike impetuousness, as she does throughout the film. She runs the house just as she cranks and drives the car, Ursula uninterested in the maintenance of either. But it is Ursula who bounds outside in bare feet after a storm, sighing, "Everything smells so fresh after the storm."

The sisters' cozy existence is interrupted when they discover that the storm has washed a twenty-something male onto the beach. Taking him into their house, the women show proprietary concern for the Polish stranger, Andrea (Daniel Brühl), who speaks no English. Ursula, however, starts showing more than concern. On the very first night of Andrea's stay, she sits at the bedside watching the beautiful boy sleep, dropping a flower onto his food tray when he finally can eat. While the practical Janet digs up weeds in the garden, Ursula secretly writes notes at a desk inside, which she later pins to various objects in Andrea's room to teach him English. When she holds to her chest a paper with "Ursula" spelled out, upside down, attentive viewers recognize this as a symbol of Ursula's uneventful life rendered upside down by the handsome Pole. In contrast, Janet's only response is that Ursula's English lesson is "making holes in the furniture."

Meanwhile, Andrea offers gifts of teasing affection from his sickbed with convincing disingenuousness. After all, these white-haired, wrinkly spinsters are probably older than his grandparents. Viewers understand his naivete, for at this point Ursula's increasing passion is ambiguous even to us. Is hers the love of a woman for a child she never had? Does her joy in Andrea's presence reflect the intense affection teachers can develop for students? Even the practical Janet has become enamored, telling Ursula that she will use her private inheritance to outfit Andrea. Ursula's impassioned response is revelatory: "Why not our joint account? . . . I saw him first!"

Andrea's background comes to light after he hears Janet's pedestrian piano playing and responds with ear-covering anguish. Signaling that he prefers the violin, Andrea is treated to a performance in his sickroom by a local fiddle player. After politely listening to the amateur, Andrea gestures for the violin and proceeds to play with extraordinary skill, intensifying his physical beauty with heavenly sound. The filmmakers intercut medium shots of Andrea playing the violin (Ursula's point of view) with low-angle shots from behind his shoulder that cause the moving bow to vertically fill the screen, with Ursula standing behind it. As we see the bow moving up and down her frame as the violin plays, attentive viewers recognize the symbolism: Andrea plays on Ursula's heartstrings.

At this point a different kind of love interest enters the film, tantalizing us with the possibility of romance as we have grown to recognize it. A beautiful woman, distracted from her landscape painting by the mellifluous violin, yells, "Bravo!" up to the sisters' window whence the music comes. Conditioned by Hollywood convention, we know that this will be the one for whom Andrea falls. Indeed, in the next scene we witness the young woman, Olga (Natascha McElhone), bathed in the warm yellows, reds, and browns of firelight, sitting alone in her cottage. Because Andrea's beautiful music plays on the soundtrack, we must exercise our power to consider whether the energy of the music is diegetic or nondiegetic. If diegetic, it has entered Olga's mind, and she contemplates its beauty. If nondiegetic, it reminds the audience of conventional romance movies, as though Olga longs for the handsome player of the music. In this unconventional movie, it seems to be both.

Indeed, as in *A Midsummer Night's Dream*, various problems impede the potential lovers from connecting. The first obstacle, as in many comedies, is another woman. Andrea, finally walking and fitted with clothes, attends the village harvest festival, where he makes eyes at a plump redhead. Warned away by a jealous boyfriend, Andrea directs his love toward the violin rather than the redhead, soon playing it to the delight of the whole room, including Olga.

The next scene visualizes the impediment of a more intense infatuation. Ursula and Andrea walk down to the shore, and, as they sit watching the ocean, Andrea lays his head in Ursula's lap. Though we recognize his action as directed toward a grandmother figure, Ursula's response is much more ambiguous. After lifting her wrinkly hand to her beating heart she lowers it toward Andrea's head, barely daring to graze his hair. Is it a gesture of profound tenderness, as of an aged woman who has found either her long-lost son or, more heart-wrenchingly, is it long-latent sexual desire?

We discover it is the latter when later we are made privy to Ursula's subconscious. She chastely dreams that a younger version of herself is rolling around in a field of wheat, captured in Andrea's embrace. Immediately before Ursula wakes, however, the filmmakers cut in the face of Olga on the embraced dream woman. Once again viewers must exercise power: Why might Ursula's subconscious replace her dream self with Olga? Power-full viewers will remember the energy of an earlier scene, in which Olga finally introduces herself to Andrea, bursting in on the ladies' private garden where he plays the violin for them. After this happens, Ursula inscribes Olga with a metaphor of romantic impediment taken straight from medieval romance: "[Olga] frightens me. She's like the witch in a fairy tale." The film thus sets up an unconventional love triangle: Ursula sees Olga as a love impediment, and viewers of conventional movies see Ursula as a love impediment, whereas Andrea primarily loves to play his violin.

Meanwhile, another obstacle develops when the village doctor, who treats Andrea's injuries, starts ogling Olga. Jealous of how Andrea has attracted the attentions not only of the geriatric sisters but also of the radiant Olga, the doctor suggests notifying the authorities about Andrea, a German-speaking stranger who has infiltrated 1936 England. Worrying over Andrea's vulnerability, Janet intercepts and burns a letter in which Olga, another German speaker, introduces herself to him.

Despite all these stones in the pathway of romance, Olga and Andrea finally have a conversation alone, and she invites him to her cottage, saying that she wants to paint his portrait. Trained by cinema convention, we expect a romantic love scene to develop as Olga paints and Andrea plays his violin. Indeed, shot-reverse-shots (shots that alternate between individual characters looking at each other) direct our attention to their beautiful eyes intensely focused on each other, a convention of the medium that often alludes to sexual desire.

*Ladies in Lavender*, however, prefers to undermine Hollywood convention. As Andrea leans in to kiss Olga's full lips, she pulls back, saying, "You must go." Andrea, as shocked as we are, leaves the cottage. What follows provides a telling commentary. We are given a shot of Olga seated alone in the cottage, her head and shoulders framed by a curtained window that provides the only light in the mise-en-scène. Olga's head thus looks like a portrait on a painter's canvas—much like the head of Andrea she has been painting on her white canvas. By thus alluding to the creation of art, the film provides a clue that its own artistry may be challenging standard Hollywood fare.

The filmmakers then insert a graphic match-cut, the shot cutting from Olga in front of her window to Ursula in front of a window, not only creating a connection between the two women but also contributing to a motif. Repeatedly in the film we see Ursula bathed in light as she looks out a window with melancholy longing. Desiring a beautiful and talented young man, Ursula is separated from uniting with the object of her desire by a pane-full barrier of glass—the old glass in her cottage as wrinkly as she. The juxtaposition of these two shots—two women in front of windows—summarizes the difference between two friends of Andrea: Olga, with the framed window behind her head, has become the beautiful *object* of Andrea's desiring eye, while Ursula, who looks through windows at what she cannot have, is the desiring *subject,* longing for Andrea's eye. The film thus suggests the film theory of Laura Mulvey discussed in the preceding chapter, wherein conventional films situate beautiful women as the object of the gaze, valued for their "to-be-looked-at-ness." Indeed, the window frame around Olga makes viewers think of the "to-be-looked-at-ness" of a painting, whereas the window frame around the wrinkly old woman makes us think of someone separated from her desire.

Another contrast between the two women appears not long afterwards. We see the practical Janet cut Andrea's hair, after which Ursula impetuously grabs and pockets one of the locks from the ground. The shot then cuts to a pub, where Andrea joins Olga and the doctor at a table. Commenting on Andrea's haircut, Olga tenderly reaches up and smooths a lock into place. Not having seen Ursula's similar gesture when his head was in her lap, Andrea is now baffled by Olga's response; after all, she had earlier rejected his kiss. But hasn't Hollywood done this to us before, setting up a potential kiss only to make us wait for the consummating moment? Perhaps he (and hence we) will get the desired eroticism after all!

We are delighted, therefore, when Olga sends for Andrea and suggests an elopement—until we discover it is no ordinary elopement. Olga tells Andrea that her brother, the famous violinist Boris Danilof, is in London and that she wants Andrea to meet him. Because Andrea considers Danilof "a god," and since the train leaves in only a few minutes, he consents to leave without packing or telling his spinster hosts about his departure. So when Ursula hears the news that Andrea and Olga have surreptitiously run off to London, she moans in despair. We see her crawl onto Andrea's bed and roll up into a fetal position—as though implying Andrea has left this bed to crawl into that of another woman, which, of course, is what Hollywood has trained us to expect.

The filmmakers, however, synthesize idea with energy, generating power that subverts Hollywood expectations. The shot cuts from Ursula on the bed to a postman delivering a package to the sisters' cottage. It is Olga's painting of Andrea. In an accompanying note Andrea apologizes to the sisters for his departure: "I am sorry. You gave me life. Now I have a chance to use it," and he tells them to listen on November 10, when he will be performing on the radio. This, we realize, is his new life, born immediately after Ursula appears in a fetal position. Rather than experiencing sexual love, she has enabled Andrea's creative love to be reborn, pro-creation in an entirely different key.

After Ursula hangs the portrait of Andrea over the fireplace of his former bedroom, the shot cuts to scruffy villagers piling into the sisters' house. The camera then pans over the working-class audience as they listen to Andrea's magnificent violin music over the wireless. Weathered, careworn faces register awe as they silently soak up the lovely sound, their power participating with the mind of the maker. The shot then cuts to a very different audience, dressed in evening gowns and tails. Listening to the live symphony where Andrea plays lead violin, these people appear as enraptured as the Cornish villagers. Crosscutting between these two audiences, the film gives us an image of the *imago Dei*. All humans, no matter their age, class, gender, nationality, or education, have power to relish the consummation of art, not only characters on the screen but also viewers outside it. As the camera pans the London crowd listening to the symphony, Olga never appears in the mise-en-scène. She has entirely dropped out of the movie, for her role is over. Subverting the expectations of Hollywood romances, Olga chose to reunite Andrea with his creative vocation rather than to unite him with herself.

The filmmakers follow their pan of the London crowd with a slow tilt that reveals Janet and Ursula in the audience, listening rapturously to Andrea's performance. The shot lingers on Ursula's face, dissolving into a montage of earlier shots from the film, obviously comprising Ursula's memories of Andrea. One memorial image, however, is new: Ursula stands at the edge of the garden and throws the stolen lock of Andrea's hair into the wind. She has let him go, releasing him into the embrace of his love, the power of his art.

The film closes with the sisters leaving the symphony hall, stop-action camera work placing them farther and farther along an arched hallway as they move toward a darkened exit. But then, in a type of graphic match, the shot cuts to them exiting from a similarly darkened arch of stone along their Cornish beach, their backs still to us. As we admire the sun-bathed, wave-washed, gorgeous rocky coast, we are struck with the beauty of their quiet lives. Associating love with creation, both that of nature and that in art, *Ladies in Lavender* challenges the cultural convention that sexual fulfillment trumps all other love.[8]

## NEED LOVE VERSUS GIFT LOVE IN FILM

The contrasting love of the aged Ursula and the youthful Olga illustrates the difference between need love and gift love as C. S. Lewis defines them. In *The Four Loves,* he describes the latter as "wholly disinterested and desires what is simply best for the beloved."[9] Most films, of course, seem to focus on the former, the phrase "I need you" often intensifying a so-called love scene. In contrast, gift love entirely sacrifices one's own comforts and needs, if not life itself, in order to serve the best interests of someone else, the most transcendent example being Christ's sacrifice on the cross. In addition to divine gift love, however, there is what Lewis calls "natural Gift-love," which "is always directed to objects which the lover finds in some way intrinsically lovable," a kind of sacrificial love that occasionally graces secular movies, though usually not box-office hits.

*The Unforgivable* (Nora Fingscheidt, 2021) provides a good example. Employing no special effects, the movie maintains a color palette as plain as its hero. Sacrificing the made-up good looks of Hollywood heroines (made-up in both senses of the term), Sandra Bullock serves as the film's protagonist, a woman recently released from prison, whose personality is as unattractive as her surroundings. Those who criticize the "unrelentingly grim story" seem to have missed the point, for the film places viewers in the same position as

---

[8]I borrow much of my discussion of *Ladies in Lavender* from Crystal Downing, "Romancing the Crone," *The Cresset* 70, no. 4 (Easter 2007): 45-48.

[9]Lewis, *Four Loves,* 177.

first-century viewers of Christ's sacrifice.[10] Looking only at surface appearances, crowds jeering at Jesus on the cross end up fulfilling the words of Isaiah:

> He was despised and rejected by mankind,
> a man of suffering, and familiar with pain.
> Like one from whom people hide their faces
> he was despised, and we held him in low esteem. (Is 53:3)

Only later did people understand Christ's sacrificial act, and the same can be said of those who watch the protagonist in *The Unforgivable*, whose natural gift love comes to light only at the film's end.

This, however, does not mean that *The Unforgivable* is a Christian allegory. Its idea might better be understood in terms C. S. Lewis presents in *The Abolition of Man*. Arguing that certain moral imperatives are universal, and hence "natural" (as in *natural* gift love), Lewis gives numerous non-Christian examples, two of which illuminate *The Unforgivable*: "Great reverence is owed to a child," from the Roman poet Juvenal, which echoes an ancient Chinese proverb, "Respect the young."[11] To say anything more would ruin the impact of a film in which idea and energy generate a Pentecost of power only after the sacrifice is over—as with Christ's sacrifice.

More can be said about the gift love that energizes *Land* (2021), in which Robin Wright, the director, also plays the protagonist, Edee. The film opens with a sequence of city shots that communicate Edee's successful urban lifestyle, an existence contrasting markedly with a rickety cabin in a remote part of Wyoming that Edee moves into after abandoning her last vestiges of civilization, her phone and vehicle. An indiscriminate viewer might assume the film's repeated shots of beautiful mountain scenery signal that Edee prefers the beauty of isolated nature to the conveniences of city life, a conclusion that would be reinforced by point-of-view shots, in which the camera cuts from the face of Edee looking off screen to the beauty she gazes on. However, the beautiful images of land in *Land* are discontinuous inserts with little visual connection to Edee's perspective. The point-of-view shots we do see, when Edee looks off screen and the shot cuts to an image, provide us with clues to her psychology, for we slowly realize that the images are memories of her past

10"The Unforgivable," Rotten Tomatoes, www.rottentomatoes.com/m/the_unforgivable.

11Quoted in C. S. Lewis, *The Abolition of Man* (New York: Macmillan, 1965), 108.

life, projections from inside her head rather than perceptions of her outside surroundings. Attention to the energy of the medium, like attention to Christ as sacrificial medium, provides the film's idea.

Reinforcing the idea, we see Edee doing chores merely to survive, almost freezing to death from injuries until a hunter named Miguel brings a nurse to save her life. When she asks Miguel why he helped her, he replies, "You were in my path," as though in fulfillment of another principle from Juvenal that C. S. Lewis presents in *The Abolition of Man*, "What good man regards any misfortune as no concern of his?"[12] Teaching Edee survival skills, the good man expects nothing in exchange, sacrificing time and his own health to keep her alive. The movie is sacrificial as well, refusing to include a conventional sex scene between Miguel and Edee in exchange for greater audience appeal. Instead, we discover that Miguel's death brings Edee new life, demonstrating what Lewis calls natural gift love, which "desires what is simply best for the beloved."

### TOWARD A REAL CONCLUSION: *LARS AND THE REAL GIRL*

An even more profound example of gift love closes this chapter. The award-winning *Lars and the Real Girl* (Craig Gillespie, 2007) not only confirms a trinitarian view of creativity but also serves as a rare example in secular cinema of real love practiced by Christians.

The film starts with a close-up on the face of the twenty-one-year-old Lars (Ryan Gosling) looking out a mullioned window, a baby-blue knitted scarf around his neck soon pulled over his mouth. Cutting to a shot from behind him and then to his side, as though the camera were trying to assess what he is doing, the director then cuts to a point-of-view shot, what Lars sees coming toward him from a big house beyond a snowy driveway. It is Karin (Emily Mortimer), whom we later discover is his pregnant sister-in-law. Rather than opening the door, Lars first hides to the side of the door, only returning to the window after she knocks, such that the glass maintains a barrier between them. Yelling through the window, "I have to go to church," in answer to Karin's invitation to breakfast, he only opens the door to hand Karin the scarf from his neck, insisting that she "put the whole thing on" as protection from the snowy

[12]Quoted in Lewis, *Abolition of Man*, 99.

weather. An over-the-shoulder shot of Lars watching Karin through the window as she runs back to the house implies some kind of interest in her. Only later do we discover that this opening montage symbolizes his pysche. Lars has barricaded himself, both physically and emotionally, from human contact. What follows are scenes of various attempts to thaw Lars's resistance to gift love.

## Different Kinds of Love

In the next scene, shot-reverse-shot captures Lars in a church pew as a pastor says from the pulpit, "Love one another. . . . Love is God in action." When Lars leaves the church, however, he pulls back from the pastor's touch. In the parking lot he throws away a flower that an older woman handed him to give a young woman who was eyeing him from the choir. Those accustomed to Hollywood's insistent portrayal of hypocritical Christians might assume these images function as clues to abuse in the church. The next scene takes place in an office, where we see that the cute and sweetly girlish choir member, Margo (Kelly Garner), is one of Lars's coworkers. Lars, however, shares a cubicle with a crass young man who searches online sites for a more vulgar kind of love, telling Lars, "You can design your own woman."

When Lars drives home from work, a point-of-view shot from Lars's perspective, this time behind his windshield glass, shows Karin running out from the house and in front of his car's headlights. Having almost hit Karin, the startled Lars gets out the car, only to have his pregnant sister-in-law tackle him to the ground while insisting he come to dinner. The shot cuts to an awkward silence around the dinner table, with Lars pushing his food around his plate while ignoring his brother's suggestion he move out of the garage and into their house. In this scene we discover that the baby-blue scarf that Lars wears around his neck was knitted for him by his mother, who died giving birth to him. The scarf thus provides a clue to Lars's strange behavior. And it gets stranger.

## From One C. S. to Another

While the previous sequence might remind Christians of three loves described by C. S. Lewis—affection, friendship, and charity—the next sequence, signaling eros, requires the guidance of C. S. Peirce, who developed triads appropriated by film theorists, not only icon, index, and symbol but also the object, representamen, and interpretant by which viewers recognize them. *Lars and the Real Girl*, as we shall see, illustrates their relevance to cinema superbly.

After a screen title announces "six weeks later," we see, via long shot, a box delivered to Lars's room in the garage. Following a brief take of the box lying on the floor as Lars dresses, the shot cuts to him approaching the door of the big house. Because it is the first time he has intentionally approached other people in the film, the box seems to have had power over him. Indeed, when Karin and her husband, Lars's brother Gus (Paul Schneider), open the door, Lars tells them he has a "visitor" that he met "on the internet": a wheelchair-bound woman named Bianca who doesn't speak much English. Telling them that "she is religious," he asks whether she could stay in a spare room at their house rather than sleeping with him in the garage. In high exuberance, Gus and Karin invite Lars and his new friend to dinner later that evening.

The next shot is powerful, a long take of Gus and Karin on a couch, both staring off camera with looks of agonized concern. The take is long enough to force viewers to exercise power, in Sayers's sense. What might Gus and Karin be seeing? What has Lars done? To answer these questions, the shot cuts to Lars sitting next to an anatomically correct, life-size sex doll. Most viewers will be as stunned as Gus and Karin, seeing in Bianca what Pierce calls an icon, the embodiment (pun intended) of a salacious sex toy. Some Christians may stop viewing at this point, thinking, "This is not the kind of movie I should be watching." Meanwhile, fans of X-rated movies might respond differently, thinking, "This boring movie is finally getting interesting." What Peirce calls the interpretant of each viewer functions according to habits of perception shaped by the community with which each identifies.

Believing that Lars needs help, Gus and Karen reach out to their family doctor, who has psychological training. Dr. Berman, played with subtle finesse by Patricia Clarkson, perceives Bianca not as a sex icon but as an index in Peirce's sense, pointing to what caused it—Lars's difficulty connecting to *real* humans. Wanting to explore that index, Dr. Berman advises the couple to "go along with" the "delusion." Gus, however, seeing Bianca as an icon of perverted eros, says, "I'm not going to do it," and scenes to follow show other people struggling with their habits of perception. In other words, *Lars and the Real Girl* is about the very act of seeing, not only for viewers in the film but also for viewers *of* it.

Immediately after Gus refuses to follow Dr. Berman's advice, the filmmakers insert significant crosscutting between two different locations associated with Lars. First, we see a group from his church discussing what to do about Lars. After one man contemptuously refers to Bianca as a "big plastic thing," the pastor responds that Lars believes "God made her to help people," a very different perception. The shot immediately cuts to Lars's workplace, where the man who showed Lars the sex doll site yells at Margo, who stole his "action figures" in retaliation for his abuse of the teddy bear she keeps by her computer. As the shot cuts back to the church group, we hear a disgusted member describe Bianca as "a golden calf." The crosscutting elicits active questioning among attentive film viewers: What is the difference, other than size, between a "big plastic thing," which Lars does not use sexually, and little plastic things like action figures, or between teddy bears showered with affection and a "love doll" showered with affection? Doesn't fighting over action figures and teddy bears turn innocent toys into golden idols as well? Indeed, interpretants can see a toy, or even a *real* person, as an idol, just as adoring fans can turn celebrity actors into idols.

Next comes a statement that will shock many interpretants. In response to Bianca as a golden calf, the pastor asks the small group, "What would Jesus do?" The shot immediately cuts to Bianca holding a hymnal while sitting next to Lars in church, followed by congregants stopping to welcome Bianca to their church. Rather than an icon or index, the pastor has encouraged his church to view Bianca as a symbol, in Peirce's sense, of God's love. Viewers *of* the movie, however, still struggle with habits of perception trained by the film industry, which usually presents Christians either as icons of hypocrisy or their faith as an index of mental or emotional instability. Indeed, at this point, some viewers might perceive the church to be as dysfunctional as Lars.

## Cutting Together the Four Loves

It is Dr. Benton's business, of course, to work with the dysfunction of Lars, and she practices what she preaches to Gus and Karen by treating Bianca as a "real girl" in order to gain Lars's trust. By spending time talking to Lars about Bianca's health concerns, Benton discovers that Karin's pregnancy has reignited Lars's memories that his mother died at his birth, a guilt he carries on his shoulders as he does the blue scarf. Dr. Benton thus changes viewer perception by eliciting what Peirce calls "collateral acquaintance," fuller knowledge about Lars's past.

After Lars allows Dr. Benton to gently touch his arm, the film cuts to an office party where Lars dances alone, eyes closed while pretending to dance with a real woman, even as the host dances with Bianca by pushing her wheelchair to the music. The scene is followed by short takes of people indulging Lars's delusion: bringing Bianca to a hairstylist, getting her a job as a model/mannequin at a dress shop, taking her to visit sick children in the hospital, and so on. Included are short takes of Gus confessing various ways he failed to love Lars over the years.

By the end of *Lars and the Real Girl,* Bianca has become a symbol of true love modeled by a Christian COMMUNITY, to use the caps Peirce employed. Indeed, by invoking Peirce's basic triad of object—representamen—interpretant, we see that Bianca hasn't changed; she is the exact same object, significantly called a "love doll" in the film. But interpretants, both in and of the film, change from seeing her as an icon of sex, to an index of trauma, to the symbol of sacrificial love. *Lars and the Real Girl* thus exemplifies what art historian and film theorist Kaja Silverman says of C. S. Peirce: "The richest signs or signifiers are always those which . . . combine iconic, indexical, and symbolic elements."[13] In fact, by the end of the film, we see Lars being healed due to the exercise of the four loves as defined by the other C. S.: *agapē,* the Christlike sacrificial love ignited by the pastor; *storgē,* the family-love that keeps Karin reaching out to Lars and Gus confessing his family failures; *philia,* as coworkers and church members share a common project, loving Lars by befriending Bianca; and finally, at the end of the film, the beginning of healthy *eros* with Margo, a "real girl" who combines all four loves.

C. S. Lewis, of course, was familiar with the famous verse from St. John: "God is love. Whoever lives in love lives in God, and God in them" (1 Jn 4:16).

[13]Kaja Silverman, *The Subject of Semiotics* (New York: Oxford University Press, 1983), 22.

Significantly, the other C. S. alludes to the same verse as he begins his pronouncement quoted in chapter six, a statement that encapsulates the love manifest in both form and content of *Lars and the Real Girl*: "Everybody can see that the statement of St. John is the formula of an evolutionary philosophy, which teaches that growth comes only from love. . . . Suppose, for example, that I have an *idea* that interests me. It is *my creation*. It is my creature; . . . it is a little person. *I love it*; and I will sink myself in perfecting it."[14] Indeed, Bianca was a creation in the mind of Lars, who worked at perfecting it as a little person through conversations with and introductions to others. It was a greater love, however, that transformed all who interacted with Lars's creation, giving them creative power to respond to Bianca as the energy (incarnation) of Lars's idea. As one of Lars's coworkers pronounces, "Bianca reached out and touched us all. She was a lesson in courage and Bianca loved us all, especially Lars."

The same could be said of the film itself, which can reach out and touch viewers willing to collaborate with what Sayers calls "the love of the artist for the artefact."[15] As she puts it in *The Mind of the Maker*, "The business of the creator is not to escape from his material medium or to bully it, but to serve it; but to serve it he must love it."[16] Though the makers of *Lars and the Real Girl* clearly loved their medium, garnering multiple award nominations, the film did poorly at the box office. All too many people refuse to exercise power when viewing creative idea and creative energy empowered on the screen by the mind of the *imago Dei*.

As testified throughout this book, creation itself is an act of love, the *imago Dei* fulfilled by human creativity on the screen. Indeed, Sayers's assertion that "a work of creation is an act of love" has been endorsed by many filmmakers, as when Francois Truffaut suggested that "the film of tomorrow will be an act of love."[17] After not too many tomorrows, C. S. Lewis was writing *The Four Loves*, where, in addition to the basic four, he acknowledges the importance of love for a beautiful "object . . . which would make a man unwilling to deface a great

---

[14]Quoted in Roger A. Ward, *Peirce and Religion: Knowledge, Transformation, and the Reality of God* (Lanham, MD: Lexington Books, 2018), 452, emphasis added.

[15]*Letters* 3:257.

[16]Sayers, *Mind of the Maker*, 66.

[17]Sayers, *Mind of the Maker*, 129; François Truffaut, *The Films in My Life*, trans. Leonard Mayhew (Boston: Da Capo, 1994), 19.

picture even if he were the last man left alive."[18] Both Sayers and Truffaut would suggest that Lewis's words also apply to the beauty of a great *moving* picture. Indeed, a movie is de-faced until we have faces to see that the real thing is the love of God, who created us to be creative, even in the way we watch movies.

[18]Lewis, *Four Loves*, 32. Lewis originally wrote essays in the book as 1958 radio broadcasts.

# Coda
# Sayers and Cinema

*Intersecting Histories*

For those who want to learn more about Sayers as well as cinema, this coda describes various ways the history of each intersects, thus preparing Sayers as an adept guide for *The Wages of Cinema*. After all, Sayers was born the same year as the world's first movie studio, 1893, and she was born into heavenly life with Christ in 1957, the year *Life* magazine proclaimed the birth of a "New Hollywood."[1] By connecting key moments and figures in the development of narrative cinema with Sayers's growth as a writer, this chapter views historical accounts of both cinema and Sayers in an entirely new light. As part of the process, it will distinguish the European from the American origins of the film industry, with Sayers as our guide.

## Social History and Cinema

Histories, of course, approach their subject matter in diverse ways, as do those about famous writers. One biography may start with the author's birth, another with her ancestors. A history of cinema may start with the invention of photography, whereas others focus on earlier displays of moving images. Either kind of narrative might celebrate evolutionary growth or emphasize impediments and wrong turns. As Hayden White argues in *Metahistory*, humans construct histories based not only on facts as they understand them but also on their assumptions about the kind of story those facts suggest. Is it a tragedy or a romance? All historians, in other words, look at the past through a particular lens, explaining why histories of Christianity may have different emphases depending on whether the author is Greek Orthodox, Roman Catholic, Calvinist, or agnostic. Though

[1] Eric Hodgins, "Amid Ruins of an Empire a New Hollywood Arises," *Life*, June 10, 1957, 146-66.

most historians aim for objectivity even as they acknowledge their goals and presuppositions, their very act of writing an historical narrative affects the way readers understand the past.[2]

Aware of this fact, scholars known as social historians gather evidence about the lives of everyday people to better understand the contexts of historical eras, defining their goals as threefold:

1. documenting large structural changes
2. reconstructing the experiences of ordinary people in the course of those changes
3. connecting the two[3]

Even though Dorothy L. Sayers can hardly be considered an ordinary person, her relatively unknown involvement with cinema places her in a position relevant to social history: someone engaging with culture-changing events while living through them.

## Precursors to Cinema: The Magic Lantern and the Zoetrope

Many histories of cinema begin with the European invention and popularization of the magic lantern in the seventeenth century.[4] Directing candlelight or torch light through pictures painted on glass, magic lanterns could project those images onto a wall. The images were often of demons, devils, and ghosts, their nimbus of light from the lantern making them appear like evil spirits hovering in a darkened room. The devices therefore became popular among magicians, who used magic lanterns for special effects.

By the late eighteenth century, magicians had embellished their magic lantern techniques, sometimes sliding one glass on top of another to create the effect of eyes moving on a face. Or they might set up two lanterns, one projecting a stationary background scene, while another would move an image into the scene. Though sounding primitive today, magic lantern shows

[2]Hayden White, *Metahistory: The Historical Imagination in Nineteenth Century Europe* (Baltimore: Johns Hopkins University Press, 1971). C. S. Lewis makes a similar point in "De Descriptione Temporum," in *Selected Literary Essays*, ed. Walter Hooper (Cambridge: Cambridge University Press, 1969), 77-91.

[3]Charles Tilly, *As Sociology Meets History* (Cambridge, MA: Academic Press, 1981), 22.

[4]Historians disagree about the inventor of the magic lantern, but most attribute the device to Dutch astronomer Christiaan Huygens (1629–1695).

delighted and sometimes terrified viewers—as Sayers attests. In an unfinished memoir called *My Edwardian Childhood,* she tells of becoming so frightened while viewing her first magic lantern show around age four that she had to be extracted from the room. Rather than a demon or ghost, the lantern projected a "clown falling off a donkey" to a group of children. Understandably, Sayers seems somewhat baffled by her childhood terror, explaining in the very same paragraph of her memoir that she liked being told horror stories at the time, often "pleading" to be told "murderous tales of ogres." Clearly, spoken or written terrors did not affect her as much as seeing visual images. And two pages after recounting her magic lantern fright, Sayers writes that her greatest worry during childhood was the possibility of going blind.[5] Sayers thus implies that visual images had far greater psychological power over her than verbal imagery, a power that explains her later attraction to photography and cinema.

Sayers repeats her magic lantern experience in a fictionalized biography called *Cat O'Mary,* which she began after abandoning her nonfictional memoir a year or two earlier. Though also never finished, *Cat O'Mary* includes another famous antecedent of cinema, the zoetrope, invented by British mathematician William George Horner in 1834. Sayers describes the big metal bowl with narrow openings below its rim, explaining, "You put in a sheet of coloured pictures round the inside, and gave the bowl a twirl on its stem, and then, when the bowl revolved, you looked through the slits and saw the pictures moving."[6]

The popularity of magic lantern and zoetrope displays led to the invention of another kind of moving picture show, this one captured on celluloid film.

## From Edison to Lumières and Méliès

Inspired by a camera he saw in Paris in 1889, American entrepreneur Thomas Edison asked his assistant William Kennedy-Laurie Dickson to invent two devices, one to film motion (the kinetograph), the other to display the moving

---

[5]Dorothy L. Sayers, "My Edwardian Childhood," in *Dorothy L. Sayers: Child and Woman of Her Time,* ed. Barbara Reynolds (Cambridge, UK: Dorothy L. Sayers Society, 2002), 11, 13. I also describe Sayers's early fascination with moving images in "Through the Screen: Dorothy L. Sayers' Journey into New Worlds," *VII: Journal of the Marion E. Wade Center* 36 (2019): 6-7.

[6]Johanna Leigh, *Cat O'Mary: The Biography of a Prig,* in Sayers, *Child and Woman of Her Time,* 27, 46. Sayers calls the device a *bioscope,* which usually names a reel-to-reel film projector designed by an American in 1897.

images. The latter machine, dubbed kinetoscope, had a peephole at the top through which a single individual might watch a continuous loop of moving images inside. To provide film strips for the machines, Dickson built a rotating cabin with a retractable roof that could follow and catch the sunlight—the world's first motion-picture studio, which began producing twenty-second movies in 1893, the year Sayers was born. By 1894, kinetoscope parlors had opened all over the United States as well as in England.

Because Dickson's kinetograph was cumbersome, an important development in cinema came when the Lumière brothers, owners of a photographic equipment factory in Lyon, France, developed a lightweight machine that not only filmed actions but also could project them through an attached magic lantern. When the Lumière invention came to England in 1896, an article in the London *Times* said it demonstrated a "higher state of development" than the Edison kinetoscope: "The spectator no longer gazes through a narrow aperture at the changing picture, but has it presented to him full size on a large screen."[7] The Lumières called their apparatus a cinématograph, thus initiating the English word for the craft of camera work today, *cinematography*. Sayers's home country embraced the film industry, introducing some of the earliest experiments in cinematography, such as splicing together bits of film, superimposing images via multiple exposures, and presenting images "as if seen through telescopes or microscopes."[8]

Though sometimes presenting brief skits, cinématograph movies did not tell stories. It took a person well-versed in illusion to imagine how, by splicing and dissolving multiple shots together, one could create narrative magic. After attending a cinématograph show, magician Georges Méliès, who had employed magic lanterns in his performances, decided he wanted to include film images. Because the Lumières would not sell him one of their machines, Méliès obtained in 1896 equipment built by British inventor and filmmaker Robert W. Paul.

By 1897 Méliès had not only built his own camera but also constructed a film studio on the outskirts of Paris. There he borrowed and embellished editing techniques inspired by British filmmakers—stop-motion photography,

[7]Reprinted in Colin Harding and Simon Popple, *In the Kingdom of Shadows: A Companion to Early Cinema* (Madison, WI: Fairleigh Dickinson University Press, 1996), 8.

[8]Kristin Thompson and David Bordwell, *Film History: An Introduction*, 3rd ed. (New York: McGraw-Hill, 2010), 16, 13.

dissolves, fade-outs and fade-ins—to create brief stories. France and England, in other words, supplied the creative minds that transformed Edison's capitalist enterprise into a narrative art form, explaining why film historians argue, "By 1897, the invention of the cinema was largely completed."[9]

France and England also fed the creativity of Dorothy L. Sayers. In 1899, the year Méliès released *Cinderella,* his first narrative film combining multiple shots, the five-year-old Dorothy produced her first narrative fiction—in a letter describing the behavior of her stuffed monkeys Jacko and Jocko.[10] Her thrill with narrative increased as she was tutored at home in French. By early adolescence, Dorothy was reading Alexandre Dumas's great work *The Three Musketeers* in the original French, loving it so much that she performed scenes from the novel for neighbors and family. In addition to costumes for the productions, which seem as extravagant as those used by Méliès for his film *The Musketeers of the Queen* (ca. 1903), Dorothy decorated her bedroom with props and drawings inspired by Dumas, signing letters to her cousin with the name Athos, one of the three musketeers.[11]

Furthermore, since her parents periodically went into London for theater, Dorothy probably heard about the 1898 stage adaptation of *The Three Musketeers,* a production so celebrated that its fencing contest was filmed by the British Mutoscope & Biograph Company. The adolescent Dorothy became infatuated with the star of the production, Lewis Waller (1860–1915), after seeing him play Henry V on stage. As she gushes in a 1908 letter to her cousin Ivy, "I have fallen madly, hopelessly, desperately in love with the splendidest, handsomest, loveliest, most magnificent man in England."[12] Several years later, at a time when she was frequenting the cinema, Sayers probably saw Waller play the title role in *Brigadier Gerard* (Bert Haldane, 1915), a British film based on stories by Arthur Conan Doyle.[13] Sayers, of course, later became famous for detective novels that repeatedly allude to Conan Doyle's famous creation, Sherlock Holmes.

---

[9]Thompson and Bordwell, *Film History,* 11.

[10]*Letters* 1:1.

[11]*Letters* 1:5. For letters signed Athos, see 6, 8, 13.

[12]*Letters* 1:13. To listen to what Sayers heard, go to YouTube and enter "Speech from Henry V by Lewis Waller c 1910." For her parents' love of theater, see Barbara Reynolds, *Dorothy L. Sayers: Her Life and Soul* (New York: St. Martin's, 1993), 18.

[13]Though the Internet Movie Database does not show a release date for *Brigadier Gerard* in England, the database also does not show a release date in England for *Quo Vadis?,* which we know Sayers saw.

### A Banner Year for Cinema and Sayers: 1908

The same year Louis Waller enchanted Sayers with his characterization of King Henry V, multiple events were influencing the development of cinema:

- Edison's film company united with American Mutoscope and Biograph, cofounded by Edison's former assistant William Dickson, forming a monopoly that standardized the production and distribution of American movies to one reel, usually lasting ten to twelve minutes.
- Storefront nickelodeons, charging a nickel for a series of one-reel shorts projected on a screen, became the primary form of film exhibition in America.
- The mayor of New York temporarily shut down all nickelodeons in the city due to their displays of sex and violence, resulting in production companies agreeing to censor their films.
- Edwin S. Porter directed D. W. Griffith in *Rescued from an Eagle's Nest*, their collaboration eventually leading to important developments in film form.
- An association of businessmen in France formed Société Film d'Art to promote multireel movies based on famous literature, thus establishing what became known as "feature films."
- German Expressionism, which would later affect cinema, began to influence theater and painting.
- Vicente Blasco Ibañez published *Blood and Sand*, the novel that Sayers sought to adapt for the screen before June Mathis turned the novel into a successful movie (see chapter seven).

One could argue that 1908 also ignited what would become Sayers's enchantment with cinema and "everything dramatic."[14] Several months before she saw Lewis Waller perform on stage, she enchanted audiences with her contributions to a pageant in Somersham, England. Newspaper reports highlighted the adolescent Dorothy for composing two of the pageant tableaux and for playing musical accompaniment on her violin.[15] Not much later in 1908, she matriculated as a boarding student at the Godolphin School in Salisbury, which was "strong in drama and music, about both of which, especially drama,

---

[14]Quoted from one of Sayers's schoolmates in Martin Ferguson Smith, *In and out of Bloomsbury: Biographical Essays on Twentieth-Century Writers and Artists* (Manchester: Manchester University Press, 2021), 230.
[15]Smith, *In and out of Bloomsbury*, 210-11.

Dorothy was passionate."[16] She also became so adept at camerawork that she won a prize in photography at Godolphin's commemoration ceremony in 1912. Before Sayers finished her adolescence, then, she had demonstrated a passionate proclivity for the three essential components of cinema: photography, music, and scriptwriting. Not surprisingly, after being awarded a prestigious scholarship to Oxford University's Somerville College, Sayers often went to the movies, the city of Oxford boasting a total of six cinemas by 1914.[17]

## The Wages of Italian Cinema

During her university years, 1912–1915, Sayers witnessed the next advance in cinematic artistry, what scholars call the "golden age of Italian silent film," its colossal movies entering "triumphantly into Great Britain" just as Sayers was entering triumphantly into Oxford.[18] In 1913, Sayers viewed what is considered the first blockbuster in the history of cinema, *Quo Vadis?* (Enrico Guazzoni, 1912). Another Italian silent, *All'ombra della Corona* (Achille Consalvi, 1913), affected her even more, perhaps because it was released in England under the title *The Three Musketeers*. In an unpublished letter to her parents, she describes it as "quite the best film I ever saw not even excepting *Quo Vadis*."[19]

Italians, like the British, embraced cinema not long after the Lumière brothers brought the cinématograph to their country in 1896. Between 1905 and 1931, five hundred Italian production companies produced ten thousand films, many of which were exhibited in specially built theaters that could seat a thousand people. Because title cards with dialogue written in any language could easily be substituted for the originals, two Italian productions made a worldwide splash as early as 1911 with *The Crusaders* [*Gerusalemme liberate*], a four-reeler directed by Enrico Guazzoni (who was later responsible for the nine-reel *Quo Vadis*), and the five-reel *L'Inferno* (Bertolini, Padovan, & De Liguoro), a celebrated silent that may well have ignited Sayers's interest in Dante.

---

16Smith, *In and out of Bloomsbury*, 222, 229.

17When Barbara Reynolds published a letter from November 10, 1912, she deleted Sayers's reference to buying new plates for her camera. The full letter is Wade 65/16. The number of cinemas in Oxford comes from a 1914 report cited by Harding and Popple, *In the Kingdom of Shadows*, 209.

18Gian Piero Brunetta, trans. and quoted in John P. Welle, "*Dante's Inferno* of 1911 and the Origins of Italian Film Culture," in *Dante, Cinema and Television*, ed. Amilcare A. Iannucci (Toronto: University of Toronto Press, 2004), 42, 47n12.

19Unpublished letter to her parents, written on Somerville College stationery, no date (Wade 78/36-37). Sayers also shared the glories of *Quo Vadis* with her friend "Jim," July 30, 1913 (Wade 22/10).

As John P. Welle explains, *L'Inferno* was the "first serious artistic encounter between the nascent film industry and the Italian literary tradition," inaugurating the transition in Italy to multireel feature films. Filled with "innovative special effects" that visualize Dante's schema for the wages of sin, the film was released in England as *Dante's Inferno* during October 1912, the very same month Sayers moved to Oxford to begin her studies at Somerville College. The longest and most costly film their country yet produced, Italians regarded *L'Inferno* as a work of art rather than mere entertainment. And the British seem to have responded similarly to the "colossal" film, *Punch* magazine publishing a cartoon about it soon after its release, and another cartoon nearly half a year later.[20] Sayers enjoyed *Punch* magazine, sometimes comparing her experiences to "a page out of *Punch*."[21] Hence, cultural references to *Dante's Inferno*, if not the film itself, might explain why Sayers chose to attend a lecture on Dante during her first term at Somerville College—not long after the film appeared on Oxford screens. As Barbara Reynolds makes clear, Sayers had not read Dante before attending this lecture.[22] As late as 1946, Sayers told a correspondent that she would love to see "the *Inferno* in Glorious Technicolor," perhaps remembering the black-and-white silent movie—or at least posters advertising it—during her first year at Oxford.[23]

Whether or not Sayers screened the 1911 *Inferno*, we do know she continued to watch Italian films. After being awarded first-class honors at Oxford University, she accepted a position teaching modern languages in the northeastern port city of Kingston-upon-Hull. Finding the job dissatisfying, Sayers took solace in the city's many cinemas. In 1916, after viewing Giovanni Pastrone's *Cabiria* (1914), she breathlessly wrote her parents about the twelve-reel film, describing it as "magnificent" and "glorious."[24]

---

20Welle, "*Dane's Inferno* of 1911," 36. For reproductions of the *Punch* cartoons, see Downing, "Through the Screen."

21Reynolds, *Dorothy L. Sayers*, 363; *Letters* 1:105.

22Sayers attended the lecture on November 16, 1912, as she recounts to Henry Sayers and Helen Sayers, November 17, 1912 (Wade 65/17); Barbara Reynolds, *The Passionate Intellect: Dorothy L. Sayers' Encounter with Dante* (Kent, OH: Kent State University Press, 1989), 18. For more information supporting Sayers's screening of *Dante's Inferno*, see Downing, "Though the Screen."

23*Letters* 3:237.

24*Letters* 1:120-21; Sayers to her parents, February 5, ca. 1916 (Wade 67/2).

Sayers's assessment of *Cabiria* matches that of film scholars, who consider it "one of the highest achievements of silent film art." Shot on location in various parts of Italy, it employed "the most monumental and elaborate three-dimensional sets yet created for a motion picture." In addition, Pastrone developed new techniques to enhance the visual impact of the medium. Rather than cutting the film to insert a close-up, as British filmmakers had been doing, Pastrone patented a dolly that allowed the camera to *move through* the monumental sets into a close-up. Often considered the first tracking shot in film history, Pastrone's innovation was known for many years as "Cabiria movement."[25]

## From Photographic Art to Cinema Scenarios

Sayers quit her teaching job after four terms and returned to the beautiful city of Oxford, where she interned at Blackwell's, the firm that published her first two books of poetry, one in 1916, the other in 1918. While working at Blackwell's she maintained her interest in photography, going to London in 1919 to have her picture taken. As she explained to her mother, "Oxford is perfectly useless for photographs."[26] Considering that Sayers was still living off her father, who paid Blackwell to apprentice his daughter, this was an amazing claim. She believed visual artistry warranted the expenditure of both time and money.

To fulfill her desire, Sayers went to the studio of Dorothy Wilding, which should amaze as well. Though Wilding was still early in her career, Sayers recognized the photographer's skill, saying, "This woman is an artist," long before Wilding became famous for taking pictures of British royalty and film stars. Born the same year as Sayers (1893), Wilding had opened her London studio on Regent Street in 1918. When Sayers went there for her sitting, she would have seen an image of Basil Rathbone, a busy stage actor whose photograph Wilding had put on display, posing him "in top hat, cape, and monocle"—looking much the way Sayers would describe Lord Peter Wimsey in her first detective novel, written only two years after seeing the image of Rathbone in Wilding's studio. Tellingly, Basil Rathbone became known for his numerous cinematic portrayals of Sherlock Holmes, whom

---

[25]Welle, "*Dante's Inferno* of 1911," 22; Cook, *History of Narrative Film*, 59-60.

[26]*Letters* 1:152.

Sayers repeatedly mentions in her first novel, along with her numerous references to photography.[27]

In Dorothy Wilding's London studio, however, Sayers was more interested in artistic photography than detective fiction. After two financially rocky years at Blackwell's, she decided to follow a love interest to Normandy, where she helped him with a foreign-exchange program at a French boarding school. Working and flirting with Eric Whelpton daily, she conceptualized their relationship in cinematic terms, telling her parents, "It would make rather a jolly movie one of these days."[28] A little over six months later, Sayers was writing film scenarios. Rather than a script, a scenario describes images as they will appear on screen for a proposed silent movie and usually includes the order, length, and mood of individual shots.

## Scripting Screen Adaptations

In July 1920, Sayers met a British film producer named Cecil Mannering on a boat crossing from France to England.[29] Enticed by his suggestion that she could make lots of money for a screen adaptation of *Blood and Sand* (the 1908 novel by Vicente Blasco Ibañez), Sayers recruited her Oxford friend Dorothy Rowe to help with the project. In little more than two months they constructed a scenario called *The Matador*, which Sayers presented to "my Cinema man," as she called him, during another visit to London. Mannering, who directed eight short films in 1920, told Sayers he was "immensely pleased" with the adaptation.[30]

Unpublished correspondence reveals Sayers's exuberance, not only about *The Matador* but also about another scenario she was writing called *The Bonds*

---

27Dorothy Wilding, *In Pursuit of Perfection* (London: Robert Hale, 1958), 39. Wilding took Rathbone's photograph before she moved to Regent Street, where she displayed her photographs (39-41). For descriptions of Lord Peter in a top hat and monocle, see Dorothy L. Sayers, *Whose Body?* (New York: Avon, 1961), 7, 16; Sayers, *Murder Must Advertise* (San Francisco: HarperCollins, 1993), 29. Rathbone appeared as Sherlock Holmes in fourteen American films between 1939 and 1947.

28*Letters* 1:162; Reynolds, *Dorothy L. Sayers*, 276n99.

29*Letters* 1:164. Barbara Reynolds identifies the "producer" as Cyril Mannering, but since the Internet Movie Database has no record of a Cyril, she most likely misread Sayers's handwriting, which is easy to do. Born in Scotland, Cecil Mannering acted in twenty-four movies between 1913 and 1937, including two in 1920 while he was directing eight shorts.

30Reynolds, *Dorothy L. Sayers*, 99. Reynolds identifies the collaborator as Dorothy Rowe, based on a letter in which Sayers consults Rowe (*Letters* 1:164), but Sayers calls it "*my* scenario" (emphasis added) in a later letter to her parents (*Letters* 1:167). For the sobriquet "my Cinema man," see *Letters* 1:166.

*of Egypt.* In a letter to college friend Muriel Jaeger, who had recently visited her in France, Sayers mentions both projects, requesting a telephone call in which Jaeger might tell her about the movies currently being shown in London. She also requests the addresses of cinema producers along with an overview of the "sort of films" they make. Then, at the end of her letter, Sayers copies out for Jaeger a letter she sent to Fox Films accompanying a scenario.[31]

Earlier correspondence with Jaeger may have contributed to Sayers's exuberance. During a bout with the mumps in France, Sayers asked her friend to send her as many Sexton Blake detective stories as possible. This resulted in a gleeful correspondence in which, as Barbara Reynolds summarizes, "they conducted a brilliant spoof analysis of the Sexton Blake saga."[32] Significantly, seven Sexton Blake movies were produced between 1909 and 1919, films that both women may have screened during their years in Oxford, perhaps even during Jaeger's visit to France when they discussed *The Matador* and *The Bonds of Egypt.*

Unfortunately, none of Sayers's scenarios saw the light of cinematic projection. Part of the problem may have been one that Sayers predicted about *The Matador*: "It is quite possible that somebody else has bagged the rights already."[33] Indeed, several months later an adaptation of the novel appeared on stage in America (1921), its playwright, Tom Cushing, most likely having obtained the rights before Sayers finished her scenario. After its theatrical success, Cushing helped June Mathis turn *Blood and Sand* into a movie that became one of the most commercially successful films of 1922, starring Rudolf Valentino.

One cannot help wondering what direction Sayers's life might have taken if she and Cecil Mannering had met and collaborated earlier. Sayers thoroughly enjoyed writing cinema scenarios, telling her mother that they were "very amusing to construct, even if they come to nothing." Indeed, a year after *The Matador* came to nothing, she still hoped to earn wages from cinema.[34] On July 16, 1921, she wrote her mother about a friend who might "be able to get

[31]Dorothy L. Sayers to Muriel Jaeger, September 1, 1920 (Wade 22/153-57).

[32]Reynolds, *Dorothy L. Sayers*, 95. The first Sexton Blake mystery story appeared in 1893, becoming a saga as more than 200 authors added over 4,000 stories about the detective, the last Sexton Blake appearing in 1978.

[33]*Letters* 1:167-68.

[34]Dorothy L. Sayers to Henry Sayers and Helen Sayers, September 3, 1920 (Wade 87/42).

me into touch with cinema people," stating two paragraphs later, "A novel seems the thing to write now-a-days. I wish I had the application for it." Clearly, her preference was for cinema. Nevertheless, less than three months later she had finished writing her first novel.[35] The rest, as they say, is history. Sayers's Lord Peter Wimsey detective fiction turned her into a bestselling author and one of the founding members of London's prestigious Detection Club, a distinction that brought her into the orbit of one of the most famous film directors of all time.

### Alfred Hitchcock and Dorothy L. Sayers

Born in England six years after Sayers, Alfred Hitchcock (1899–1980) has ties to Sayers through Helen de Guerry Simpson (1897–1940), an associate member in London's Detection Club who became one of Sayers's dearest friends. A novel coauthored by Simpson and Detection Club member Clemence Dane, *Enter Sir John* (1928), was adapted by Hitchcock for two 1930 talkies, *Murder!* in English and *Mary* in German. Five years later, Simpson collaborated on the dialogue for Hitchcock's film *Sabotage*, socializing with the director during an era when she was also socializing with Sayers.[36] The year *Sabotage* premiered, 1936, was the same year both Hitchcock and Sayers got offers from MGM—he to make movies for the studio in London, she to grant film rights for one of her novels set in London.

Thanks to Helen Simpson, the chances that Sayers saw Hitchcock movies, if not Hitchcock himself, are all but certain.[37] Both Sayers and Hitchcock grew up attending live theater in London with their parents, retaining into adulthood a passion for productions on stage, and both avidly read and admired the same writers: Charles Dickens, Wilkie Collins, Arthur Conan Doyle, and G. K. Chesterton.[38] Furthermore, even though Sayers became a mystery novelist and Hitchcock a mystery filmmaker, in 1920 both were writing film scenarios, Hitchcock with greater success since he worked for the British arm

---

35*Letters* 1:178.

36Charlotte Chandler, *It's Only a Movie: Alfred Hitchcock, A Personal Biography* (London: Simon & Schuster, 2005), 105. For Hitchcock's relationship with Helen Simpson, see Donald Spoto, *The Dark Side of Genius: The Life of Alfred Hitchcock* (Boston: Da Capo, 1999), 295.

37Helen Simpson to Dorothy L. Sayers, June 10, 1936, (Wade 240/18). Helen casually mentions a comment made by "Mr. Hitchcock" as though Sayers and she have discussed the director often before.

38E. R. Gregory, introduction to Dorothy L. Sayers, *Wilkie Collins: A Critical and Biographical Study* (Toledo, OH: Friends of the University of Toledo Libraries, 1977), 8n3; Spoto, *Dark Side of Genius*, 504.

of an American cinema company (Famous Players—Lasky), that eventually become the juggernaut known as Paramount. He got his foot in the door, however, by offering to create intertitles for the company's silent films, having developed graphic skills by designing advertisements and brochures for a London telegraph and cable company. Advertising, in other words, intensified Hitchcock's appreciation for visual imagery.

The same could be said of Sayers. Having trouble landing a publisher for her first novel, Sayers began working, in 1922, as a copywriter for the S. H. Benson advertising firm in London, a job that inculcated increased awareness about the framing and positioning of visual images. In fact, Sayers's interest in photography was reignited not long after advertisers started using photographs taken by Dorothy Wilding, in 1923. Having once been photographed by Wilding and now working in advertising, Sayers wrote her mother about getting out her camera again, proclaiming with delight, "*it needs no words*!!"[39] Her attraction to nonverbal images parallels that of Hitchcock, who firmly believed, according to Gene Adair, "that the art of film was more about images than about spoken words."[40] Almost all film theorists emphatically agree.

## Hitchcock, Sayers, and German Expressionism

As discussed in chapter two, Hitchcock was powerfully influenced by German Expressionism, and the same could be said about Sayers. *The Cabinet of Dr. Caligari* (1920) carries the distinction of being one of only two movie titles mentioned in Sayers's fiction, the other being *The Student of Prague* (1913), a film that also "impressed" Hitchcock during his adolescence and that many scholars consider a precursor to German Expressionism.[41] Sayers alludes to the two German films in a short story based on an actual historical event, the fall of a German bomb near London's Covent Garden on January 28, 1918. In the story, called "The Image in the Mirror" (1928), Sayers's protagonist, Duckworthy, is cutting through Covent Garden on his way "to see a film at the Stoll" when the bomb falls.[42] Because Sayers once "trumped" through "half London" while looking for a movie that her friend John Cournos might like, she

[39]*Letters* 1:216, emphasis original. See also Terence Pepper, *Dorothy Wilding: The Pursuit of Perfection* (London: National Portrait Gallery, 1991), 16.

[40]Gene Adair, *Alfred Hitchcock: Filming Our Fears* (Oxford: Oxford University Press, 2002), 40.

[41]Spoto, *Dark Side of Genius*, 422.

[42]Dorothy L. Sayers, "The Image in the Mirror," in *Hangman's Holiday* (New York: HarperCollins, 1933), 4.

certainly knew about the Stoll Picture Theatre, which provided full orchestra accompaniment and could seat over two thousand people.[43] The largest production company in Britain, Stoll Pictures started releasing a series of popular movies about Sherlock Holmes in 1921, just as Sayers was composing her first Peter Wimsey story. This may explain why Sayers mentions film rights when she writes home about marketing her first detective novel.[44]

It was over a decade later, however, before Sayers published her story mentioning Stoll Pictures. In "The Image in the Mirror" (1933), Duckworthy tells Lord Peter about nightmares after the bombing, comparing them to German movies: "I'd be stumbling for hours through a queer sort of world—all mist and half-lights, and the walls would be all crooked like they are in that picture of 'Dr. Caligari.'" This description appears three paragraphs after the man tells Lord Peter about being traumatized as a child when his mother took him to see *The Student of Prague,* "about a young fellow at the university who sold himself to the devil, and one day his reflection came stalking out of the mirror on its own, and went about committing dreadful crimes."[45] At first Duckworthy simply dreams of seeing his reflection in a long mirror, but soon he experiences doppelgänger images in real life, coming to believe his mirror self has committed a serious crime, as in *The Student of Prague.*

Given her interest in cinema, Sayers probably saw the German remake of *The Student of Prague* (1926), which, premiering two years before the publication of "The Image in the Mirror," was hailed as director/actor Henrik Galeen's finest German Expressionist film. If she did see Galeen's adaptation, it would have elicited memories of the 1913 silent that she, like her story's protagonist, saw years earlier, eliciting from Duckworthy, "I forget the details, it's so long ago."[46] Certainly screening one if not the other rendition, Sayers recognized in *The Student of Prague* a dramatic retelling of the Faust legend that connects her early cinematic hopes with her later theatrical career. For, in her exuberant 1920 letter to Muriel Jaeger about her two screenplays and cinema producers, Sayers shares that she is "constructing a story about a man who sold his soul to the devil."[47] One can only wonder whether she used some of

---

[43] *Letters* 1:237.

[44] *Letters* 1:182.

[45] Sayers, "Image in the Mirror," 11, 10.

[46] Sayers, "Image in the Mirror," 10.

[47] Sayers to Muriel Jaeger, September 1, 1920 (Wade 22/157).

the material from that story for her 1939 Faust-like play *The Devil to Pay*. Indeed, as in *The Student of Prague*, a mirror is essential for Sayers's staged play.

Hitchcock also valued mirrors. After witnessing how Murnau used them in *The Last Laugh*, he became convinced of their "enormous emotional power," as they suggested not only split personalities but also "the need for introspection." As Donald Spoto recounts, Hitchcock put mirrors "wherever possible" in both *Vertigo* (1958) and *Psycho* (1960), two of his most revered films.[48] Cinematographers continue to play with mirrors to this day. Especially common are shots capturing people's eyes in automobile rearview mirrors, as well as views in cars' side mirrors even as the camera captures the surrounding scene, multiple viewpoints simultaneously rendered in one shot. As Sayers puts it in the closing line of "The Image in the Mirror," "There's something queer about mirrors. Uncanny, a bit, don't you think?"[49]

It was during the height of German Expressionism that both Sayers and Hitchcock saw their dreams fulfilled. In May 1923 Sayers welcomed the publication of her first detective novel, *Whose Body?*, which contains over a dozen references to photography, including specific descriptions of camera equipment. Several months later, Hitchcock saw the completion of the first film for which he had major creative input, serving as screenwriter, assistant director, and set designer. Called *Woman to Woman* and considered "one of the first international British successes," the film deals with the birth of an illegitimate child and thus touches on an issue that wrenched Sayers's life.[50]

## Sayers's Si(g)ns

While Hitchcock was reveling in the wages of cinema, Sayers was agonizing over the wages of sin. In 1923 she discovered she was pregnant, a rebound romp with a car salesman (who relished cinema) after the demise of a "hero-worship" relationship with an intellectual who would occasionally "condescend to see" movies with her. Believing she must hide "so bitter a sin," Sayers took a leave of absence from Benson's advertising agency and journeyed to the southern coast of England to deliver her baby in secret.[51] During her lifetime,

---

48Spoto, *Dark Side of Genius*, 422.

49Sayers, "Image in the Mirror," 30.

50Michael Powell, *A Life in Movies: An Autobiography* (New York: Knopf, 1987), 117.

51*Letters* 1:223, 237. See also Reynolds, *Dorothy L. Sayers*, 121, 163.

only four people seem to have known about Sayers's child: the man she would eventually marry; her cousin Ivy Shrimpton, who fostered unwanted children with her mother; Bill White, who took no responsibility for the child he sired; and John Cournos, the intellectual who broke Sayers's heart. (Revealingly, Sayers named the baby John, not Bill.)

Several weeks after the birth of John Anthony on January 3, 1924, Sayers transported the baby to Ivy's home, five days before *Woman to Woman* premiered in America.[52] When Sayers returned to London, she discovered that the person who had been staying in her flat had unintentionally locked her out. Rather than passing the time by window shopping or browsing in a bookshop, Sayers chose to go to the movies. Several months later, she entertained a visiting great aunt by taking her to a film.[53] Clearly, cinema provided an important outlet for the thirty-year-old author who carried a burden of sin, a burden so great that her parents died never knowing they had a grandchild.

### The Integrity of Film: *Wuthering Heights*

During her pregnancy, Sayers continued to work on her second novel, *Clouds of Witness,* which, unlike her first, not only focuses on several sexual affairs but also explicitly refers to cinema. While writing a letter, Lord Peter comments to a servant waiting to take out the mail, "Wish I could write at the rate people do on the cinema [screen]." He proceeds to mock the movie convention in which a detailed letter is accomplished "in one scrape of the pen."[54] Later in *Clouds of Witness,* Lord Peter experiences what is described in the novel as a "cinematographic episode," one that echoes elements from Emily Brontë's famous 1847 novel *Wuthering Heights.* Like Brontë's Lockwood, Lord Peter visits a remote house in Yorkshire, having to rely on "stout white posts" to avoid falling into the surrounding bogs. Inside the houses, both of which contain a "high oak settle" in front of an "immense fireplace," Wimsey and Lockwood interact with surly owners before discovering a highly attractive woman sequestered within. Both must fight off vicious dogs, Peter with a

52 Sayers transported John Anthony to Ivy on Wednesday, January 30, 1924; *Woman to Woman* opened in the US on February 4.

53 *Letters* 1:209, 215.

54 Dorothy L. Sayers, *Clouds of Witness* (New York: HarperCollins, 1995), 60.

walking stick, Lockwood with a fire poker. Sayers even calls a servant in the house Jabez, echoing the Jabes who enters Lockwood's dreams while he sleeps at Wuthering Heights. Nevertheless, even though Sayers had read *Wuthering Heights* more than once, mentioning Emily Brontë while discussing *Clouds of Witness* in a letter, she describes Lord Peter's experience not as literary or Brontë-like but as "cinematographic."[55]

Why single out that episode as cinematographic? Other events in the novel seem more the stuff of cinema, as with Lord Peter's unusual transatlantic flight in a two-seater biplane, by which he transports evidence exonerating his brother, who is being tried for murder. The incident, in fact, gives clouds and witness in *Clouds of Witness* extra meaning: "Lord Peter peered out through the cold scurry of cloud. The thin struts of steel, incredibly fragile, swung slowly across the gleam and glint far below, where the wide country dizzied out and spread like a revolving map."[56] Sayers thus describes the perspective from a biplane much as viewers would soon see it in the first film to win the Academy Award for Best Picture, *Wings* (William Wellman, 1927), a celebrated silent about fliers during World War I. Though *Clouds of Witness* came out while *Wings* was still in production, earlier newsreels (which appeared on cinema screens as early as the 1910s) offered perspectives that must have influenced Sayers's description of Lord Peter's flight, since she never flew on an airplane.[57]

So, once again, why designate the Brontë-like narrative as the cinematographic one?

Given her enjoyment of cinema, Sayers may have seen the first ever film adaptation of *Wuthering Heights*, a British movie released in 1920, the year she was constructing her own cinema scenarios and probably seeing as many movies as possible. Tellingly, the scenario for *Wuthering Heights* was written by Eliot Stannard (1888–1944), who composed or adapted eight of the nine scripts that Alfred Hitchcock made into films between 1925 and 1929. Even before his work with Hitchcock, Stannard was respected not only for the

---

[55]For relevant passages in *Clouds of Witness*, see 82-91; see also Emily Brontë, *Wuthering Heights* (San Francisco: Ignatius, 2008), 10, 14, 17, 38, 88. For Sayers's familiarity with *Wuthering Heights*, see *Letters* 1:69-70. For her mention of Brontë in the context of *Clouds of Witness*, see *Letters* 1:215.

[56]Sayers, *Clouds of Witness*, 242.

[57]See, for example, *Fighting the War* (Donald C. Thompson, 1916), a documentary that includes shots taken from war airplanes; www.silentera.com/PSFL/data/F/FightingTheWar1916.html.

integrity of his work but also for his essays about the artistry of filmmaking, so the 1920 *Wuthering Heights* must have been visually stunning. This would explain why Sayers felt the need to visit Yorkshire while finishing *Clouds of Witness*—she wanted to make sure that her cinematographic image of the moors, perhaps based on the 1920 *Wuthering Heights*, was accurate. After all, earlier in *Clouds of Witness*, she had referenced the problematic portrayal of letter writing in movies.

Unfortunately, the 1920 *Wuthering Heights* is lost, as are many movies made before the transition, in 1951, from nitrate film stock to the acetate base of safety film. Not only does nitrate celluloid disintegrate over time, but it is so flammable that cinema projection booths had to be fireproofed. During the era that Hitchcock was making his British films, city officials had to outlaw the transportation of movies on the London Underground for fear of spontaneous fires. Sayers, as we have seen, had a very different kind of interest in spontaneous fires.

## Devilish Fires

As discussed in chapter four, Sayers developed her Christian aesthetic while writing a play about the rebuilding of Canterbury Cathedral after a devastating fire. *The Zeal of Thy House* (1937) was so successful, in fact, that Canterbury Festival organizers asked Sayers to write another play. Called *The Devil to Pay*, Sayers's 1939 work, perhaps not coincidentally, alludes to cinema. In act 3, set in 1527 Innsbruck, Faustus and Mephistopheles, the devil to whom Faustus has sold his soul, entice an emperor to wage war on the pope. As part of their enticement, Faustus offers a "magical device" that will project on a screen the emperor's army defeating Rome. After Faustus states, "Let's have the show," Mephistopheles explains how to watch the display:

> Turn your back to the light, and look up northward,
> Where the pale clouds lie like a silver screen;
> See where the shadows waver, cast by the sun.

"Silver screen," a common metaphor for cinema, was already in use when Sayers was screening movies as an Oxford University student. It denoted a place where people turned their backs to the light of the projection booth to view black-and-white images moving on a screen like shadows, color film not becoming commercially viable until over a decade after *The Devil to Pay* premiered.

To reinforce that her characters are watching a war story on the silver screen, Sayers has characters comment on what they are seeing, starting with the emperor proclaiming, "I see! I see!" and with Faustus once again referring to a dramatic production: "Is the show ended? / I was enjoying myself." By aligning the silver screen with Mephistopheles and the soulless Faustus, Sayers comments on people who use film for profit rather than see it as art. Indeed, not long before the show begins, she has Mephistopheles refer to profit and Faustus mention wealth while they are tempting the emperor to conquer Europe.[58] Like a Phoenix rising from the ashes, *The Devil to Pay*, like *The Zeal of Thy House*, served as Sayers's response to the shoddy work of Phoenix Films.

## Fired Up by Sybil Thorndike

*The Wages of Cinema* rises from ashes as well: those scattered by biographers asserting that Sayers renounced cinema. As a final (fire)proof, this coda closes describing a friendship Sayers developed with one of the most famous British stage and screen stars of her day. In 1956, Sayers dined with Dame Sybil Thorndike (1882–1976), whose ashes are interred at Westminster Abbey. Joining the two famous women for lunch was a mutual friend, Rev. Aubrey Moody, who gave Sayers "Victorian transparencies," probably employed by a magic lantern, that she was planning to make into a type of slide show. Moody reports that, during his lunch with Sayers and Thorndike, he "suddenly became aware that the restaurant was rather quiet. Everyone was listening enthralled to the two great ladies' audible conversation. 'Where's my hat?' said Dorothy, as they rose to go. She had been sitting on it and just pulled it on, flattened as it was."[59] Sayers was probably too enchanted by all she had in common with Thorndike to worry about her hat.

Sayers and Thorndike, both daughters of clergymen, relished going to London with their parents to see live theater. And they both adored famous stage actor Lewis Waller, Sybil so charmed that she asked her father to let

58 Dorothy L. Sayers, *The Devil to Pay* (London: Gollancz, 1939), 82-86.

59 Sayers refers to the transparencies in two unpublished letters to Moody: April 4, 1955 and August 24, 1956 (Wade 380/7, 3); Moody's comment about the lunch appears in *Letters* 4:324n4.

her sit through the same Waller play a second time. The fifteen-year-old Dorothy not only described Waller as the "most magnificent man in England" but also hung up four photographs of him on her bedroom wall, kissing them every night.[60]

Over a decade later, Sayers wrote the famous 1921 letter to her parents in which she mentions an idea that turned into her first Peter Wimsey novel. But she also shares that she is joining friends at the Little Theatre to see a Grand Guignol play, which reputedly "surpasses everything else in grisliness." Sybil Thorndike appeared in every program for the Little Theatre that ran from September 1920 through June 1922, which means that Sayers witnessed her perform on stage.[61] One cannot help wondering, therefore, whether she saw the Grand Guignol in which Thorndike's character was murdered and stuffed in a trunk, thus influencing Sayers's commission for Phoenix Films, *The Silent Passenger* (Reginald Denham, 1935), wherein Lord Peter finds a murdered man stuffed in a trunk.

Sybil and Dorothy also shared an admiration for Harcourt Williams, director of the Old Vic Theater in London from 1929 to 1932. Sybil not only acted under his direction but also did a European tour with Williams and other Old Vic actors soon after VE Day in 1945. As for Sayers, she so respected Old Vic productions that she suggested the Canterbury Festival organizers recruit Harcourt Williams to direct *The Zeal of Thy House*.[62] Sayers's dreams were fulfilled when Williams not only directed but also starred in the play, doing such a fantastic job that he reprised his roles to great acclaim during the London run of *Zeal* the following year. Not surprisingly, festival organizers recruited Williams to take on both direction and the lead role for Sayers's second Canterbury play, *The Devil to Pay*, performed in summer of 1939. When Sayers published the script for the latter, she appended a sonnet titled "To the Interpreter HARCOURT WILLIAMS," praising the integrity of Williams's work as an "interpreter" of a playwright's work.

Harcourt Williams also appeared on screen, taking minor roles in a score of films, including two directed by and starring his protégé Sir Laurence Olivier, with whom Thorndike also appeared on stage and screen. It seems only

---

[60]*Letters* 1:13; Jonathan Croall, *Sybil Thorndike: A Star of Life* (London: Haus Books, 2008), 26.
[61]*Letters* 1:174; Croall, *Sybil Thorndike*, 144-45, 528.
[62]*Letters* 1:406.

appropriate, then, that the only extant film footage of Sayers includes Harcourt Williams. In 2011, a collection of film reels was discovered in a house near Canterbury, having been made by amateur documentary filmmaker Sidney Bligh, who ran an electrical shop. On the reels are images from the Canterbury Festival plays, such as a costumed Harcourt Williams joining other actors for brief outdoor reenactments from the Canterbury plays. Bligh also filmed the Canterbury playwrights T. S. Eliot, Charles Williams, and Sayers. One black-and-white clip shows Sayers standing in front of Canterbury Cathedral, holding her London *Times* while smiling and blinking at the camera. Another clip, in color, shows her in furs holding a play program outside the cathedral.[63]

Equally dear as Harcourt Williams to both Thorndike and Sayers was film actor and screenwriter Val Gielgud, the brother of Sir John Gielgud. Both women worked with Val when he served as head of productions for BBC radio. When Sayers and Thorndike met for lunch, both still considered Gielgud a good friend, Sybil boasting to him in 1953 about her film work, which included over a dozen movies by then, including Alfred Hitchcock's *Stage Fright* (1950).[64] Sayers and Thorndike may have discussed their common connection to Hitchcock during their restaurant-hushing lunch, as well as director Michael Powell, who met with Sayers in 1945 to talk about Peter Wimsey film adaptations and who directed Thorndike in *Gone to Earth* (1950).

Sayers and Thorndike had many other people in common, such as author Clemence Dane, who won the Academy Award for Best Story for *Perfect Strangers* (1945); birth control specialist Charis Barnett Frankenburg; and Robert Speaight, an actor who performed on stage with Sybil in 1944 after having played the voice of Jesus in Sayers's radio cycle, *The Man Born to Be King*.[65] Sayers's name even appears in a biography about Thorndike, the author noting that "Along with T S Eliot, Dorothy L Sayers and Marie Tempest, [Sybil] was a vice-president of the Oxford Pilgrim Players."[66]

---

[63]For a film about Sidney Bligh and his filming of Canterbury events, including the Canterbury festival plays, watch "Seeking Sidney," https://vimeo.com/403972225. Members of the Dorothy L. Sayers Society were first shown the black-and-white shot of Sayers and play reenactments on June 15, 2013, at a special gathering in Canterbury. For details about the gathering, see *The Dorothy L Sayers Society Bulletin* 228 (July 2013): 3-6.

[64]Croall, *Sybil Thorndike*, 393.

[65]See Mo Moulton, *The Mutual Admiration Society: How Dorothy L Sayers and Her Oxford Circle Remade the World for Women* (New York: Basic Books, 2019), 117.

[66]Croall, *Sybil Thorndike*, 342.

The connections between Thorndike and Sayers are more than fun coincidences. They highlight the important ways both theater and film provided a means for women to gain recognition for the integrity of their work. What Harcourt Williams proclaimed of Thorndike parallels what many said of Sayers: "I came to appreciate the amazing vitality of Sybil Thorndike. Every day she seemed to be speaking here, giving a recital for some good cause there, attending early service, dealing with correspondence, and acting at night with undiminished vigour. And always in such good spirits and high humour."[67]

Most important of all, Sayers and Thorndike never totally renounced the Christianity they inherited from their clergymen fathers, even though they similarly denounced the use of stage or screen for evangelistic purposes. In an essay called "Religion and the Stage," commissioned in 1928 by Earnest Benn, who published Sayers's *Tristan in Brittany* the very next year, Thorndike writes, "A religious system that patronises art and claims to teach the artist what to see and what to say is on the side of darkness, not of light." She proceeds to argue that the "artist accepts life as it is and claims the gift of a clearer vision of it, and the power of so presenting it that others also may see his vision." But "the nearer it gets to direct preaching, the worse it is likely to be as drama." Sayers wrote something similar in a letter to Rev. Aubrey Moody, the friend who joined her and Sybil for lunch:

> Instead of concentrating on writing good plays, people try to write pieces that shall "go further in evangelistic effort," or "make the Christian Faith exciting." . . . Any work of art is false to its interior truth if it proceeds, not from the love of the work per se, but from an intention to manipulate the minds of the spectators. And you cannot serve God, or anybody else, with falsehood.[68]

Inspired by Sayers, *The Wages of Cinema* celebrates the love of work as well, not only that of filmmakers, including actors such as Dame Sybil Thorndike, but also the creative work of those who watch movies, thus contributing power to idea and energy on screen.

---

[67]Quoted in Croall, *Sybil Thorndike*, 338.

[68]Quoted in Croall, *Sybil Thorndike*, 217; *Letters* 4:171.

# Index

*2001: A Space Odyssey*, 186
Academy Awards, 29, 31, 32, 33, 55, 83, 99, 124, 162, 180, 196, 233, 237
Acker, Ally, 176
Adair, Gene, 229
Adorno, Theodor W., 96-97, 103, 119, 156-57
Aeschylus, 25, 29, 39, 41, 42, 74
*Age of Innocence, The*, 36
Allen, Woody, 33
Althusser, Louis, 158, 161
American Mutoscope and Biograph Co., 49, 222
Andreyev, Leonid, 51
angled shots, 50, 64, 68, 78, 80, 82, 87, 88, 140, 170, 186, 195, 204
*Apocalypse Now*, 183
Apostolos-Cappadona, Diane, 36
apparatus theory, 158-62, 165, 166, 179
Aquinas, Thomas, 83, 114, 117
Aristophanes, 30-31, 33, 66, 68
  *The Birds*, 66-68
Aristotle, 29, 31, 43
Arnheim, Rudolf, 97
Astruc, Alexandre, 151-52, 155
Athanasius, 128
Augustine, 23, 83, 115, 126, 131, 133, 168, 182
Austen, Jane, 188
auteur theory, 151-57, 159, 160
Balázs, Béla, 8, 11, 147-48
Balthasar, Hans Urs von, 11, 23, 38
*Barbie*, 185-90
Barrie, J. M., 5, 96
Barth, Karl, 131-35, 141
Barthes, Roland, 65, 161
Barzun, Jacques, 3, 145
*Batman* movies, 57
*Battleship Potemkin, The*, 54-55, 148
Baty, Gaston, 39
Baudry, Jean-Louis, 158
Baugh, Lloyd, 32
Baumbach, Noah, 186-88
Bayer, William, 83
Bazin, André, 23, 46, 62, 149-50, 153
*Becket*, 55
Belton, John, 166-67
Bergman, Ingmar, 23, 124-25
Bernhardt, Sarah, 21, 51
*Birdman: The Unexpected Virtue of Ignorance*, 55-68
bird's-eye-view shot, 78, 79
*Birth of a Nation*, 134-35
*Black Panther: Wakanda Forever*, 185
*BlacKkKlansman*, 36, 135
*Blood and Sand*, 175, 177, 222, 226-27
Bogart, Humphrey, 150, 196
Bordwell, David, 99, 151, 166
Brando, Marlon, 183, 188
breaking the fourth wall, 57, 59, 154
*Breathless*, 156
Bresson, Robert, 29, 152, 155
*Brick Lane*, 199-202
*Bridge on the River Kwai, The*, 76-86, 88, 91-92, 95
*Brief Encounter*, 75, 87-88
*Brigadier Gerard*, 221
British Film Institute (BFI), 4, 75-76, 186
Brody, Richard, 56, 60
Brown, David, 45
Bullock, Sandra, 208
*Cabinet of Dr. Caligari, The*, 52-53, 229
*Cabiria*, 124, 224-25
*Cahiers du cinema*, 152-53, 156
Callaway, Kutter, 133-34
Calvin, John, 133, 152
Calvinism, 132-33
*Campaign, The*, 30
Cannes Film Festival, 135, 154, 172
Carroll, Noël, 166, 167
Carver, Raymond, 57
*Casablanca*, 196
*Cavalcade*, 74
Champlin, Charles, 42
Chaplin, Charlie, 4, 100-102, 127, 147
Chase, Canon William Sheafe, 24
Chastain, Jessica, 185
Chesterton, G. K., 5, 122, 151, 188, 228
chiaroscuro, 122, 151
Chibnall, Steve, 109
Christian orthodoxy, 5, 13-14, 93-94, 126, 143-44
*Chronicles of Narnia* movies, 72
cinématograph, 220
*City Lights*, 101-102
classical vs postclassical film style, 59, 61, 68, 86, 90
cliched conventions in movies, 18, 36, 60, 88, 90, 96, 129, 130, 161, 192, 195-99, 204-6, 210, 232
close-up shots, 49, 53, 54, 59, 72, 87, 88, 89, 90, 130, 136, 147, 154, 159, 182, 197, 199

cognitivism, 166
comic book movies, 71, 128
computer-generated imagery (CGI), 128
Conrad, Joseph, 183
Constantine, 163-64
Cook, David A., 48, 51, 106
Coppola, Sophia, 195-96
*Corpus Christi* plays, 40, 44
Coward, Noël, 74-75, 87
Cranston, Bryan, 130
Croall, Jonathan, 70
crosscutting, 48, 50, 81, 163, 207, 213
Cruise, Tom, 201
*Crusaders, The*, 223
Cukor, George, 22
Daguerre, Louis, 22
Dalle Vacche, Angela, 126-27
*Dark Knight, The*, 35
Day, Barry, 74
*Death at Broadcasting House*, 103
deep focus, 149
Deleuze, Gilles, 165
DeMill, Cecil B., 22
Derrida, Jacques, 92
Detweiler, Craig, 133
deus ex machina, 31-34, 68, 136, 140
*Dialectic of Enlightenment*, 96, 97, 119
Dickens, Charles, 122-23, 228
Dickson, William Kennedy-Laurie, 219-20, 222
diegesis, 60-61, 64, 87, 182
  diegetic sound, 60-63, 163
  internal diegetic sound, 63, 204
  nondiegetic sound, 60-63, 186, 204
digital technology, 166-67
Dionysus, 24-25, 28-30, 32
dissolve, 46, 47, 59, 190, 220-21
Docetism, 12-13
*Doctor Zhivago*, 76
*Documents in the Case, The*, 100
*Dodgeball: A True Underdog Story*, 33
dolly shots, 59
Doubting Thomas, 6, 47
Douglas, Michael, 179
dream screen, the, 158-60
*Dream Street*, 98
Dulac, Germaine, 104
Dyer, Richard, 88
*Easy Virtue*, 74
Ebrahimian, Babak, 46
economy of exchange, 92-94
Ecumenical Councils, 1, 13, 24, 128, 163-64
Edison, Thomas, 47, 123, 219-22
Ehrat, Johannes, 165
Eisenstein, Sergei, 22, 53-55, 59, 60, 148, 149
Eliot, T. S., 111, 183, 237
Epimenides, 27
Epstein, Jean, 147
Euripides, 25, 28-32, 33, 42
Eusebius of Caesarea, 27, 37
*Ex Machina*, 135-42
*Eyes of Tammy Faye, The*, 185
fade-in/out, 46, 47, 221
Fassbinder, Rainer Werner, 23
Fellini, Frederico, 124
feminist film theory, 170, 175, 178-81, 184-85, 188, 206
film noir, 150-51, 154
film theory, 16, 54-55, 65, 146-70
  *see also* feminist film theory
*films d'art*, 51-52
Firth, Colin, 87, 89, 188
flashback, 86
*Four Horsemen of the Apocalypse, The*, 176
*Four Hundred Blows, The*, 154
Francis of Assisi, 45, 47, 103
freeze-frame, 154, 189
French Impressionism, 147
French New Wave, the, 154-57
Fujimura, Makoto, 3, 11-12, 117
gangster movies, 110
Gatins, John, 184
German Expressionism, 52, 147, 151, 228-29
Gerwig, Greta, 185-88
Getino, Octavio, 157-58
Gielgud, Sir John, 55, 237
Godard, Jean-Luc, 156-57, 158-59
*Godfather, The*, 188
Goldwyn Pictures, 9-10, 107, 176
*Gone to Earth*, 237
Goodwin, Richard Vance, 6
grand theory, 166
graphic match, 81, 182, 186, 187, 206, 208
*Great Dictator, The*, 102
*Great Expectations*, 75
*Great Train Robbery, The*, 48
*Greed*, 106-107
*Green Mile, The*, 36
green screen, 167, 189
*Greenland*, 129
Griffith, D. W., 22, 49-51, 53, 98, 122-23, 134-35, 222
happy endings, 130-31, 140, 151, 154, 191, 199, 201
Harp, Richard L., 121
Hart, William S., 147
Hayes Code, the, 194
*Heart of Darkness, The*, 183
Hepburn, Katharine, 32
history of cinema, 46-55, 166, 217, 234
  England, 16, 23, 47, 70, 74-75, 108-110, 220-21, 228, 230-31, 234
  France, 21-22, 29, 47-48, 52, 147, 153-57, 175, 220-22
  Germany, 23, 52, 222, 228-31
  Italy, 16, 124, 223-25
  Japan, 97
  Latin America, 157
  Soviet Union, 22, 53-55
  Sweden, 23, 124
  United States of America (USA), 9-10, 21, 22-23, 47-51, 108-110, 150-51, 175-76
history of theater, 21-42, 109, 111
  and Bible authors, 24-29, 31, 34
  and Christian theology, 37-38, 40, 44-45
  Greek, 24-32, 34, 39, 41-42, 45, 66-68, 69, 119-20, 136

Medieval, 39-42
Roman, 34-38, 66
Hitchcock, Alfred, 4-5, 8, 10, 52, 55, 73, 74, 84, 97, 103, 105, 112, 117, 153, 156, 176-77, 228-29, 231, 233-34, 237
Hoffman, Michael, 192-93
Horace, 31
Horkheimer, Max, 96-97, 103, 119, 156-57
*How Men Love*, 5
*Hunger Games* movies, 57
*Hurt Locker, The*, 57
Huston, John, 150
*imago Dei*, 11-12, 111-112, 114, 117, 118, 125, 133, 141, 144, 168, 181, 191, 215
*In Which We Serve*, 74, 75, 87
Iñárritu, Alejandro González, 55-57, 62-63, 68
Incarnation, the, 2, 12, 19, 28, 40-41, 43, 44, 126
independent filmmaking, 167
*Infiltrator, The*, 130
Ingram, Rex, 176
intercutting, 53-54, 90, 91, 93, 163, 204
intertitles, 97-98, 102, 107, 147, 223, 229
*Intolerance*, 53
*Invasion, The*, 32-33
Jackson, Peter, 36, 181
Jacobs, Lewis, 176
*Jazz Singer, The*, 98
Jenkins, Henry, 166
Jerome, 27
*Jerry Maguire*, 201
Jesus Christ, 1, 2, 5, 6, 14, 25, 37, 39-42, 45, 47, 83, 94, 115, 126, 127, 129-30, 150, 162, 190, 208-9, 210
Johnston, Robert K., 7
Jolson, Al, 98
Kauffmann, Stanley, 46
Kazan, Elia, 112
Keaton, Michael, 56, 57
Kelly, Herbert, 113-114
*Kid, The*, 101, 127
Kidman, Nicole, 33-34
kinetograph, 219-20
kinetoscope, 220
*King Kong* movies, 180-84
Koch, Howard, 23
Kubrick, Stanley, 186
Kuleshov, Lev, 53-54
*Ladies in Lavender*, 202-8
Lake, Christina Bieber, 136
*Land*, 209-10
Lang, Fritz, 52, 112
*Lars and the Real Girl*, 210-15
*Last Duel, The*, 192
*Last Laugh, The*, 52, 231
Lauste, Eugene, 98
*Lawrence of Arabia*, 75
Lean, David, 75-76, 79, 81, 85, 87
Lee, Spike, 36, 135, 153
*Legend of Bagger Vance, The*, 36
Lenin, Vladimir, 53
Lewin, Bertram D., 158
Lewis, C. S., 3, 9, 68, 72, 77, 94-95, 118, 144-46, 153, 169, 180-81, 191, 198, 199, 208, 209-11, 213-16
*The Four Loves*, 208, 209, 211, 213-16
Lindsay, Vachel, 51-52
*Little Fockers*, 35
*Lives of Others, The*, 162-63
*Lone Ranger* movies, 35
*Lone Survivor*, 71-72
*Lonely Villa, The*, 50-51
long shot, 49, 59, 64, 149, 170, 212
long/short take, 50, 59, 60, 66, 90, 91, 93, 149, 212, 214
*Lord of the Rings* movies, 36, 72, 181
*Lost in Translation*, 195-96
low-key lighting, 122, 151, 197, 199, 201
Lumière brothers, 220, 223
Luther, Martin, 152
Lynn, Ralph, 107
MacCulloch, Diarmaid, 12, 132, 133
McNutt, David, 132-33
magic lantern, 218-20, 235
magical realism, 63-65
*Maltese Falcon, The*, 150
Mankiewicz, Joseph, 31
Manovich, Lev, 167
Marcion, 12
Mary, the mother of Jesus, 14, 37
Mathis, June, 175-78, 222, 227
*Matrix* movies, 34
medium shot, 49-50, 90, 163
*Meet the Fockers*, 35
*Meet the Parents*, 35
Méliès, Georges, 46, 47, 48, 220, 221
Menander, 34-35
Metro-Goldwyn-Mayer (MGM), 10, 74, 107
*Metropolis*, 52
Metz, Christian, 8, 10, 160
*Midsummer Night's Dream, A*, 192-93, 204
*Mighty Aphrodite*, 33, 36
mise-en-scène, 22, 57, 58, 59, 64, 66, 80, 102, 137, 149-52, 156, 161, 167, 188, 192, 205
Mitchell, William J., 167
*Modern Times*, 102
modernism, 145-47, 153, 160
Moltmann, Jürgen, 133
Monaco, James, 13, 22, 150, 156
Monroe, Marilyn, 4
montage, 53-54, 58-59, 80, 90, 102, 136, 149, 152, 156, 170, 207
Moody, Aubrey, 235, 238
motifs in movies, 56, 66, 136-38, 206
Mulvey, Laura, 178-79, 206
Münsterberg, Hugo, 146, 147
Murnau, F. W., 52, 231
musicals, 31, 99
Nero, 37
*New Kind of Love, A*, 193-95
Newman, Paul, 193-94
nickelodeons, 48-49, 51, 222
*Nights of Cabiria*, 124
Nolan, Christopher, 35
*Nosferatu*, 52

Nyong'o, Lupita, 185
*Oliver Twist*, 76
Olivier, Sir Laurence, 4, 23, 236
*On with the Show!*, 99
Origen, 15
Oscars: see Academy Awards
outlaw heroes, 129, 159, 195
over-the-shoulder (OTS) shot, 59, 78, 90, 159, 204, 210
  traveling OTS shot, 59
Pagnol, Marcel, 21-22
panning shots, 48, 49, 78, 89, 90, 163, 207
Panofsky, Erwin, 97-98
Paramount Pictures, 229
*Passion of the Christ, The*, 37
Pastrone, Giovanni, 224-25
Paul, Robert W., 220
Peirce, Charles Sanders, 162-66, 168-69, 211-15
  habits of perception, 162-64, 200, 212-13
  icon, index, symbol, 163-65, 168, 212-14
*Perfect Strangers*, 237
*Peter Pan*, 5, 96
*Phantom of the Opera*, 66
pharmakon, 193, 197
*Pinocchio*, 4
Plato, 5, 29, 119-20
Plautus, 34-35
*Pleasure Garden, The*, 105
point-of-view (POV) shot, 50, 130, 136, 137, 159, 186, 209, 210, 211
  traveling POV shot, 59, 183
Porter, Edwin S., 47-49, 222
postmodernism, 145-46
Powell, Michael, 4, 46, 54, 75, 98, 99, 101, 117-18, 176, 237
*Private Lives*, 74
*Psycho*, 231
pull-back, 83
*quem quaeritis* plays, 39
*Quo Vadis?*, 223
quota quickies, 108-9
rack focus, 91
*Raiders of the Lost Ark*, 71
*Railway Man, The*, 85-95, 122
Ray, Robert B., 129
reception theory, 166
*Reine Elizabeth, La*, 51
Renoir, Jean, 22
Richards, I. A., 145
Riefenstahl, Leni, 11
Robey, George, 100-101
*Romancing the Stone*, 179
Romanowski, William, 18
*Sabotage*, 105, 112, 228
*Saboteur*, 103
*Salmon Fishing in the Yemen*, 196-99
Saussure, Ferdinand de, 160-61, 164
Sayers, Dorothy L., 2-19, 217-38
  and Ackland, Sir Richard, 73
  and Adams, Pauline, 177
  "And Telling You a Story," 9
  and architectural/structural beauty, 8-9, 10, 15, 111-12, 118, 135, 167, 190
  "Are Women Human?," 172, 178, 180, 188
  and Arianism, 128-30
  and Barton, Eustace, 99-100
  and BBC Radio, 4, 6, 41, 55, 76, 86, 94, 104, 188, 237
  *Begin Here*, 83-84
  and Bligh, Sidney, 237
  "Blood Sacrifice," 110-11
  and Brabazon, James, 3
  *Bridgeheads*, 84, 95
  *Busman's Honeymoon*, 3, 69-70, 74, 106, 107
  and Byrne, Muriel St Clare, 23, 84, 104, 106, 108, 111
  and Canterbury Festival, 111, 174, 236-37
  *Cat O'Mary*, 219
  and Cecil, Lord David, 84
  *Clouds of Witness*, 232-33
  and Coomes, David, 3
  and Cournos, John, 220, 232
  and Dane, Clemence, 74, 237
  and Dante Alighieri, 2, 3, 4, 9, 10, 11, 15-16, 17, 18, 43, 153, 223-24
  and Denham, Reginald, 108-9
  and Detection Club, 4-5, 74, 150-51, 228
  "Detective Stories for the Screen", 113
  *Devil to Pay*, 231, 234-35, 236
  *Emperor Constantine, The*, 14, 128
  *Five Red Herrings*, 102
  and Fleming, John Anthony, 231-32
  "Forgiveness and the Enemy," 94
  *Gaudy Night*, 106-7, 149
  "Gaudy Night" (essay), 139
  and Gielgud, Val, 55, 56, 61, 66, 104, 237
  and Gnosticism, 127
  and Godolphin School, 222-23
  and Haddon, Peter, 103-4, 109
  *Haunted Honeymoon*, 69
  *Have His Carcase*, 170-71
  *He That Should Come*, 104
  and Higham, David, 104
  and Holmes, Sherlock, 221, 225
  "The Human-Not-Quite-Human", 174-75, 189-90
  "Image in the Mirror", 229-31
  *Inferno, L'*, 16, 223-24
  and Jaeger, Muriel, 227, 230
  and Loder, John, 105
  *Love All*, 173-74, 178, 194, 197
  *The Man Born to Be King*, 6, 14, 41, 76, 77, 94-95, 104, 185, 237
  and Manichaeism, 126-27
  *The Mind of the Maker*, 3, 81, 114-18, 120-23, 125-28, 131-33, 137-41, 143-46, 148, 153, 178, 190, 215
  *Murder Must Advertise*, 102
  "My Edwardian Childhood," 219
  *The Nine Tailors*, 43
  and Nott, Kathleen, 143-45
  and Oxford University, 3, 10, 16, 70, 84, 175, 177
    Somerville College, 16, 175, 223-24
  and Pelagianism, 131-33, 141
  and Pentecost, 148-49
  and Perceval, Hugh, 103-5
  and Phoenix Films, 103-4, 106, 108-110, 112-13, 117, 118, 149, 235, 236

and *Punch* magazine, 224
and Rathbone, Basil, 225
and Reynolds, Barbara, 15, 16, 73, 101, 104, 224
and Sexton Blake movies, 227
*The Silent Passenger*, 104-6, 107-110, 114, 149, 236
and the silver screen, 234-35
and Simmons, Laura, 11, 44, 121
and Simpson, Helen, 4, 73, 74, 84, 105, 110, 112, 117, 228
and Speaight, Robert, 237
and stigmata of theater, 43-45
and Stoll Picture Theatre, 229-30
"Striding Folly", 108
*Strong Poison*, 98, 100-101, 170, 171
"Target Area", 95
and Thorndike, Dame Sybil, 4, 235-38
and Thurmer, John, 114
"Towards a Christian Aesthetic", 119-21, 123, 126, 149, 157
and trinitarian creativity, 113-15, 119-21, 124-25, 134, 136, 143, 146-48, 153, 155-59, 167, 195, 207, 209, 210, 212, 215, 238
"The Triumph of Easter", 131-32
and Vane, Harriet, 100, 102, 106, 111, 170-71
and Virgil, 2, 4, 15, 17, 18, 170
and Waller, Lewis, 221, 222, 235
and Welch, Claude, 115-16
*Whose Body?*, 7, 10, 15, 99, 176, 231
and Wilding, Dorothy, 225-26, 229
and Williams, Charles, 9, 237
and Williams, Harcourt, 236, 238
and Wimsey, Lord Peter, 7-8, 10, 15, 70, 74, 98, 99, 100, 102-5, 107, 109, 131, 139, 151, 170-71, 228, 232-33, 236
and Yancey, Philip, 115-16
*Zeal of Thy House*, 111-14, 117, 135, 139, 142, 167, 172-74, 234, 235, 236
Scorsese, Martin, 4, 36
Seldes, Gilbert, 123-24
semiology, 160-62, 166
semiotics, 162-66
Seneca, 37
*Seventh Seal, The*, 124
Shakespeare, William, 31, 35, 36, 51, 62-63, 123, 152, 174, 192, 194, 195, 199
shot-reverse-shot, 205, 211
*Sight and Sound*, 4, 113, 118, 124, 152, 178
silent film, 97-102, 106-7, 109, 175-76, 223-27, 229-31, 233
Silverman, Kaja, 164-65, 214
*Singing in the Rain*, 99
Slide, Anthony, 176
Smith, James K. A., 148
Solanas, Fernando, 157-58
Sontag, Susan, 10-11, 19
Sophocles, 25, 39
Spielberg, Steven, 31, 71, 150
Spoto, Donald, 109, 231
spy movies, 130
*Stage Fright*, 237
Stannard, Eliot, 233
Steiner, Wendy, 145-46
Stroheim, Erich von, 105-7, 149-50
*Student of Prague, The*, 229-30
*Suddenly, Last Summer*, 32
superheroes, 56-59, 64-67, 70, 72
synecdoche on screen, 62, 78, 136
talkies, 96-103, 108-9, 148, 171, 228
*Taming of the Shrew*, 36
Taylor, Elizabeth, 32
Terence, 35
Tertullian, 23, 38
Thalberg, Irving, 22
Thanouli, Eleftheria, 59
Thespis, 25
Thiede, Carsten Peter, 25
Third Cinema, 157-58
Thompson, Kristin, 99, 151
*Three Musketeers, The*, 221, 223
"Thus Spake Zarathustra", 186
tilt, 59, 60, 78, 207
Tocqueville, Alexis de, 129
Tolkien, J. R. R., 36, 72
*Total Recall* movies, 34
Toynbee, Arnold, 68
tracking shots, 59, 64, 154, 225
*Tramp, The*, 101
Trinity, the, 38, 113-15, 129, 143, 144, 148, 162, 168
*Trip to the Moon, A*, 48
Truffaut, François, 153-56, 160, 169, 215, 216
Turner, Kathleen, 179
Turvey, Malcolm, 146
*Unforgivable, The*, 208
Valentino, Rudolf, 176, 227
Varda, Agnès, 175
Venice Film Festival, 172-73
*Vertigo*, 231
Vertov, Dziga, 112
Vietnam War, 182-83
voiceover, 87, 93
Wagner, Richard, 183-84
Warner Brothers, 30, 98, 99, 181, 185
Watt, Ian, 77, 84-85, 92
Welle, John P., 224
Welles, Orson, 23
*West Side Story*, 31
westerns, 32, 35, 71
White, Hayden, 217
Wiene, Robert, 52
*Wild Strawberries*, 124
Williams, Tennessee, 32
*Wings*, 233
*Witness*, 182
Wollen, Peter, 162-65, 168
*Woman to Woman*, 231
Wood, Christopher W., 152
Woodward, Joanne, 193-94
World War I, 52, 70-71, 177
World War II, 10-11, 52, 69-70, 71, 73-95
Wright, Robin, 209
*Wuthering Heights*, 232-34
Zeffirelli, Franco, 36
zoetrope, 167, 219

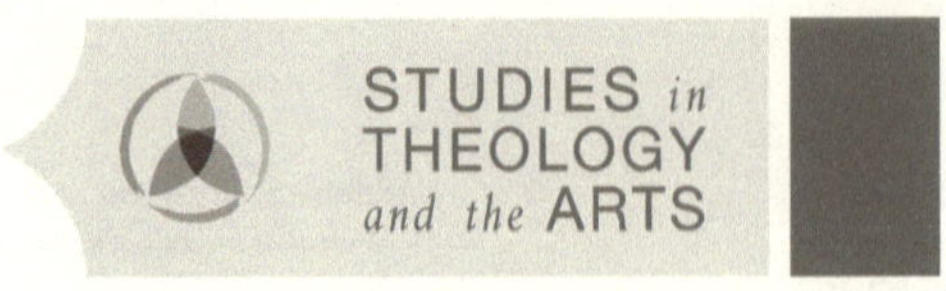


IVP Academic's Studies in Theology and the Arts (STA) seeks to enable Christians to reflect more deeply upon the relationship between their faith and humanity's artistic and cultural expressions. By drawing on the insights of both academic theologians and artistic practitioners, this series encourages thoughtful engagement with and critical discernment of the full variety of artistic media—including visual art, music, literature, film, theater, and more—which both embody and inform Christian thinking.



**Also available in the**
**Studies in Theology and the Arts Series**

*Modern Art and the Life of a Culture*
by Jonathan A. Anderson and William A. Dyrness

*The Faithful Artist*
by Cameron J. Anderson

*Contemporary Art and the Church*
Edited by W. David O. Taylor and Taylor Worley

*A Subversive Gospel*
by Michael Mears Bruner

*God in the Modern Wing*
Edited by Cameron J. Anderson and G. Walter Hansen

*Resisting the Marriage Plot*
By Dalene Joy Fisher

*The Art of New Creation*
Edited by Jeremy Begbie, Daniel Train, and W. David O. Taylor

*Seeing Is Believing*
By Richard Vance Goodwin

www.ingramcontent.com/pod-product-compliance
Lightning Source LLC
LaVergne TN
LVHW091125080826
845145LV00008B/2048

* 9 7 8 1 5 1 4 0 0 8 8 0 5 *